THE LOVE OF GOD

THE LOVE OF GOD
AND SPIRITUAL FRIENDSHIP

Bernard of Clairvaux

Abridged, Edited, and Introduced

by James M. Houston

Chancellor, Regent College

General Editor—Classics of Faith and Devotion

MULTNOMAH PRESS
PORTLAND. OREGON 97266

This edition of *The Love of God* is adapted freely from two main sources: chapters four and five are translated from Ravelet's French text, *Oeuvres de Saint Bernard*, 1866-70; the remaining chapters are abridged from the English translation of Jean Mabillon's book, *Life and Works of Saint Bernard*, translated by Samuel J. Eales, 1889. Credit is also given to Cistercian Publications, Inc., Kalamazoo, Michigan, for permission to consult and make use of their publications, *The Golden Epistle* by William of St.-Thierry, translated by Theodore Berkeley ocso, 1971, and *Spiritual Friendship* by Aelred of Rievaulx, translated by Mary Eugenia Laker, S.S.N.D., 1974, © Cistercian Publications, in the compilation of chapters two and nine. These sources were used by permission.

Scripture references in this volume are the original author's own translations (Bernard of Clairvaux, Aelred of Rievaulx, and William of St.-Thierry).

Pen and ink drawing of Bernard of Clairvaux: Sarah Chamberlain

THE LOVE OF GOD
This abridged edition
© 1983 by Multnomah Press
Portland, Oregon 97266

Printed in the United States of America

First Printing 1983

Library of Congress Cataloging in Publication Data

Bernard of Clairvaux, Saint, 1090 or 91-1153.
The love of God, and spiritual friendship.

(Classics of faith and devotion)
Translated from the Latin.
Includes writings of William of St.-Thierry and Aelred of Rievaulx.
Bibliography: p.
Includes indexes.
1. God—Worship and love—Early works to 1800.   2. Bible. O.T. Song of Solomon—Sermons.   3. Love (Theology)—Early works to 1800.
4. Spiritual life—Early work   231 BER 1983
1922-   II. William, ‹
1085-1148?   III. Aelred, ‹
V. Series
BV4817.B382   1983
ISBN 0-88070-

Bernard, of Clairvaux,
The love of God, and
spiritual friendship /

85-219

CONTENTS

Free choice—Threefold freedom of nature, glory, and
grace—The image and likeness of the Creator expressed in this threefold freedom—Human merits are
solely the gifts of God—Grace and free choice, together the work of salvation.

Part II: The Nature and Greatness of God's Love

PREFACE TO THE CLASSICS OF FAITH AND DEVOTION

With the profusion of books now being published, most Christian readers require some guidance for a basic collection of spiritual works that will remain life-long companions. This new series of Christian classics of devotion is being edited to provide just such a basic library for the home. Those selected may not all be commonly known today, but each has a central concern of relevance for the contemporary Christian.

Another goal for this collection of books is a reawakening. It is a reawakening to the spiritual thoughts and meditations of the forgotten centuries. Many Christians today have no sense of the past. If the Reformation is important to them, they jump from the apostolic Church to the sixteenth century, forgetting some fourteen centuries of the work of the Holy Spirit among many devoted to Christ. These classics will remove that gap, and enrich their readers by the faith and devotion of God's saints through all history.

And so we turn to the books, and to their purpose. Some books have changed the lives of their readers. Notice how Athanasius's *Life of Antony* affected Augustine or William Law's *A Serious Call to a Devout and Holy Life* influenced John Wesley. Others, such as Augustine's *Confessions* or Thomas à Kempis's *Imitation of Christ*, have remained perennial sources of inspiration throughout the ages. We sincerely hope those selected in this series will have a like effect on our readers.

Each one of the classics chosen for this series is deeply significant to a contemporary Christian leader. In some cases, the thoughts and reflections of the classic writer are mirrored in the leader's genuine ambitions and desires today, an unusual pairing of hearts and minds across the centuries. And thus these individuals have been asked to write the introduction on the book that has been so meaningful to his or her own life.

EDITING THE CLASSICS

Such classics of spiritual life have had their obstacles. Their original language, the archaic style of later editions, their length, the digressions, the allusions to by-gone cultures—all make the use of them discouraging to the modern reader. To reprint them (as was done on a massive scale in the last century and still so today) does not overcome these handicaps of style, length, and language. To seek the kernel and remove the husk, this series involves therefore the abridging, rewriting, and editing of each book. At the same time we sought to keep to the essential message given in the work, and to pursue as much as possible the original style of the author.

The principles of editing are as follows. Keep sentences short. Paragraphs are also shortened. Material is abridged where there are digressions or allusions made that are time-binding. Archaic words are altered. Spelling is that of Webster's Dictionary. Logical linkage may have to be added to abridged material. The identity of theme or argument is kept sharply in mind. Allusions to other authors are given brief explanation. And marginal readings are added to provide concise summaries of each major section.

For the Christian, the Bible is the basic text for spiritual reading. All other devotional reading is secondary and should never be a substitute for it. Therefore, the allusions to Scripture in these classics of devotion are searched out and referenced in the text. This is where other editions of these books may ignore the scriptural quality of these works, which are inspired and guided by the Bible. The biblical focus is always the hallmark of truly Christian spirituality.

PURPOSE FOR THE CLASSICS: SPIRITUAL READING

Since our sensate and impatient culture makes spiritual reading strange and difficult for us, the reader should be cautioned to read these books slowly, meditatively, and reflectively. One cannot rush through them like a detective story. In place of novelty, they focus on remembrance, reminding us of values that remain of eternal consequence. We may enjoy many new things, but values are as old as God's creation.

The goal for the reader of these books is not to seek information. Instead, these volumes teach one about living wisely. That takes obedience, submission of will, change of heart, and a tender, docile spirit. When John the Baptist saw Jesus, he reacted, "He must increase, and I must decrease." Likewise, spiritual reading decreases our natural instincts to allow His love to increase within us.

Nor are these books "how-to" kits or texts. They take us as we are—that is, as persons, and not as functionaries. They guide us to "be" authentic, and not necessarily help us to promote more professional activities. Such books require us to make time for their slow digestion, space to let their thoughts enter into our hearts, and discipline to let new insights "stick" and become part of our Christian character.

James M. Houston

Dr. James M. Houston was born to missionary parents who served in Spain. Dr. Houston served as University Lecturer at Oxford University, England, from 1949-1971. He was a Fellow of Hertford College during the period between 1964-1971, and held the office of Principal of Regent College from 1969-1978. From 1978 to the present he has served as Chancellor of Regent College.

Dr. Houston has been active in the establishment and encouragement of lay training centers across the continents. These include the C. S. Lewis Institute in Washington, D.C., and The London Institute for the Study of Contemporary Christianity. In addition to his work with the Classics series, he has published a book entitled, I Believe in the Creator (Eerdmans, 1978.)

Bernard of Clairvaux
1090-1153

EDITOR'S NOTE
ABOUT BERNARD OF CLAIRVAUX
AND HIS FRIENDS

The choice of Bernard of Clairvaux, with his two friends, William of St.-Thierry and Aelred of Rievaulx, is deliberate. They stand like a medieval triptych, the central, dominating figure of Bernard with his two companions—William the great theologian of love and Aelred, the simple exemplar of friendship. Bernard stands between the two, the synthesizer of contemplation of the Divine. He was perhaps the greatest organizer of the Middle Ages. Together these men represent that balance between the love of God and the love of man in friendship which animated their theology and gave it life.

Only since the 1920s has William of St.-Thierry gradually become his own man. Even his writings have been traditionally attributed to Bernard. Without this association to Bernard, his writings might never have been preserved. Aelred's nickname has been "The Bernard of the North," representing the Bernardian influence in England.

All of these men contribute an inexhaustible source of spiritual materials today for contemplation as well as for theological and exegetical thinking.

BERNARD'S FRIENDS

Bernard had an irresistible charm with people. When he was only twenty-two, he decided to enter the monastic community of Citeaux. At that point he persuaded his uncle, four of his five brothers (the youngest then being too young), and twenty-five other friends to accompany him in this way of life. Later he would be a regular correspondent with the most influential leaders of Christendom—kings, popes, the feudal nobility. But of all his friends, William his senior and Aelred his junior were as close as any. They loved him as both their spiritual mentor and dear friend.

William of St.-Thierry (ca. 1080, 1090-1148) was born of noble family in Liège. Little is known about his early life. He was possibly educated at Laon under the famed Schoolman, Anselm, and maybe became a student friend of Peter Abelard, the important scholastic theologian. He then entered the Benedictine monastery of St. Nicasius, near Rheims. About the age of thirty-four, he was elected Abbot of St.-Thierry, where he remained in charge of administrative duties for the next fifteen years or more.

William first met Bernard in the winter of 1118 as Bernard lay ill in his primitive hut, broken with fasting and overwork. "In that hut, like the shelters assigned to the lepers at the crossroads, I found him radiant with joy, as though he had been caught up in the delights of paradise," records William. "Bending my gaze upon the kingly dwelling and its inhabitant, I was filled with such awe— God is my witness—as though I had drawn near the altar of God. I conceived such a fondness for the man that I longed to share the poverty and the simplicity of his life." He added, "Had I then been granted one wish, it would have been to stay with him forever, as his servant."[1]

• Subsequent meetings with Bernard and correspondence with him only intensified this desire in William, but for many years Bernard dissuaded William from either joining him or the Cistercians. In 1135 he did join the dozen members of the new Cistercian community at Signy in the forests of the Ardennes and renounced his dignity as an abbot for the humble, contemplative life of a simple monk.

The inspiration from William's first visit to Bernard probably motivated him to write his first serious work, *On the Nature and Dignity of Love*, in 1119-1120. He further wrote a meditation on union with God entitled *The Sacrament of the Altar* in 1128. But after joining the community at Signy, William obtained the quiet and solitude he had longed to have. Illness kept him from sharing in the hard manual labors of his brothers, so he was able to give himself to the writing of his major works, *The Mirror of Faith, The Enigma of Faith,* and *The Golden Epistle.* In addition he penned commentaries on parts of the epistle to the Romans, The Song of Solomon, and Isaiah. He also collected two series of *Meditations.* William was a first-class theologian. Increased recognition should be given to him in the future. He had an acute sense of the heresy that his old friend Abelard was propounding on the nature of the Trinity, and William became Bernard's mentor in the ensuing controversy that Bernard led at Sens against Abelard's arrogant scholasticism. Yet William was given to mental depression due to a low self-image and desire to remain anonymous. Had he not declared in a letter to the Carthusian community of Mont-Dieu—this letter is now the preface of *The Golden Epistle*—we might still have remained uncertain about his authorship of this and many other works.

Humble, devout, and wise, William's great desire was simply to be the friend of Bernard and the lover of God. He had the privilege of first reading Bernard's meditations on *The Song of Songs* and was also asked by Bernard to evaluate his work *On Grace and Free Will.* Like Luke's dedication to Theophilus, William was likewise dedicated to Bernard. His two-volume work *On the Nature of Body and Soul* carries an inscription to Bernard.

Hungry for God, William could only be a dissatisfied man, seeking no other face than the face of God.

Aelred of Rievaulx (ca. 1110-1167) was a younger and more distant friend of Bernard. Indeed he may only have met him on one occasion when Aelred was on his way to visit Rome in about 1142. Bernard had been impressed by Aelred's literary abilities and requested him to write his classic, *Spiritual Friendship.*

Aelred was born in the north England town of Hexham. His family had for several generations been in honorable church positions. He was educated within the royal court of David I of Scotland, and his Anglo-Saxon name of Ethelred was softened. There his manners became worldly-wise. Aelred would describe the feeling of alienation he felt in the court even though he was much loved by the king. "How lucky he is. How lucky. But they do not know that there was evil in me where only good should be. Terrible was my distress within. Tormenting me, it corrupted my soul with an intolerable stench. And unless You had stretched out Your hand and helped me to tolerate myself, I might have taken the most desperate remedy of despair."[2]

While still suffering in this way, Aelred was sent on a mission to York. Two years before, the Archbishop of York had founded Rievaulx as a colony of Cistercian monks. There at the gates of the monastery, Aelred offered himself as a monk. He was an immediate success, and, seven years later, he was appointed Master of Novices. Just prior to his York trip he had met Bernard. Bernard subsequently contacted Aelred and asked him to write up his notes on the talks to novices. This become known as *The Mirror of Charity*.

In 1143, Aelred was sent to found a new monastery at Revesly. Four years later he was appointed Abbot of Rievaulx. He remained there for the rest of his life. At Rievaulx he wrote *Jesus at the Age of Twelve*, and, soon after, *Spiritual Friendship* (1160). His *Pastoral Prayer* is a beautiful confession that reveals his soul. Suffering much from arthritis and other ailments, he died in much pain. Shortly before his death, he wrote *On the Soul* which lacks the polish of his earlier works.

BERNARD'S PLACE IN HISTORY

An extraordinary man, Bernard is complex—if not paradoxical. Named Bernard of Clairvaux (1090-1153) to distinguish him from Bernard of Cluny or Bernard of Chartres, he was undoubtedly the most dynamic figure of the twelfth century, if not the whole of the Middle Ages. For he dominates all other voices in his own century and changed more patterns of thought and sentiment than anyone else.

Although Bernard was not the founder of the Cistercian Order, it scarcely existed before he entered the Order, and at his death the Order possessed 350 abbeys. Bernard stood for the antithesis of Christendom during that time. Simply stated, Bernard's belief was: Knowledge of God comes only through devotion to God, in poverty, in simplicity, and in solitude. Within his own generation, the Cistercian movement—based on these principles—was the greatest success story of the Middle Ages.[3]

Bernard was born around 1090 at the court of the Counts of Burgundy. He was a member of a wealthy Burgundian family. His godly mother Aleth died when Bernard was about fourteen. Later when he was tempted to pursue learning for reasons of vain glory, his mind filled with the reproachful vision of his mother saying that "she had not brought him up with such love and care so that he could adopt this kind of empty existence, and that it was not for the fulfillment of such worldly ambitions that she had brought him into this world."[4] Praying in chapel one day at some later date, he contemplated the verse: "If therefore thine eye be single, thy whole body shall be full of light" (Matthew 6:22). Thence there was started a light, says Bernard, "like the flame which turns the forest into a roaring blaze and then goes on to burn the mountains black."[5] It was also a serene as well as reforming light, for it shone in him, and through him, and with him.

Thus the lasting reputation of Bernard has been that of godliness, as a man passionately in love with God. Earthly honors and comforts he despised, with a total lack of self-interest. "To be poor with Christ" was his one concern. So despite his father's opposition, he and his friends lived in the primitive huts in the marshy valley of the river Aube, at Citeaux. It was relocated in a more substantial structure twenty years later. Bernard admits: "I chose Citeaux in preference to Cluny (the wealthy Benedictine monastery) not because I was not aware that the life there was excellent and lawful, but because . . . I was conscious my weak character needed a strong medicine."[6]

From 1127 until his death, Bernard was called upon to give counsel on temporal affairs all over Christendom. He dealt with relations between the Count of Champagne and the King, Louis VI, and between the King and Eleanor of Aquitaine. He patched up the papal schism, and in 1145 Eugene III, one of his "sons," was elected Pope. He related with Roger of Sicily, Henry I of England, and the Hohenstaufen rulers. He traveled to Flanders, the Rhine valley, Rome, and Salerno in Italy. It is probable he spent no more than a third of his time at Clairvaux because of his travels. Yet he was sick from continual gastric illnesses.

His first biographer has suggested that it was measureless immoderateness, *nimia nimetas,* which was both Bernard's strength and weakness. The phrase applies to his self-castigation, so that he was in poor health all his life. It applies also to the relentless struggle he had against rationalistic thinking, the worldly corruption of the church, and the call to fulfill all his political concerns, including the organization of the Second Crusade. " 'My burdened conscience, and my life, resemble,' he admitted in a letter, some kind of fabled monster . . . a chimera of the century, acting neither as a monk nor as a layman . . . driven about through the abysses of the world.' "

Bernard has had the ferocious reputation of a mental puritanism, who, as an anti-intellectual, attacked personally Abelard at Sens in 1140. Viewed biblically, however, he was simply following his mentor, the Apostle Paul, in attacking the worldly wisdom of those who only teach vanity. Instead of that wisdom, Bernard substituted the simplicity of "Jesus Christ and Him crucified."

But the greatest contemporary scholar on medieval monasticism, David Knowles, has said that to tackle Bernard's own learning is to discover "a speculative theologian of wide reading, and great intellectual power; a literary genius of the first order, the greatest master of language in the Middle Ages, who alone of all this age, has a power equal to that of Demosthenes, Cicero, and of Burke, to carry us along with him on the gale of his eloquence."[7]

The paradox about Bernard continues today. Most Christians only know Bernard because of the hymns he is supposed to have written. Yet it is unlikely that Bernard ever wrote "Jesus, the Very Thought of Thee," "Jesus, Thou Joy of Loving Hearts," or "O Jesus, King Most Wonderful." But the sentiments of Bernard are clearly there, showing perhaps the impact he did make on anonymous hymn writers.

Likewise, others may think of Bernard as a great preacher, with eighty-six sermons on the Song of Solomon alone! (Rather, the sermons are on only the first two chapters and the first verse of chapter 3 of that biblical book of love.) Yet it is much more likely that Bernard only used the genre of the sermon for the careful writing he has given us in these meditations.

I am convinced that no greater writer of the Church's past needs recovering more today than Bernard. This is not only because of ignorance about "the last of the Fathers," but, as we shall see, it is because of what he can still teach us today.

THE PLACE OF BERNARD'S VOICE IN HISTORY

Certainly, Dante thought so highly of Bernard that, in his pursuit of Beatrice into Paradise, he reached the tenth sphere of the heavenly mysteries, saying:

> "I thought I should see Beatrice, and saw
> An old man, habited like the glorious people;
> O'erflowing was he, in his eyes and cheeks
> With joys benign, in attitude of piety,
> As to a tender father is becoming."

Later, Bernard taught Dante to look beyond Beatrice, even beyond the Virgin Mary,* to the One Beyond:

> "Bernard conveyed to me what I should do
> By sign and smile; already on my own
> I had looked upwards, as he wished me to."

Eventually, Dante saw what Bernard had spoken to him about:

> "Eternal light, that in Thyself alone
> Dwelling, alone dost know Thyself, and smile
> On Thy self-love, so knowing and so known.
>
> My will and my desire were turned by love
> The love that moves the sun, and the other stars."[8]

The Italian humanists of the Renaissance were enamored with Bernard. Traversari, a Florentine scholar of the early fifteenth century, ranked his *Sermons on the Song of Songs* alongside Augustine's *Confessions* and Jerome's *Letters* for its power of exhorting its readers to faith.[9] Pope Eugenius IV pondered over Bernard's *On Consideration* and sought to reform his administration accordingly.[10]

The first Reformers referred repeatedly to his statements . . . at least to those they knew. For they saw him also as a reformer of church malpractices.

Was it through Tauler, Ruysbroeck, and Thomas à Kempis—who had all been influenced by both Bernard and William of St.-Thierry—that Luther first met with Bernard's writings? We do not know, but Luther was to acknowledge Bernard in his *Sermons on the Gospel of John.* "I regard Bernard as the most pious of all the monks and prefer him to all the others, even to St. Dominic. He is the only one worthy of the name 'Father' and of being studied dili-

---

*Bernard did not accept what later became the Roman doctrine of the Immaculate Conception.

gently."[11] Luther also said: "I love Bernard as the one who, among all writers, preached Christ most charmingly. I follow him wherever he preached Christ, and I pray to Christ in the faith in which he prayed to Christ."[12]

Luther's emphasis on justification by faith through grace because of Christ was what drew Luther's pietism and Bernard's mysticism together.[13] In the decades that followed, Lutherans so popularized Bernard that the printed circulation of his works in German far exceeded any other of the Fathers—including Augustine—until modern times.

In France, Louis XIII built a church over Bernard's birthplace at Fontaine, and in 1652 the same king gave the Abbot of Clairvaux the title of "Protector of the Crown." Francis de Sales, the devout bishop of Geneva, was much inspired by Bernard's writings, as were also Fénelon and Bossuet. In 1691, Abbot Mabillon published in French the works of Bernard and some of those of William of St.-Thierry. He declared that, next to the Scriptures, the books most familiar to the people of France were those of Bernard. These books nourished "their lives in a life-long way." Pascal was much affected by Bernard; his famous dictum, "You would not seek me, if you had not already been found of me," is a direct quotation from Bernard's *On the Love of God*.[14]

In England, selections of Bernard's and William's works were edited and circulated widely in the early seventeenth century by Francis Burton. The Puritans quote Bernard almost as frequently as Augustine. John Owen quotes him at least sixteen times in his works, especially in his understanding of justifying faith. John Bradford, Richard Baxter, John Flavel, and Thomas Manton, representative of the Puritan tradition, all quote him frequently. In the eighteenth century, there appears a loss of interest in him, and only erudite men like Jonathan Edwards infrequently quote him. So, among English Protestant readers, Bernard seems henceforth to have been lost.

Several Roman Catholic revivals of interest in Bernard have continued. Two important biographies of Bernard were published, one by the Count of Montalembert in 1835 and another by Abbot Vacandard in 1895. To celebrate the eighth centenary of Bernard's birth in 1891, P. Janauschek published a bibliography of works on Bernard which amounted to 2,761 references. In 1953, to celebrate the eighth centenary of his death, a second bibliography was begun and finally published in 1957. It listed another 1,000 references. Meanwhile, a new impetus to Bernardian studies has been made by the scholarly revision of the texts of his works by Jean Leclerc in six volumes. It was completed in 1970. The recent monographs on the works of Bernard, William, Aelred, and other early Cistercians have given a whole new interest in these writers today. *

HIS WORKS

To understand and appreciate the following works, one must know the milieu and genres of the early Cistercian literature. Three things need to be pointed out.

First, this is monastic literature, matured in the school of silence.

Monks live in a milieu of silence. In the Middle Ages, monastic silence contrasted with the atmosphere of disputation and much discussion in the secular lecture halls. These secular school lectures evolved into what was to become university life. The monastic art of speaking developed thus in writing, not in debate and lecture. Their letters and sermons were carefully written in reflection and meditation to engender meditation before God. Silence was the space worthy of the mystery of God. Writing done prayerfully did not intrude into this God-filled world.

Second, the new monasticism of the "white monks," notably the Cistercians and Carthusians, developed as a school of the laity.

Whereas the traditional monasticism of the "black monks" had largely fostered the young recruits in unquestioning traditionalism, a new recruitment policy was deliberately developed by the white monks. The reason was primarily to reform monasticism with more asceticism, that is, with more emphasis on poverty and devotion to God. So adult recruitment of a wide range of social classes was developed: nobility, scholars, and a broad range of craftsmen and artisans, as well as knights. A new use of convents was also initiated so that virgins, widows, and prostitutes all mixed inside these walls. [15]

*Cistercian Publications; Kalamazoo, Michigan, 49008.

Historians are now realizing that the twelfth century saw a developing sense of concern for the individual which was new and emphatic. [16] All of these social changes and the extraordinary social admixture of these new communities presented a great challenge to pastoral instruction. The communities needed nurture and the restructuring of their psyche from the ways of the feudal world. Similarly, the modern Born Again Movement, which is largely secular paganism, needs nurturing and reeducating. The treatises of men like Bernard and William thus assume that diverse stages of spiritual development are needed by their readers.

Third, the Cistercian reform was *a school of love.*

Only one thing could possibly bind such social diversity together—namely, the love of God. Since many of the new recruits had known carnal love, only one further experience could cleanse them, and that was experiencing the chaste love of Christ.

Bernard was the herald of this new literature of love. He revived the theology of desire from the sermons of Origen and Gregory. His own experience of the sweet tasting of the Song of Songs was also part of this written revival. Love as charity was the focus of a whole new emphasis in literature, prayers, and hymns.

In the circles of knighthood now recruited, a "love" literature of what would become in the next century "courtly love" was appearing. Bernard created a counter to this in his own literature of desire and love for God. It is these writings which are his great contribution to the church.

We have represented here, then, three distinct literary genres of this literature of love: sermons, letters with their extended treatise form, and *florilegia* or collected maxims. [17]

The sermon is the genre most often represented in this monastic literature. The sermon genre's patristic origins and the two daily talks given to the monks account for the sermon's widespread representation in this literature. Not all sermons were circulated in written form, however, nor were all written sermons ever verbally delivered. There is good evidence to believe that these excerpts of Bernard's *Sermons on the Song of Songs* were devised only in a written, meditative form. Their length, their complexity in the attempt to refute error, their polished Latin cadence, their linkage of one to the next, and the deep and personal nature of the author's confessions all suggest careful, written elaboration.

The letter was a form much prized in monastic communities.

Letters were valued because of the silence practiced, because of their value in communicating between scattered communities of the same order, and because of the authority they had in the long tradition traced back to St. Benedict himself. Bernard greatly enhanced letter writing by his own extensive and influential correspondence and by the emphasis on friendship that his teaching and theology reflected.

The treatise form—the main form represented in this book— was an extension of the letter form. It was usually a reply or an acknowledgment of a personal request. It placed matters mutually discussed into an expanded or written form. Thus, many of the prefaces of these treatises are letters that accompanied the treatises. Moreover, as public letters, they became letters of spiritual direction or exhortation since the whole monastic community would hear them read aloud in public assembly. Similar in some ways to the New Testament letters, these epistles were saturated in the biblical material they most closely represented.

The *florilegium*, or collection of sayings, dates back to classical teaching. As used by the monks, however, its intent was to savor and meditate at leisure over spiritual readings that helped one's devotions. The metaphor which paints the picture of this deep devotion is that of bees who suck out nectar for the honeycomb. Bernard, the soft-spoken and warmhearted doctor, has appropriately been given the symbol of a beehive even though he incorporated most of his material in sermon and treatise form rather than in florilegia as such. But the *Meditations* of William of St.-Thierry are in florilegia.

The translation presented in this book is adapted freely from the English translation of Mabillon's text made by Eales in 1889.[18] Two exceptions to that statement include the treatises of William of St.-Thierry, "On Contemplating God" (Chapter Five), and "The Nature and Dignity of Love" (Chapter Four), which have been translated from Ravelet's French text.[19] The excerpt entitled "The Dignity of Man's Soul" (Chapter One) has been rewritten from Stanhope's *Pious Breathings*.[20]

I am much indebted, however, to the modern, critical editions of the Cistercian Publications for my more loosely worded renderings in the abridged forms of William of St.-Thierry's *The Golden Epistle* (here called "Three Stages of the Spiritual Life"—Chapter Two) and Aelred's *Spiritual Friendship* (Chapter Nine), © Cistercian Publications. I have also consulted other editions of texts such as those published by Mowbrays, a religious division of C.S.M.V., 1952, and Hugh Martin's *On Loving God by Bernard of Clairvaux*, S.C.M. Press, 1959. The bibliographical notes indicate my indebtedness to much contemporary Cistercian scholarship, especially to the edited works now being published by the authoritative series of Cistercian Publications.

The styles of the three writers represented here are distinctive. William of St.-Thierry has the tightest style. It is heavy with meaning, closely argued, and difficult to paraphrase. It is difficult to abridge his material and still maintain the flow of his thought.

Aelred is easier to condense, for his thought is more conversational.

Bernard can be digressive and therefore abridged more readily, but the translation of his Latin cadences and the skillful play on words is almost impossible to preserve in another language. Even still, one can sense the almost poetic form of his prose and the ardor and devotion of a writer who is living and breathing the words and thoughts that he is communicating.

In all the texts, the numerical side references are kept from the Mabillon text. Chapter titles are somewhat modified from either Mabillon or from the modern critical editions.

James M. Houston

[1]*Life of Bernard*, I, 7, 32-34, quoted in Jean Marie Dechanet, *William of St.-Thierry* (Spencer, Mass: Cistercian Publications, 1972), p. 24.

[2]Aelred, *Mirror of Charity*, I:79.

[3]R. W. Southern, *Western Society and the Church in the Middle Ages* (London: Penguin, 1970), pp. 250-72.

[4]*Vita Prima Bernardi*, translated by Geoffrey Webb and Adrian Walker (A. R. Mowbray, 1960), p. 24.

[5]Ibid, p. 25.

[6]Quoted in Bruno S. James, *Saint Bernard of Clairvaux* (London: Hodder & Stoughton, 1957), p. 23.

[7]David Knowles, *The Evolution of Medieval Thought* (Toronto: Random House, 1962; Vintage Books), p. 147.

[8]Dante, *The Divine Comedy; Vol. 3: Paradise*, trans. by Dorothy L. Sayers and Barbara Reynolds (London: Penguin, 1962), p. 329, 331.

[9]Giles Constable, "The Popularity of Twelfth Century Spiritual Writers in the Late Middle Ages," in *Renaissance Studies*, ed. A. Molho and J. Tedeschi (Dekalb, Ill.: 1971), pp. 3-28.

[10]Charles L. Stinger, "St. Bernard and Pope Eugenius IV (1431-1447)," in *Cistercian Ideals and Reality*, ed. John R. Sommerfeldt (Kalamazoo, Mich.: Cistercian Publications, 1978), pp. 329-343.

[11]Quoted in Carl Volz, "Martin Luther's Attitude Towards Bernard of Clairvaux," in *Studies in Medieval Cistercian History*, presented to Jeremiah F. O. Sullivan (Cistercian Publications, 1971), p. 188.

[12]Ibid., p. 197.

[13]Bengt R. Hoffman, *Luther and the Mystics* (Minneapolis: Augsburg, 1976).

[14]Jean Leclerc, *Bernard of Clairvaux and the Cistercian Spirit* (Kalamazoo, Mich.: Cistercian Publications, 1976), p. 110. See the excellent study on monastic culture and literature by Jean Leclerc, *The Love of Learning and the Desire for God* (New York: Fordham University Press, 1974).

[15]Jean Leclerc, *Monks and Love in Twelfth Century France* (Oxford: Clarendon University Press, 1979), pp. 8-26.

[16]See for example, Robert W. Hanning, *The Individual in Twelfth Century Romance* (New Haven, Conn.: Yale University Press, 1977).

[17]Jean Leclerc, *The Love of Learning*, pp. 187-232.

[18]Jean Mabillon, *Life and Works of Saint Bernard, Abbot of Clairvaux*, trans. by Samuel J. Eales (London: John Hodges, 1896).

[19]Armand Ravelet, *Oeuvres de Saint Bernard*, 5 tomes (Paris: Victor Palme, 1866-70).

[20]George Stanhope, *Pious Breathings, Being the Meditations of St. Augustine, St. Anselm, and St. Bernard*, 4th ed. (London: J. Knapton, 1714).

INTRODUCTION

In 1953, the eighth centenary of Bernard's death, Pope Pius XII issued an encyclical. It celebrated Bernard as the Doctor Mellifluous, not in any sickly sweet sentimentality, but as a true Father of the church. And it claimed him as one who gives life.

In his book *The Last of the Fathers*, Thomas Merton associates Bernard with Psalm 46:4 as a stream of the river making the City of God joyful.[1] In our information society today, a society which does not have the wisdom and humility to know always how to use that knowledge, Bernard and his friends give us renewed perspectives in five major areas of life. If we followed these men of God, they would radically change our lives today by giving faith, hope, and love with abundant fruitfulness.

I. Knowledge and the Existential Experience of God

Historians speak of the "renaissance of the twelfth century." This period saw the recovery of classical literature and Roman law, Greek science and its Arabic additions, and much of Greek philosophy and its scholastic applications to academic theology. The age was marked by a new realism about the observable world of nature and about the real events in the chronology of history. It also saw a new sense of the identity of the individual through romantic love and chivalry.

In such a cultural milieu, Anselm's dictum, *Credo ut Intelligam*,

"I believe in order that I may understand," could become abused to mean that faith was one step towards theological intellectualism. Knowledge for knowledge's sake was the threat to the Christian faith that William of St.-Thierry and Bernard saw so clearly. This they pointed out in their attacks on men like Peter Abelard. Boldly Bernard emphasized *Credo ut Experiar* instead: "I believe that I may experience," that is, experience the reality of God.

The early Cistercians argued that we are "in the school of Christ." Bernard emphasizes this clearly in his *Sermons on the Song of Songs*. The first page begins by saying: "The instructions that I address to you, my brothers, will differ from those I would address to those out in the world; at least, the manner would be different . . . it is Paul's method of teaching . . . a more nourishing diet to those who are enlightened spiritually. . . . We teach," he says, "not in the way philosophy is taught, but in the way the Holy Spirit teaches us; we teach spiritual things spiritually"[2] (1 Corinthians 2:13). Bernard adds this in his 36th sermon: "Peter, Andrew, the sons of Zebedee, and the rest of the disciples were not chosen in the school of rhetoric or philosophy, yet it was through their ministry that the Savior brought the work of redemption to fulfillment for the rest of the world."

Christ and His Word are so interchangeable in Bernard's thought that neither can be separated. He is not anti-intellectual. "I am far from saying that the knowledge of literature is to be despised, for it provides culture and skill. It enables a man to instruct others. But the knowledge of God and of one's self must come first, for they are essential to salvation. . . . Know yourself and you will have a wholesome fear of God. Know God and you will also love God. In the first, wisdom has its beginning; and in the second, it has its crown. For 'the fear of the Lord is the beginning of wisdom' (Psalm 111:10), and 'love is the fulfilling of the law' (Romans 13:10). You must avoid both kinds of ignorance, because without fear and love salvation is not possible" (Sermon 37, I, II).

The fear of the Lord is, for Bernard, the biblical concept of fear. It is as if one were living in the very presence of God, and the love of which he speaks is the love of God in Christ. These truths, then, can only be learned in Christ.

In his *Treatise on Humility and Pride*, Bernard gives three steps that lead to truth. These are, in fact, the essence of the Beatitudes. First, the sinner needs to have his intellect humbled by

Christ—to be "poor in spirit"—so that he learns to know himself and become a disciple. Second, he needs to have the Holy Spirit so change his will that he is merciful towards other people, learns to know others, and becomes a friend of God. Third, he needs God the Father to so enrapture him in contemplation that he is purified in heart to know or "see God."

Thus the goal of humility, the basis of this learning, is to know the truth. Pride in contrast leads only to ignorance and foolishness, and the proud person is without God in the world.

Bernard's friend William of St.-Thierry also upheld the supernatural character of faith, a stance that opposed the critical spirit of Peter Abelard. The latter defined faith as "an opinion concerning things unseen that are not perceptible to the bodily senses." In denying the supernatural character of faith, Abelard rebutted William and left one's soul prey to the cankerworm of doubt. There were disastrous consequences. Yet William contended against such thought. "Faith does not dwell in a man's heart as an opinion or as a conjecture. A man is fully conscious of it as he is of other unquestionable knowledge. God forbid that Christian faith should in any way resemble those opinions or assessments of the Academicians which teach that a man should believe nothing and know nothing but conjecture about everything" *(Disputation Against Abelard I).*

Sacred learning as these early Cistercians saw it was nurtured by a monastic culture of desire for God as a lifelong preoccupation. They cultivated their worshipful quest by silent meditation on the Word of God and by prayer. Scripture was studied for its own sake.

These early writers saturated their works in Scripture as the materials in this book clearly show. Scripture was "masticated" by the constant repetition and memorization of verses. It was daily recited in their services. They united Scripture with meditation and prayer. Each writer's thought flowed naturally from his public communication with his readers to the presence, once more, of God.

In his last and unfinished sermon on the Canticles, Bernard speaks of our communion with God on "the bed of his weakness" and in "the night of his ignorance." In such a posture, the seeking soul, like the Bride, will seek the Word as the power and the wisdom of God.

II. The Primary Importance of Love

There can be no spiritual literature without spiritual experience. Had Bernard and his friends merely collected the *florilegia* of others, they would have been assessed as writers—but not as saints. Sanctity can only be expressed by deeds.

So in the sermon that might be considered to contain Bernard's secret of living—his last completed sermon on the Canticles—he makes the statement that follows. "Now someone may ask me what it is like to enjoy the Word. My answer is, 'Look for someone who has had actual experience and ask him. Yet do you think that if I had been granted that experience, that I could describe to you what is beyond description? . . . The tongue does not teach this; grace does. It is hidden from the wise and the prudent, and it is revealed unto babes (Luke 10:21). . . . It is the virtue of humility, then, which is counted worthy to possess what it does not possess.' In its unworthiness, the soul experiences God's worthiness, 'because it pleases the Father of the World, the Bridegroom of the soul, Jesus Christ our Lord, who is God above all, blessed for ever. Amen' (Romans 9:5)." This language of love summarizes his whole theology.

Pascal would say during his life, "It is the heart, not the reason, which experiences God. This then is faith: God perceived by the heart and not by reason."

But in the twelfth century, Bernard had already begun his theology of love. "Love is the fountain of life, and the soul which does not drink from it cannot be called alive." This is the beginning and the end of life, for "God is love." Since love is of God, the experience of love in God can come only through Jesus Christ His Son.

It is the gift of love that orients the soul to God. Thus love is not something that is just desirable and pleasant to experience, as one option among others. It is man's whole reason for existing at all. That is why the figure of the bride in the Canticles appealed to these theologians of love. It is the proper imagery of the soul before God. In his treatise *On The Love Of God,* Bernard examines our universal obligation to love God "because He is God," and he finds that the measure of our love is "to love Him without measure."

If man is made to be a lover, then that means that he is created free, free to choose. But by reason of the fall of man, man chooses the wrong things in idolatry, absolutizing created things instead of the Creator. He loves also selfishly, loving himself in the place of God. Man, therefore, has by grace to grow out of such baser and perverted forms of love and come to love God for His own sake and to also love himself as God loves him. Then he shall relate to God not by fusion, as water may identify in a barrel of wine, but as a bride to a bridegroom, free to choose the one loved.

Bernard's treatise *On Free Will and Grace* is, therefore, fundamental to his theology of love. This is only another way of seeing once more that man is made to love God. But to love God with disinterested love, he must first be free. Relating to God, then, becomes a progressive growth in freedom.

William of St.-Thierry sees that "the art of arts is love. It is jealously taught by nature and God, the author of nature. Developed in the very depths of the human soul by the Creator, this love has its native land in God."

Thus William prefaces the beginning of his treatise *On the Nature and Dignity of Love* with discussion about the art of loving. Drawing much from Augustine, he sees that the exercise of love lies in the will. But in the willfullness of sin and its rebellion against God, love is impure and deflected from loving God. So William says, "Only those who humbly obey God are really docile to love." It needs the Will or Spirit of God to transform our own wills in order to love God as we should. The will, then, may lead either to ruin or to blessing in willing to love God.

In the experience of the love of God within our hearts, we may be granted specific evidences of God in our soul. These are encouragements for us to practice charity that we might realize the love "being shed abroad in our hearts by the Holy Spirit" (Romans 5:5). We shall then begin to find that love and reason give us bifocal vision on life; we are given depth to reality that is beyond mere intellectualism as love enlightens reason and reason instructs love. Without love, reason leads only to pride, while love without reason is passion. This bifocal view, then, provides wisdom. Indeed it is the love of God within us that is true wisdom, for wisdom is only another name for the enjoyment of God. None less than Christ Himself "is made unto us wisdom," says the apostle. So William is also telling us that the loving and contemplating of God in enjoyment is only possible in and through Christ.

As Aelred examines the natural tendency of man to love, called *affectus,* which man is inclined toward, he sees that the longing of man for love is the longing for a beatific life. This life is what God really created man to have. Just as it is natural for a stone to fall or for a fish to swim, so it is for man to love. This inclination to friendship may thus be extended to see that God is friendship. Aelred consequently raises no objection in his dialogue with Ivo when the latter ventures to paraphrase the Apostle John's text, "God is friendship. . . . He who dwells in friendship dwells in God and God in him."

The flowering of friendship in our lives makes us more fully human. The deepening of love for a friend also shows us that infinitely greater possibilities we see again for our communion and union with God. Aelred opens up for us the exciting possibilities we have of enriching our vertical relationship with God by the horizontal embodiment of friendships with others. "Friend of man can become friend of God" *(Spiritual Friendship).* But this is no mere humanistic friendship, for Aelred would remind us he is talking about "spiritual friendship," a gift of God's grace through Jesus Christ our Redeemer. Man's love needs first to be redeemed and restored if it is to be this kind of friendship.

III. A BIBLICAL UNDERSTANDING OF SCRIPTURE

Friendship with God was sustained and nurtured in these early Cistercians by meditation on the Scriptures. As we have seen they were saturated in the Scriptures. Their desire for God was one with their desire to know and to obey His Word. "Christ in all the Scriptures" was a reality to them. This was made possible because their *hermeneutic* was more complex than ours today. By that we mean that their interpretation of the text of Scripture was fourfold whereas ours today tends to be only on one level.

Our literary interest tends towards mastery or at least a strong grasp of the text. Medieval monastic learning was rather one of compunction, that is, of desiring to communicate with God and to be at one with Him. They wanted rather to "taste" God than to talk about Him. Since God was their desire, and God dwells in heaven, they sought to be heavenly-minded scholars. They were not preoccupied, then, with the Ph.D. or its theological equivalents in academia, which is the bane and secularization of much theology today.

To be elegant in literary style was recognized as homage to God, and, in this respect, the Latin of Bernard is "mellifluous." But the Cistercians believed that the interpreter of Scripture should be more than a man of letters or scholarship. Above all, he should be a spiritual man.

Biblical scholarship needs to be rethought today, for it has largely become empirical inquiry of historical criticism. The focus is on the exercise of textual, historical, and literary criticism to find what is supposed to be the precise meaning and intent of what the author really wanted to say. But in the contemporary quest for meaning as such, the response of the reader may be quite overlooked. The method may fail to involve the reader in the intent of the message.

The oversight mentioned above is why biblical scholars of our day and age can be world renowned for their expertise with Scripture and lack any personal or moral engagement with the truth at all. This would have horrified men like Bernard, and he would have questioned whether even as a matter of scholarship this could be possible. For, like his contemporaries, he interpreted the Bible in a fourfold way: (1) literally, in terms of the historical context of the text; (2) allegorically, in seeing Christ in all the Scriptures; (3) tropologically, in obedience to the correction or instruction in morals; and (4) anagogically, in that Scripture is still to be fulfilled, so that the reader is exhorted to heavenly contemplation. It was a system of understanding the Bible that went back to Cassian, Gregory the Great, and continued through the Reformation. Certainly there could be abuse with this fourfold approach to Scripture, but as David C. Steinmetz has said, "The medieval theory of levels of meaning in the biblical text, with all its undoubted defects, flourished because it is true, while the modern theory of a single meaning, with all its demonstrable virtues, is false." The early Cistercians saw godliness as an aspect of biblical scholarship itself, an aspect which is seldom emphasized today. Somehow, then, the return to biblical authority must be more than a doctrine of inerrancy, a doctrine which may simply reinforce an empirical approach to Scripture that is koranic and not truly biblical.

It was the contemplation of the truth of Scripture that made Bernard learned, and it was the contemplation of justice that made him wise. Such knowledge was more than intellectual

knowledge. It was volitional since it involved obedience and response to the Word of God. The metaphorical language of the
bride, that is to say, the metaphorical language of the desire for
God, meant the union of love and knowledge to Bernard. Therefore, just as Bernard attacked Abelard for a lack of true scholarship, so too we should attack the blindness of rational thought. In
its perversity of will, it does not deliver truth to man today without
a humble and repentant heart.

IV. Biblical Anthropology as the Basis of True Humanness

Bernard implicitly taught that man was created in the image
and the likeness of God (Genesis 1:26). (William and Aelred
taught this more explicitly.) They and other medieval writers read
this also in Augustine, although each had their own detail and emphasis in teaching this doctrine. God created man to be a noble
creature, argued Bernard, but man exchanged the divine image for
an earthly one (Romans 1:23). This evil decision of Adam's is now
hereditary so that man is born corrupt.

Bernard associates "the image" more specifically with man's
will. Man still has freedom of choice, so "the image" remains. But
when man willed to lose the freedom not to sin, and the freedom
not to have the misery of an impotent will, then his likeness to
God was lost. Man is not happy, then, for he remains in "the land
of unlikeness." He is an exile from the intentions of God for him.

William of St.-Thierry sees that journey home to the Father as
the story of the prodigal son. In the far country, the son remembers
who he once was, so he places the emphasis not on freedom of will,
but on the memory of what God has made man originally.

Moreover, William is more concerned about the restoration of
the "image" by the action of the Holy Spirit. He connects memory
with the Father, reason with the Son, and the love which proceeds
from both in the Holy Spirit. The Trinity is needed for man to recover his status. Since the Holy Spirit is the union of the Father
and the Son, only by the Holy Spirit will that union between man
and God be restored also. This only occurs in man's exercise of
faith in God.

Aelred thinks also of the return journey of man, the exile, to the image and likeness of God. Aelred sees the need of the image being healed. Now man's memory is forgetful of God, man's knowledge is full of self-deception, and man's love is self-centered. Like Bernard, Aelred sees the will as being crucial to counter the weight of self-interest if man is to become more like God.

Contemporary Roman Catholic writers make perhaps too much of the distinction between the "image" and "likeness" of Genesis 1:26. For example, Odo Brooke, who has written a series of articles on William of St.-Thierry, argues that the "image" gives man the potential for realizing the "likeness" by the process of sanctification. This sanctification comes as a result of man's self efforts. This seems to be reading more into the texts than is warranted.

The early Cistercians do not see man as having any latent potential in himself to achieve this likeness to God. William's own emphasis is rather that this process is all the operation of the Holy Spirit, from His initiative to His active agency. Man's capacity for God is rather in terms of his need and not his own efforts for self-actualization.

The biblical teaching on the "image" suggests less emphasis on the idea of resemblance and more on the idea of being God's representative, His steward over resources, or His viceroy deputized to rule over a kingdom. Indeed, the idea of "domination" is explicit in the same text of Genesis 1:26. This is more of an ethical reality than merely a matter of resemblance; it is more of what is required of man rather than what man himself can achieve. It also links up more clearly with the New Testament emphasis of Christ as the image of God. He is the head of the new humanity that still has an eschatological dimension of fulfillment to come.

Limited as the doctrine of the "image" was for these early Cistercians, it clearly established the dignity that man had before God and of man's responsibility to God. Their understanding is therefore much needed today with all the false humanism that prevails in the narcissistic cult of self-fulfillment. This cult of the human personality has no fear of God nor love for Him. The less that we concentrate on self-development and the more we love Christ unabashedly like these Cistercians did, the more truly human we shall become. Man becomes most human when he becomes most godly, and this can only begin when he forgets himself to be in love with God.

V. Spiritual Friendship

A modern writer has asked wisely, "If theologians cannot speak perceptively about the mystery of human love, how can they hope to communicate the meaning of divine love as an existential power?"

Reversing this, Aelred argued that if Jesus must be loved as the dearest of friends, then every human friendship that is spiritual and according to Christ is an excellent way of encouraging devotion to Christ. "As soon as a man is a friend of another, he is the friend of God." The reason clearly is because God is love.

Was Aelred too optimistic about the possibility of human friendship being so exalted? Yes, we might be tempted to say so, unless we remember his insistence upon "spiritual" friendship.

Aelred's writing on *Spiritual Friendship*, the third part of his treatise on *The Mirror of Charity* (which spells out the principles of true friendship), along with the whole genre of letter-writing among his friends teaches us that the School of Love must be a community of friends also.

In an age when self-realization leads to intense alienation and few people have the experience of real friendships, Aelred's message is refreshing and challenging. "I call them more beasts than men," he says bluntly, "who say life should be led without the need for others, without the need for consolation, without time or patience for those who may cause trouble or distress for others, and, therefore, are persons who take no pleasure in the good of others, who believe their failure is no one else's business, and who therefore seek help from no one and want no one else's love."

Aelred speaks from personal experience about the need to have real friends. In the Prologue to *Spiritual Friendship*, he speaks of his adolescent need of friends. Like the young Augustine who authored *Confessions*, his delight was to love and be loved.

Aelred also tells us that he read Cicero's book *On Friendship*. At first he was delighted with it, but as he began to compare it with the Scriptures, he began to realize that the two did not contain the same language. "Nothing had been sweetened with the honey of the beloved Jesus; nothing that had not been seasoned with the salt of the holy Scriptures could quite hold my heart," admitted Aelred. Without the authority of the Scriptures, he realized there could be no foundation for spiritual friendship. The fact was that the stoicism of Cicero knew nothing of the love of God. Nevertheless, the prudence of the world often does teach us much. And so Aelred culled from this literature, from the writings of the Fathers, and from his own lifetime's experience what he considered to be rules for a pure and holy love.

In three dialogues among friends, Aelred used the genre of friendship to talk about friendship.

In the first dialogue, he deals with the origin and essence of friendship. In the second dialogue, he considers the value and limits of friendship. In the third, he more randomly considers some of the practical difficulties about friendship.

As a fallen sinner, Aelred is well aware that friendship cannot be idealized. Instead, friendship has to be tested, pruned, weeded, and cleansed of false motives and self-seeking relations. Moreover, unless friendship is constantly looked at from a divine perspective, it will become corrupted. So it must constantly be seen as coming from God.

We must always be on our guard against false friendships, such as friendship for carnal pleasure or friendship for material gain. The one offends against "good will" since we indulge in sexual pleasures willfully, and the other offends against "charity" since it pretends to be real affection for the other person when, in fact, it is a love of material goods. The only true friendship is that which combines both "good will" and "true charity." To do this really combines the love of God with our love of others.

The cultivation of such spiritual friendship is not an end in itself. Aelred sees it as a part in the process of becoming like Christ. Quoting from the Gospel, Aelred writes, " 'I have appointed you that you should go forth,' says the Lord, 'and should bring forth fruit.' That fruit is love for one another. For in true friendship one travels by making progress and receives the fruit of the experience by the delight of its perfection. Thus spiritual friendship is begotten between the good who have lives, habits, and interests that are alike, which is in accord in benevolence and charity on things human and divine." Such true friendship is only one step away from heaven as one loves in Christ, on behalf of Christ, and for one's friend who is in Christ. "Thus," concludes Aelred, "from the holy love with which he embraces his friend, one rises to that by which he embraces Christ."

I would urge our generation to recover a deep, loving interest in the writings of Bernard and his friends, William and Aelred. For those brought up in evangelical families, the knowledge of doctrine has often been too cheaply available. It needs the slow, personal experience of God and His ways to nurture real faith, and not the rapidity with which theology is taught in the classroom or read in "how to" books. To those who fear the encroaching secularism of faith by professionalism within the church today, these writers are a good antidote. Against this spirit of religious technocracy and scholasticism some of us have fought hard, and suffered accordingly.

Today we may not have the obsession of medieval romantic love, but we are still confused about the reality of love. A spiritual renewal among us today must include a new reverence for love, the reality of the love of God, and the practical demonstration of God's love in our personal relationships. Performance must become once more subservient to authentic relationships. The dimension of the heart needs to be reinstated as more fundamental than the cleverness of our brains. The faculty of the desire for God and the gardening we need to do in a contemplative, interior life are essential to recover—if we would live more genuinely before God. We have overrated the role of reason because we have been seduced by the wonders of science and technology. To turn one's back on academia for the love of God seems anti-intellectual to those who do not know the spirit of the early Cistercians, but it is reassuring to those who take the risks of truly loving God and one another today.

Biblical authority today is in much confusion. Scripture must be interpreted, not just as a text, but in reverence, love, and obedience as the medieval scholars did. When this fuller interpretation takes place, then scholarship will be one again with godliness. Perhaps the reform of the hermeneutical endeavor is one of the greatest challenges of our day for biblical scholarship. Renewed attention to the early Cistercians may help in this respect.

From many quarters one senses a desire for the interpretation of the Christian faith in terms of genuine humanness. Secular anthropology, psychology, and sociology are being found wanting in their prescriptions about man. The lack of reverence for human life and the lack of sacredness for the individual in our society challenge us to reconsider the dignity of man before God. Divorce, sexual immorality, unemployment, superficial relationships, lack of compassion—all would challenge us to renew acquaintance with the biblical understanding of man held by previous generations of God lovers such as the Cistercians.

Finally, I am convinced that these writers had far more sense than we have today about the reality of friendship with God and with other human beings. Yet it is the suffering of betrayal, of mourning the superficiality of personal life, and of the indifference to the needs of others in our society that may once more alert us to the meaning of what "spiritual friendship" is all about. Should we as Christians be awakened to these realities, then we might indeed experience another Renaissance of the Holy Spirit in our dying culture.

James M. Houston

---

[1]Thomas Merton, *The Last of the Fathers* (New York: Harcourt, Brace, and Co., 1954), p.11.

[2]See for example M.—D. Chenu, *Nature, Man and Society in the Twelfth Century* (Chicago: University of Chicago Press, 1968), pp. 1-48.

Part I
THE DIGNITY OF THE SOUL BEFORE GOD

I

THE DIGNITY OF MAN'S SOUL*

ANY ARE DEEPLY LEARNED IN THE VARIOUS disciplines of the Arts and the Sciences. Yet they continue to remain profoundly ignorant about themselves. They are inquisitive about the affairs of other men, and yet they remain void of thought or care about themselves.

Indeed, even in their essential and best studies where God is the subject of inquiry, these scholars still assume God is to be found only in the external world. They overlook the evidences of Him within their own breasts. They do not realize that no one else can be so intimate to them as God Himself. So I desire to look within, rather than to the outside world. . . .

Now when I turn my eyes inward, I discover three distinct faculties of my soul that enable me to remember, contemplate, and desire God. These are the faculties of memory, understanding, and will.

Three faculties of the soul

By the first of these faculties, I recollect. By the second, I discern. By the third, I love and embrace God. When I reflect upon God, I find Him in my memory and delight in Him by those memories which He has been pleased to im-

*This essay was written by William of St.-Thierry as *The Nature of Body and Soul.* These excerpts are from book eight. It is uncertain when this work was composed.

3

part to me. By my intellect, I see what God is in Himself. I see what are His angels and His saints, what man is, and indeed what are the other works of His hand. Each of these contribute to show His excellence.

But God in Himself is incomprehensible, the Beginning and the End. He is the Beginning without conclusion, and the End without any more excellent End. When, then, I reflect upon myself, I realize God must exceed all comprehension because I find that I cannot even know myself. Yet I am but one of God's creatures. If I consider God's relationship to the angels, then He appears lovely and infinitely desirable because their constant employment and bliss is to behold and to look upon Him. The saints themselves find God full of delight as their blessed spirits rejoice in Him.

In men, God is the most worthy object of love because He is *their* God and they are His people (Exodus 5:1). He dwells in them as His own house. They are His temple in which His divine presence resides (2 Corinthians 6:16). He does not disdain mankind nor any single individual. Rather whoever remembers, understands, and loves Him, the same is with God. We ought to love God "because He first loved us" (1 John 4:19).

He made us after His own image and in His own likeness, a privilege given to no other creature. Now when we are said to be made after God's image (Genesis 1:27), the meaning may be that we are made to understand and to be acquainted with the Son. By the Son we come to understand and know the Father and gain access to God.

So near is the relation between us and the Son of God that the Son of God Himself is the express image of the Father (Colossians 1:15). We are made after that image of Him. This nearness of relationship is further signified by use of the express phrase made "after His likeness" (Genesis 1:26) rather than the words "after His image." That which is made after the image of another must agree with the original model. But it has only an empty name unless it also has a real likeness to justify it.

Let us then be careful to express both the image and the likeness of God by desiring peace, contemplating truth, and loving charity. Let us keep God in our remembrance, having Him in our consciences and behaving ourselves with the deference and reverence that is becoming to those who believe God to be always present in them. For if our mind reflects His image, then it is capable of receiving and partaking of Him. It is *His* image because it is capable also of rising still higher to remember, consider, and love its Maker. In doing so, there consists true maturity and wisdom. Nothing comes so near to that perfect wisdom above as the rational mind. By its three faculties of memory, understanding, and will, it subsists in that ineffable Trinity of the Godhead as an image does to its original.

Preserving the image of God

Let us therefore be careful to remember this. Let us endeavor to love Him by whom man is endowed with the capacity to be forever blessed.

Blessed, then, is that soul with whom God takes up His residence and makes it the place of His rest. Blessed is he who can say, "He that formed me has lodged and dwelt in my tabernacle." For to such a one God cannot deny the rest of heaven.

Why, then, do we go outside of ourselves to seek God in external objects when all the while He is with us and in us, if we will only make it our preoccupation to be with Him and in Him? For He is certainly with us and in us when we have a living faith in Him. This is all the union we can ever want unless it be that of seeing Him "face to face" (1 Corinthians 13:12). The Apostle assures us that "Christ dwells in our hearts by faith" (Ephesians 3:17). For Christ is our faith.

By faith, then, I reflect upon and remember God as my Creator. I adore Him as my Redeemer. I wait for Him as my Savior. I believe I see Him in all His creatures and that I have Him within myself.

Above all else, I know Him as He is. For to know the Father, the Son, and the Holy Spirit is life eternal (John 17:3). This is infinite delight and the fullness of all joy. No mortal can conceive how bright, how sweet, and how ravishing that vision shall be when we shall see God face to face. This is the Light of them who shine by His reflection. This is the Rest of those who have been exercised by labors and sufferings. This is that Country of them who are called home from their exile. This is the Life of those who live and the Crown of them who have overcome.

The mind, as the likeness of God

In the meanwhile, the image of that blessed Trinity—which I find in my soul—teaches me that I ought to make the main motive of all my actions the realization that memory, understanding, and the love of God reflect Him. For the mind is the likeness of God in which there are three powers: memory, understanding, and will. We attribute our advance in knowledge to memory, even though, strictly speaking, it is not the faculty by which we think. We attribute all our knowledge to the understanding, also, by thinking we find out the truth. When we find truth, we commit it to the custody of our memory.

The Triune likeness

Memory is more particularly our resemblance to our Father. Understanding is more so related to the Son. Our will is likewise related to the Holy Spirit. No part of us is more like the Holy Spirit as is our will or love. For kind affection is nothing else than a modification and exaltation of the will in which is its proper excellence. Love is not only a gift but it is the best gift of God (1 John 4:9, 10). For that love which is of God, and which God is, is properly called the Holy Spirit, by which the love of God is shed abroad in our hearts (Romans 5:5) and all the Trinity dwells in us.

Let then that Image of God which is in you be awakened. Preserve such reverence for your person as is due to God's temple. For the greatest honor we can ever give to God is our worship and our imitation. Every devout, heavenly-minded Christian is an imitator of God. For a devout mind is like a temple consecrated to God's service, and a pure heart is the altar that sanctifies every gift. Moreover, you worship God with reverence when you are merciful as your Father in heaven is merciful. For the apostle has declared that to give and to do good for God's

sake are sacrifices with which He is well pleased (Hebrews 13:16).
 In all things submit yourself to be a child of God so that you reproach not His Sonship. He has adopted you by His wonderful mercy. In all you do be sure to consider and act as one who is aware that God is always with you and by your side. Take heed, then, not only to your external senses but also to your most secret imaginations of thought so that none will possess you with lust or other sinful desires.

Nothing can be so restless and fleeting—no part of my nature can be so changeful—than my heart. How exceedingly vain, trifling, wandering, and unsettled is this vagabond. Never fixed on the will of God, never stirred by divine guidance and counsel, it follows instead its own whims. It is in perpetual motion, without any principle of rest within it. It is under a thousand different determinations at once and flies about after innumerable quests. It makes experiments but to no purpose. It seeks rest everywhere but it finds it not. Happiness flies away from it.
 My heart's pursuits are endless. It is not even consistent with itself as it changes its proposals, inclinations, and aversions. It starts fresh projects, sets them up, and then it pulls them down; and it runs the race over and over again. All this is from its own mercurial nature that can lie still nowhere. It must always be in motion although its actions are in self-contradiction.

The restlessness of the heart

So when the soul falls away from worthy causes, and it becomes bewildered by sordid affections—then vanity seizes it, curiosity distracts it, covetous desires allure it, pleasure seduces it, luxury defiles it, envy racks it, anger ruffles it, and grief afflicts and depresses it. The soul is then overwhelmed and sinks into all manner of vice. All this happens because it forsakes God, for He alone is the answer to all the heart's wants and desires. Thus the mind is dissipated and scattered among a multitude of trifles. Although it seeks anxiously for satisfaction, yet it cannot attain any until it returns to the All-Sufficient object of

The vulnerability of the soul

the heart. . . .

The conditions of my being are such that I cannot live in subjection to myself but only in being subject to Him. I can never have the mastery of my own heart. Only God has that. So long, then, as I am not united to God, I am divided within myself and at perpetual strife within myself. Now this union with God can only be secured by love. And the subjection to Him can only be grounded in humility. And the humility can only be the result of knowing and believing the truth, that is to say, having the right notions of God and of myself.

How necessary it is to inquire diligently about the true state of my soul. Then I will discover how vile, weak, fickle, and corruptible I am. Then I will discover also how vital it is to lay hold of God and to hold Him fast, for it is from Him that I derive my being and without Whom I am nothing. And because it is of sin that I have departed from my God, the way back to God is by true confession and repentance of those sins which set me at such a distance from Him.

II

THREE STAGES OF THE
SPIRITUAL LIFE*

S ONE STAR DIFFERS
FROM ANOTHER, OR AS
one cell from the next, so the spirit of the
beginner, the spirit of the one making
progress, and the spirit of the mature can be distinguished.
The state of the beginner may be called "animal," the
state of the one making progress "rational," and the state
of the mature "spiritual."

Every religious institution is made up of these three
categories of men. Those in the state called "animal" are
those who are not yet governed by reason nor yet by the affections. They are stimulated by authority and good example or are led by teaching. But they are still like blind
men led by the hand, acquiescing in the good where they
find it, and following and imitating others.

Then there are the "rational" who judge by their reason
and the discernment that comes from natural learning.
They know the good and are desirous of it. But they are
still without love.

Finally, there are the spiritually mature who are led by
the spirit and are more abundantly enlightened by the
Holy Spirit. They are called "spiritual" because the Holy
Spirit rests upon them as He dwelt with Gideon (Judges
6:34).

*This essay is from *The Golden Epistle* by William of St.-Thierry.

9

Each state of man
can progress.
The first state is concerned only with the body, the second with the soul, but the third finds rest only in God. Each can make progress of sorts as each has its own development.

Progress of the first state is by perfect obedience so that control is gained over the body as it is brought into subjection. Its climax is when this becomes a pleasurable habit.

The rational state advances as the knowledge learned is that of faith. Thus progress is made as it lives according to the teaching of faith.

Maturity is reached as the soul passes from the judgment of reason to that of spiritual affection. Maturity of the rational state leads into the beginning of the spiritual state. Progress in the spiritual state is looking upon the glory of God with uncovered face (2 Corinthians 3:18). Its fullness is to be transformed into the same likeness, from glory to glory, as it is enabled by the Spirit of the Lord.

THE FIRST, OR ANIMAL STATE

Animality is a form of life which is dominated by the senses. It is engrossed in the pleasure afforded by material things that it loves, and thus it feeds its sensuality. Since it is accustomed to think only of the bodily senses and to assume that nothing exists except what it has left outside or it has brought back into itself, it finds its happiness is possible only in living with bodily pleasures.

This state turned away from God becomes folly when it is excessively turned in upon itself. It is so wild that it is ungovernable. When it is controlled, it can appear to be wise—yet it is still folly. As the apostle declares: "Claiming to be wise, they were made fools" (Romans 1:22).

However, when turned towards God, this animal state can become holy simplicity. It is the simplicity of the will wholly turned towards God in conversion which seeks only one thing of the Lord—to dwell with Him (Psalm 27:4). Such simplicity then possesses in itself some of the beginning of God's creation (James 1:18) and enables God to act within the soul. Together with "the fear of the Lord which is the beginning of wisdom," it can begin to develop all the fullness of virtues. These virtues are justice, because it defers to a superior; prudence, because it does not trust itself; temperance, because it refrains from deciding for itself; and fortitude, because it submits itself wholly to obedience and is concerned not to judge but to do only what it is told to do.

Reaching the maturity of the "animal" state, or of the spiritual novice, is not a quick event. It is not a task completed after the moment of conversion nor in a day. Rather, it demands a long time and much labor and sweat. It depends also upon God's mercy and grace as well as on man's willingness and alacrity (Romans 6:16).

Maturity of the "animal" state

Spiritual disciplines will demand the cell of solitude as a workshop and enduring perseverance in that shop. In it, anyone who is on good terms with his own sense of inner poverty is rich. Whoever possesses good will is endowed with all that he needs to live well. Yet good will is not always to be trusted, for it must be kept in check and controlled—especially by a beginner. Rather let the discipline of holy obedience be good will, and let good will rule the body.

In the morning, demand an account of yourself for the night which is past and draw up a program for yourself for the day that lies ahead. In the evening, call a reckoning of the day that is now past and lay down a rule for the night that is coming. If you are strict in this way, you will not have the leisure for inordinate pleasures. Anyone who has the mind of Christ (1 Corinthians 2:16) knows also how profitable it is to Christian piety, how fitting and profitable it is to God's servant—the servant of Christ's redemption—to devote at least one hour to an attentive review of the benefits of Christ's passion and redemption. This causes one to savor these benefits in spirit and to store them away faithfully in the memory. This is spiritually to eat of the body of the Lord and to drink His blood in re-

108 By meditation

membrance of His commandment: "Do this in remembrance of Me" (Luke 22:19).

By reading   At fixed times, hours should be given to specific reading. For haphazard reading, constantly varied, and done as if by chance, does not edify, but makes the mind unstable. Taken into the memory lightly, it only goes out even more lightly. You should concentrate upon certain authors and let your mind grow accustomed to them.

The Scriptures need to be read in the same spirit as the way in which they were written. You will never enter into Paul's meaning until, by reading him with constant application and by giving yourself to constant meditation, you imbibe his spirit. Likewise, you will never understand David until by your own personal experience you have made the very sentiments of the Psalms your own.

This insight applies to all Scripture. There is the same gulf between attentive study and mere reading as there is between real friendship and mere acquaintance, or between deep companionship and a passing and chance encounter. Some part of your daily reading should also be committed to memory.

126   The reading should also stimulate the desire to pray which should interrupt the reading. Yet it is an interruption which in fact restores the mind to even more purified understanding. For reading serves the purpose for which it is done. If the reader truly seeks God in his reading, then everything that he reads tends to promote that end. The reader makes the mind surrender in the course of that reading and brings all that is understood under captivity to Christ (2 Corinthians 10:5).

By desire for God   Next, the beginner in the "animal" state, as Christ's raw recruit, should be taught to draw near to God so that God may draw near to him. Such is the apostle's exhortation: "Draw near unto God and He will draw near unto you" (James 4:8). [As a relational being], man has not only to be created and formed but he has also to be breathed into by the breath of God so that he becomes a

living spirit (Genesis 2:7). The formation of man as a
human is his mortal training. The formation of man as a
spiritual being is the love of God.

Now the love of God in man which is born of grace is
fed with the milk of [Scripture] reading, nourished with
the food of meditation, and strengthened and enlightened
by prayer. The best and safest reading matter for the meditation of the "animal" man—the one newly come to
Christ—is that which trains him in the interior life with
the outward actions of the Redeemer. In these actions he
will find an example of humility and a stimulant to love
and devotion. He should also be given the lives of the
saints and the accounts of their martyrdoms. He should
not trouble himself with historical details, but he should
always find something to stir him up to love God and to
despise himself.

The novice should be taught to raise his heart in prayer **By prayer**
in order to pray spiritually. He should stay as far as he can
from material objects when he thinks of God. He should
be exhorted to direct his attention with all the purity of
heart that he can give when he is offering the sacrifice of
his prayer. May he forget himself and appreciate what is
his offering, and what is its quality.

To the extent that the novice is able to see or understand to Whom he is making his offering, so he will reach
out to Him with his affections. Love will be his true understanding. For prayer is the affection of a man who clings to
God with an intimate and devout conversation. It is a
state in which the enlightened mind enjoys God as long as
it is permitted. Thanksgiving is an unwearying and undis-
tracted attention on the good will of God. It is the unin-
terrupted prayer of thanksgiving of which the apostle says:
"Pray without ceasing" (1 Thessalonians 5:17). This
prayer is constantly absorbed in thanksgiving because it is
the state of always being in the joy of the Holy Spirit.

THE SECOND, OR RATIONAL STATE

195   Passing from the state of "animal" to the rational state in our progress to the spiritual is an advance toward full reality. We have seen above that the spiritual progress of the "animal" state requires specific discipline of the body so that the outward man is prepared for the pursuit of virtue. Likewise, the "rational" man must busy himself with the spirit, either to bring it into existence if it does not already exist, or else to develop and to regulate it.

First of all, this question must be asked: Who or what is the spirit itself which makes the reason rational? What is the reason which makes a mortal animal a rational being and which brings him to maturity?

Maturity of the "rational" state   Man endowed with spirit becomes good and rational when he "loves the Lord His God with his whole heart and his whole soul, and all his mind and all his strength" (Deuteronomy 6:5). Only in God can he also love his neighbor as himself. He has that good spirit that fears God and keeps His commandments. This is the whole duty of man (Ecclesiastes 12:13).

Now if man excels the "animal" and the other parts of himself, then there is no worthier or more useful exercise for him to perform than to reach out to what is most excellent. There is nothing worthier to seek or sweeter to find or more useful to possess than what is only superior to man himself—God alone. Nor is He far from any of us, "for it is Him in whom we live and move and have our being" (Acts 17:27f.).

We live in God through faith; we move and progress in hope; and we have our being as in a permanent dwelling through love. For it was by Him, and for Him, that the rational spirit was created in order that its inclination might be toward Him (Song of Solomon 7:10), and that He should be its good. For it was from His goodness that the rational spirit was created to be His image and likeness (Genesis 1:26, 31) in order that, as long as man lived his life here, he should resemble God as nearly and as truly possible. Thus man should be holy as God is holy (1 John

3:3) and in the next life be as blessed as God is blessed.

In a word, all the greatness and goodness of the Spirit consists in looking upon and wondering at the aspiring for what is above. In this way the devoted image hastens to cling to its exemplar. For it is the image of God, and the fact that it is His image, which enables man to understand that he can and should cling to Him whose image he is.

By aspiring upwards

While on earth, memory, understanding, and love rule the body which has been entrusted to rational man. Above all, he loves always to be engaged in the sphere from where he knows he has received whatever he is and whatever he has (1 Corinthians 4:7). Here it is that his spirit's gaze is fixed from where he depends. While living with men, he does so not simply to live this mortal and human life but to share with them God's life and to seek and to obtain things of God.

Because of his spiritual nature, rational man loves to raise himself always to the things which are highest in the spiritual order—God and the things of God. This cannot be done by savoring proud thoughts but by loving devoutly, and living soberly, justly, and piously (Titus 2:12). These pursuits love silence, long for tranquillity of heart amidst bodily toil, accept poverty of spirit and peace when in outward distress, and cultivate a good conscience with complete purity of both heart and body.

It is the above pursuits which make the spirit what it is, whereas those empty studies are trifling, verbose, and wrangling, and are only designed to feed curiosity, dissipation, and corruption of the spirit. Similarly a will that has grown proud through habit often inflates the spirit with pride when the heart has dried up. From such a state of affairs there proceed vainglory, trust in one's self, neglect of God, boasting, disobedience, scorn, presumption, and other diseases of the spirit which arise from conceit and the habit of pride.

16   The Love of God

251
Maturity of the
"spiritual" state
When the object of man's thought is God and the things which belong to God, then the will reaches the stage when it becomes love. Then the Holy Spirit, the Spirit of life, makes His presence felt by way of love and gives life to all. The Spirit lends His assistance in prayer, in meditation, or in study in the midst of human weakness. Immediately the memory becomes wisdom and tastes with relish the good things of the Lord.

Now the thoughts which arise from the good things of God are brought to the intellect and are formed into the affections. The understanding of the one thinking, then, becomes the contemplation of the one loving. These thoughts are shaped into certain experiences of spiritual or divine sweetness which are brought before the gaze of one's spirit. And the spirit rejoices in them.

As much as it is possible for man, worthy thoughts are now entertained of God, if indeed "thought" is the correct term. For there is no *cognitatio* where there is no impelling principle or *cogit*, nor is anything impelled, *cognitur;* but there is only the awareness of God's abundant sweetness. This leads to exultation, jubilation, and a true experience of God's goodness on the part of the man who has sought Him in simplicity of heart.

By ridding one's
soul from false
attachments
This way of thinking about God does not lie at the disposal of the thinker. It is a gift of grace. It is bestowed by the Holy Spirit who breathes where He chooses (John 3:8), how He chooses, and upon whom He chooses. Man's part is simply to prepare his heart continually by ridding his will of foreign attachments, his reason of anxieties, and his memory of idle or absorbing business (though that business be of extreme necessity).

In the Lord's good time, and when He thinks fit, the elements of thought may be freed to do their proper work. Each element contributes its share to the outcome of joy in the soul. Then the will displays pure affection for the joy which the Lord gives. The memory yields faithful material. And the intellect affords the sweetness of experience.

A will that is neglected gives rise to thoughts that are idle and unworthy of God. A will that is corrupted yields thoughts that are perverse and alienated from God. A rightly ordered will leads, however, to thoughts that are necessary for the living of this life. A dutiful will engenders thoughts which are rich in the fruit of the Spirit and bring enjoyment to God. "Now the fruit of the Spirit," says the apostle, "is love, joy, peace, longsuffering, kindness, goodness, faithfulness, gentleness, self-control" (Galatians 5:22, 23).

252
By the exercise
of the will

In every kind of thought, the intention of the will determines its nature. By the intervention of God's mercy, the just is made more just; by His judgment, the bedeviled is still more defiled (Luke 6:45). Therefore, the man who desires to love the Lord or does already love Him should always question his spirit and examine his conscience about the motive and desire he has within himself. He needs also to ask what else the spirit hates or wills, and what are the false desires the flesh entertains in opposition to it (Galatians 5:17).

253

254

Consider first the object of the will's desire. Then examine the extent of the desire and the way in which the object is desired. If it is a man's basic desire to love God, then he should examine how much and in what way he desires God. Does he do it to the point of despising himself and everything else? Does this happen only in accordance with the judgment of reason or with the inclination of the mind as well, thus reinforcing the will by love, delight, charity, and unity of spirit? For such is the way in which God is to be loved.

By desiring God

"Love" is the strong inclination of the will toward God. "Delight" is a clinging to Him or a union with Him. "Charity" is the enjoyment of Him. But "unity of spirit" with God is for the man who has his heart in heaven, and it is that term for the will's progress toward God. No longer does he desire what God desires, or love God, but the soul is perfect in its love so that he can only will what God wills.

To will as God wills is to be like God. To be able to will only what God wills is already to be what God is. This is because for God, to will and to be are one and the same. Therefore, it is well said that we shall see Him fully when we shall be like Him [an inversion of 1 John 3:2]. Those who have become the sons of God have been enabled—not to be God—but to be what God is in holiness and in blessing. The source of their present holiness and their future blessedness is God Himself, Who is their holiness and their blessedness.

Likeness to God   Resemblance to God is the whole of man's perfection. There is a likeness to God which is lost only with life itself. This has been given to man by the Creator as evidence of the better and more sublime likeness which has been lost. It is possessed regardless of man's acceptance or refusal since it is derived from nature, not by will or effort.

But there is another likeness to God which is closer to God, because it is willed freely. This likeness consists of the virtues which inspire the soul to imitate the greatness of the Supreme Good, His greatness in goodness and His greatness in the eternal unwearying of His goodness.

There is yet one more likeness to God of which something has already been said. It is so close to God that it is better described as unity of spirit. It makes man one with God, one spirit. Not only is the unity of the "willing" the same, but even the inability to will anything else but what God wills is identical. It is called unity of spirit not only because the Holy Spirit inclines man's spirit and brings about this unity, but because this unity is the presence of the Holy Spirit Himself in the believer.

The Holy Spirit is charity. He is the love of the Father and of the Son. He is Their unity, sweetness, good, kiss, embrace, and whatever else They have in Their supreme unity of truth and truth of unity. The soul in its blessedness is caught between Their embrace and Their kiss as Father and Son. So the soul receives as the Son receives from the Father or as the Son gives to the Father.

In a manner that exceeds description or thought, the man of God receives what God is by grace.

Hitherto alone, man now becomes one with God and his bodily solitude is changed into unity of spirit. Our Lord's prayer for His disciples summed up all the character of spiritual maturity. It is fulfilled in Him. "Father, I will that as You and I are one, so also they may be one in Us" (John 17:21).

Since this inexpressible reality—man becoming one with God in Christ—can only be seen in an inexpressible way, the man who would experience it must cleanse his heart. For the truth of John 17 cannot be seen or understood by means of bodily likeness in dreams or in one's consciousness or by any investigation of one's mind. It can only be found by humble love from a clean heart (Matthew 5:8). This reality is the face of God which no man can see when he lives as part of the world (Exodus 33:20). This is the beauty which, when contemplated, brings sighs from the soul who would love the Lord his God with his whole heart, his whole soul, his whole mind, and his whole strength (Deuteronomy 6:5). Nor will this lover of God cease from arousing his neighbor to do the same if he loves him as himself (Mark 12:31).

III
TREATISE ON GRACE AND FREE CHOICE *

Dedicated by Bernard to William, Abbot of Saint-Thierry

Y THE GRACE OF GOD, I HAVE BEEN ABLE TO FINISH this meditation on grace and free choice which I began on an occasion that you know. I *am* aware that I may have done less than justice to the great issues of this subject and possibly have done so in futility. Others of the past have already succeeded in writing about it so much better. So please read it in private. Reading it out publicly would only advertise the foolish boldness of the author rather than edify the piety of the reader.

However, if you later judge that it is useful for the public, then note specifically any obscurities of the text and any ways in which the material could be said more clearly or with more conciseness. Do not hesitate to correct it. Or else send me back your own corrections and changes. Remember the dictum: "Those who give me more light will have one day eternal life" (Ecclesiasticus 24:34).

---

*This essay was written by Bernard of Clairvaux, probably about 1128. It may be viewed as his commentary on the epistle to the Romans, or rather his understanding of the issues of grace and freedom which arise in the epistle to those in Rome.

I. THE GRACE OF GOD

1   Once in conversation I was referring to my experiences of the grace of God. I mentioned how I saw that I was accompanied by the grace of God in all my actions and felt carried along by it. So helped was I by grace that I knew I could attain spiritual maturity.

Someone in the meeting then asked me, "If it is all God's doing, what part do *you* have to play? What do you hope for as *your* reward?"

My reply to him was, "What is your own answer to your questions?"

"I wish," he replied, "you would glorify God (John 9:24) who has gone before you in the grace that has already expected what your actions will be. He has taken all the initiative in your actions toward Him, and He has given you a holy and virtuous life. Let your public worship, then, be an acknowledgment that you are not ungrateful for all His graces received by you and which you ever receive anew."

"Certainly," I replied, "that is wise advice. If only you could give me the power to pursue it. For it is easier to know theoretically what to do than to actually do it. To lead a blind man on his way, and to provide a carriage for him to travel in, are two very different things. It is one thing to advise, and it is another thing to furnish all that he needs so that he does not fall by the wayside."

In holy living we need two forms of help.   Thus it is with our subject of grace. Not all who show us the way of holiness provide the helps that we need to go in that direction. For I have absolute need of two things: to be instructed, and to be helped to live out the instruction. You can give me very wonderful teaching that clears up my ignorance by your advice. But the sentiment expressed by the apostle is very true: "It is the Spirit of God who helps us in our infirmities" (Romans 8:26).

Moreover, the One Who really guides me by advice must also assist me through His Holy Spirit, to succor me to be able to do what you advise. It is already by His help that I even will to want to do what is right. Unaided, I do not even want to do that (Romans 7:18). Otherwise I would have no ground to believe that I could go further and to do what I know I should. "God is at work . . . both to will and to do of His good pleasure" (Philippians 2:13). "But," you say, "if it is all God's doing, where then lie our merits? On what are our aspirations founded?" Listen to what St. Paul teaches us: "Not by works of righteousness which we have done, but by His mercy He saved us" (Titus 3:5). What! Do you really think you could ever be the author of your own merits? Do you believe that you will be saved by your own righteousness? Why, you cannot even say "Jesus is Lord" without the Holy Spirit (1 Corinthians 12:3). Is it possible that you have forgotten the words of Jesus Christ? "Without me you can do nothing" (John 15:5), and again, "It depends not upon man's will, nor of him who runs, but of God that shows mercy" (Romans 9:16).

"But," you interject, "what then is the role of free choice?"

I reply in one phrase: "To be saved." Take away the freedom to choose, and there is nothing to be saved. Without the two bound together, the work of salvation cannot be done. It is necessary to have a cause which produces it as well as a subject in which it is produced. God is the author of salvation. The faculty of free choice is the unique subject of it. God alone can give this, and free choice alone can receive it.

From this we conclude that what is received alone by free choice could no more occur without the recipient's consent than could the act of giving occur without the giver's consent. It is in this sense that it is true to say that free choice cooperates with grace to provide our health— by the act of consent. To consent, then, is to be saved (Acts 2:47; 2 Corinthians 6:2).

Free choice is one thing; animal appetite is yet another. That is why the brute beast is incapable of having this spiritual wholeness, because it is destitute of the necessary consent by which it may gently obey the will of God. It

2
The role of free choice

Animal appetite

cannot acquiesce to His command, nor can it believe in His promises, nor can it give thanks for His benefits. There *is* a great difference between voluntary consent and animal appetite. The latter we share in common with the animals. Ensnared by the pleasures of the flesh, animal appetite has no power to consent freely to the Spirit. That is why the apostle refers to it with another name, "the wisdom of the flesh," when he says to the Romans, "The carnal mind is enmity against God" (Romans 8:7). The appetite of the flesh does not submit to the law of God; it is even incapable of doing so. But even if the natural appetite relates us to the animals, free choice distinguishes us completely so from them.

The Meaning of Free Choice

Free choice is a distinctive and habitual spirit which frees a man. It cannot be either forced nor constrained. It stems from the will and is not the result of necessity. It is neither given nor extorted, except by the freedom of choice. If free choice is forced in spite of itself, then it is no longer freedom of choice. It then becomes enforcement.

Where the will is absent, so is the consent. For only what is freely given can be called consent. Hence when there is consent there is also free choice. Where there is free choice, there is freedom itself. I believe this is what is properly called free choice.

II. What Is the Nature of Freedom?

3   I will give greater clarity to what we have said and proceed with a more systematic understanding of our purpose. It is a constant in the natural world that life is not identical with the senses, the sense perceptions are not identical with the appetites, and the appetites are not identical with consent. This should become more obvious by the specific definition of each of these categories.

Definition of Life

Life in any body is an internal and natural dynamic which has existence only within the confines of that body.

Definition of the Senses

A sense is a vital dynamic in the body which is also seen outside the body.

Definition of an Appetite

An appetite is a natural attribute of any animal which coordinates all the senses with order and promptitude.

Definition of Consent

Consent, on the other hand, is an act of agreeing which comes from the full expression of the will. As I have said above, it is a self-determining habit of spirit that is freedom itself.

Definition of Will

Finally, will is a rational movement that governs the senses and the appetites. In whatever direction it turns, the will always has reason as its inseparable companion. It is not that will is invariably motivated by reason, nor through means of reason; but it never moves without reason. The will may in fact reason against reason, that is to say, use reason as its counsel and judgment. But the will never operates without the instrumentality of reason.

In the same sense that the will never operates without the reason, the Evangelist says that "the children of this world are wiser than the children of light" (Luke 16:8). Again, "They are wise in doing evil" (Jeremiah 4:22). Indeed, freedom of wisdom in this sense cannot be present in a creature—even to do wrong—unless it uses reason to do so.

4   Now reason has been given to the will to instruct it and not to destroy it. However, reason will lead to the destruction of the will if the will is hindered from moving freely in accordance with its own judgment, even if the will is hindered by the least necessity. Such necessity might push the will to consent to an appetite or to a spirit which urges toward what is wrong (which will make an animal of such a consenter, alien and even hostile to the Spirit of God).

On the other hand, necessity might force reason to seek out what is good in following the illuminations of grace. By such means, reason may become wholly spiritual, capable of judging all things, and not subject to the judgment of others (Romans 14:4; 1 Corinthians 14f.). If, then, reason prevents the will from doing what it chooses, then free choice cannot exist alongside of necessity.

Without Free Choice, Rational Man Cannot Be Found Just or Unjust

Rational man cannot become just or unjust out of necessity or without free consent of the will. (So man ought not to be dejected or elated on this account.) In either case, the faculty needed to be happy or unhappy—namely, the will—is lacking.

The other elements that we have noted above—life, the senses, the appetite—cannot of themselves make one either happy or unhappy. If this were not so, then trees, because of their life, or animals, because of their senses and appetites, would also be subject to sorrow or blessing. But this is out of the question. Thus it is what we call "will" which distinguishes us as human beings from these other things.

Free will experiences well-being.

It is free choice and not necessity of will which makes us capable of experiencing a sense of well-being or of misery. These senses are related to whether we are found in a state of happiness or evil. That is why I value consent or free choice, because of the inseparable connection between freedom and will.

It is only right that judgment should be associated with reason and never separated from it. This consent is truly free in itself because of the will, and truly judged of itself because of reason.

It is only right that judgment should also be associated with freedom. For whatever has the free disposal of itself—should it fall into sin—judges itself in the very act of sinning. And it is a true judgment. For if a man will suffer justly, he will merit what he wills. But if he does not will something, then he will not be condemned for it.

How can man have anything imputed to him, whether 5 it be good or bad, if he is not free to choose one from the other?

Necessity excuses one from either good or bad being imputed to him. For the presence of necessity implies the absence of freedom. And where there is no freedom, there can be no merit nor any judgment apart, of course, from original sin. This is clearly quite another subject. It is necessary to see the indubitable logic of this. All action which is not accompanied by freedom of consent is totally denuded of merit and cannot be considered as either good or bad. Hence all things that pertain to man—his life, senses, appetites, memory, spirit, and other faculties—are subject to necessity to the degree that all of them are not fully subject to the will.

But as to the will, since it cannot disobey itself, no one wills what he does not want to will. So it is impossible to be deprived of the freedom of choice.

An Act of the Will Can Only Be Changed by the Will

An act of the will can be changed. But it takes another act of the will to do so. Thus freedom is never lost.

Judgment arises out of will.

The will can no more deprive itself of this freedom than it can deprive itself of willing. Should it ever happen that a man wills to do nothing—or to submit to something that is not his own will—then he could lose the faculty of will. That is why we impute no judgment of right or wrong on those who are infants, who are mentally defective, or who are just asleep. In these conditions, they are no longer masters of their own reasons, and retain neither the use of their own will nor the judgment of freedom.

Since the will knows no freedom other than itself, it is right that its judgment should arise only out of itself. For neither do heaviness of spirit, nor lack of memory, nor restlessness of appetite, nor obtuseness of the senses, nor the languor of vitality in and of themselves constitute one to be charged guilty. Their opposites do not make one innocent, and so their exercise should not count one guilty. This is because it is known that these conditions are on occasion necessary conditions of man and can never occur without any consent of the will.

III. THE THREEFOLD FREEDOM OF NATURE, GLORY, AND GRACE

6   Only the will is inherently free. It is not to be forced or made necessary. It cannot be forced to deny itself nor to consent to other things by force.

It is this freedom that makes man a being who is righteous or unrighteous, capable and deserving of being just or unjust, of being happy or sorrowful. It is consent which leads to one of these conditions. This is what is entailed in free will. At the same time, free will is not the freedom that the apostle speaks about when he says: "Where the Spirit of the Lord is, there is liberty" (2 Corinthians 3:17).

Freedom from Sin

In the Corinthians passage, Paul means freedom from sin as he points out elsewhere: "When you were the slaves of sin, you were free from righteousness. But now being made free from sin, and become the servants of God, you have your fruit unto holiness, and the end everlasting life" (Romans 6:20, 22). Yet who can attribute such excellent freedom to those who live under the sentence of death? (Romans 8:6). So I certainly cannot believe that free choice takes its freedom from this kind of liberty.

Freedom from Sorrow

There is also a freedom from sorrow, of which the apostle also says: "The creature itself also shall be delivered from the bondage of corruption, into the glorious liberty of the children of God" (Romans 8:21). But who could attribute to himself in this mortal condition even this kind of freedom? Therefore, we have also to deny that free choice takes its name from this freedom.

Freedom from Necessity

There is, however, a third kind of freedom which seems to be more appropriate than the other two above. This is what we may call the freedom from necessity, because necessity is what is opposed to freedom. What is done by necessity does not derive from the will and vice versa.

Threefold Freedom

There are, then, these three forms of freedom. They 7 are: freedom from sins; freedom from misery; and freedom from necessity. The last of these reflects on our human condition. The first reflects on how we are restored by grace. The second is what is reserved for us in heaven, our true Homeland.

The Three Liberties: Of Nature, Grace, and Glory

These three freedoms result in the liberties of nature, grace, and glory. In the liberty of nature, we were created with free will to will freedom as a creature noble in God's eyes. In the liberty of grace, we are recreated to be reestablished as blameless, as a new creation in Christ (2 Corinthians 5:17; Galatians 6:15). In the liberty of glory, we are raised up to glory where we are blessed by the Holy Spirit to be a perfect being.

The first liberty is thus a title of considerable honor.

But the second grants us even greater dignity. The last gives us total joy. By the first, we surpass all the other animals on earth. By the second, we have dominion over all flesh. By the third, we triumph over death itself (1 Corinthians 15:26).

To express this in another way, it may be said that in the first liberty of nature, God gave man dominion over sheep and cattle and the beast of the field (Psalm 8:8).

In the liberty of grace, God likewise crushed and laid low beneath our feet those spiritual "powers of the air," of whom it is said: "Lord, do not deliver the souls of those who trust in you to the wild beasts" (Psalm 74:19).

Finally, the liberty of glory will enable us to triumph fully over ourselves, giving us the complete and absolute victory over corruption and death. Then when death is itself overcome (1 Corinthians 15:26), we shall pass over into "the glorious liberty of the sons of God" (Romans 8:21). This liberty will be given to us by Jesus Christ when He presents us to God His Father and establishes us in His eternal kingdom (1 Corinthians 15:24).

Freedom from sin

I think it is concerning the prospect of that eternal kingdom as well as of the present condition that He calls us to be free from sin. It is of this which Christ speaks when He said to the Jews: "If the Son shall make you free, you will be free indeed" (John 8:36). He wanted the Jews to understand by these words that even free choice needs a liberator who can deliver—not from necessity—but rather from the sin into which free choice had fallen both freely and willingly.

Deliverance from the penalty of sin is also implied in this liberty of grace. Free choice had incurred the penalty by its foolishness and endured it with much impatience. Free choice could never have been liberated from these other two evils except through Him Who, alone of all men, was made free from among the dead (Psalm 88:5). Free, that is to say, from sin in the midst of sinners.

8
Christ alone frees from sin.

Indeed, He alone among the children of Adam was free from sin, "who did no sin, nor was guile found in His mouth" (1 Peter 2:22). He also possessed liberty from the misery which is the penalty of sin, but this He possessed only in potency and not in actuality. For according to the Apostle John, He said, "No man takes it from me, but I lay it down (my life) of myself. I have power to lay it down, and I have power to take it again" (John 10:18). The prophet Isaiah had also foretold that the Son would be offered up because God willed it so (Isaiah 53:10). Thus when He chose to do so, He was "born of woman, born under the law, to redeem those that were under the law" (Galatians 4:4, 5).

Thus Christ, too, was subject to the law of suffering. But it was only because it was His full desire to identify with sufferers and sinners in order to liberate them and to lift from the shoulders of His brothers the yoke of both sin and suffering.

The Savior Possessed These Three Liberties

Christ, therefore, possessed in His own person these three liberties. He had the first because of both His human and divine nature, and He had the other two by His divine power. Whether indeed the first man, Adam, was endowed with the last two liberties in paradise, or how or to what extent he had them—these things we shall discuss later.

IV. WHAT IS THE LIBERTY OF THOSE HOLY SOULS IN THEIR DISEMBODIED STATE?

It is a certain truth that the holy souls who are freed of this mortality rejoice fully and perfectly before God, Jesus Christ, and the angels. They are freed from sin and are liberated from suffering. While they have not yet received their resurrected bodies and undoubtedly lack some measure of glory, yet they experience no trace of suffering.

Freedom from Necessity Characterizes Both Good and Rational Beings

Freedom of choice is shared by both God and man. It is not lost either by sin or by suffering. It is not greater in a righteous man than in a sinner, nor is it fuller in the angel than in man. For as the consent of human will which is directed by grace toward what is good enables man to do so freely in goodness, so in the good the will is free. For it is freely given and not by constraint.

In the same way, when free choice inclines willingly toward what is bad, it still makes a man do evil spontaneously and freely so. Man is not forced to do evil by some other cause than his own free choice. He simply chooses to do so at the instigation of his own free will.

Likewise the angels in heaven, and even God Himself, remain freely good. They do so by their own will and not from any extrinsic necessity. So, too, the devil freely chooses to do evil or to persist in it, not by external coercion, but of his own free choice.

Freedom of the will thus continues to exist—even when the mind is held captive—as fully so in the bad as in the good, yet more consistently so in the good. So, too, the freedom of the will of the creature is as complete in its own way as in the Creator, although, of course, the Creator has such freedom infinitely and more powerfully so.

10
The bondage of sin

However, when someone complains and says: "I *wish* I could have a good will, yet I cannot manage it," this cannot prejudice the freedom of will as if it could be violated or subjected to necessity. Rather what this person says is evidence of the fact that he lacks the freedom that is called freedom from sin. Indeed this desire to have a good will clearly proves that he has a will since his desire is aimed at what is good only through his will. If he is unable to have a good will, yet he wants to have one, he shows that he lacks freedom, i.e., freedom from sin. It is that lack of freedom which is opposing, though not suppressing, his will.

Indeed, it is more than likely that in a person's desire to have a good will, he has one already. Likewise, if he wants to do evil, he will desire so because he already has a bad will. So when we desire good, we can see we have a good will; and when we desire evil, the will is already evil. In either case, the will is what there is, and freedom is also there, for necessity yields before the will. If we are unable to will what we want, then freedom itself has been taken captive by sin.

I believe, then, that free choice takes its name from **11** that freedom alone by which the will is either free to judge itself as good—if it has consented to what is good—or as bad—if it has consented to what is evil. It is only by choosing to be that the will can consent to either good or bad.

Of the two liberties (freedom from sin and freedom from suffering), the former might more appropriately be called free counsel, and the latter free pleasure. Free choice is another matter as we have seen.

Judgment, Counsel, and Pleasure

Choice is an act of judgment.

It is the business of judgment to distinguish between what is lawful and what is not. Likewise, it belongs to counsel to examine what is expedient and what is not, as it is to pleasure to experience what is pleasant and what is unpleasant. Would to God that we took counsel for our profit as freely as we judge our deeds! Then we might freely distinguish the things that are right and wrong and choose the licit and reject the illicit as harmful to us. We would then be free to choose and enjoy free counsel, as well as become freed from sin.

But suppose if we did not have this blessing to choose only what is permissible and profitable; then we would possess perfectly the liberty of good pleasure. Then we would be freed from everything that displeased God, and thus we would be completely free of all sorrow.

We discern by means of judgment that there are many

things to be done or omitted. Nevertheless we choose or reject through counsel that which may be quite contrary to the conscience of our own judgment. We do not freely embrace as pleasing all that we observe with counsel to be right and good. Rather, we endure it all impatiently, something that is hard and burdensome to bear. So it is evident that we possess neither the counsel that frees nor the pleasure that liberates.

12   We have still another question to examine which we shall do more particularly later on. Before the sin of Adam, did man possess these two liberties?

One thing is certain: We *shall* possess them fully one day when by God's mercy we shall pray the petition of Our Lord: "Thy will be done on earth, as it is in heaven" (Matthew 6:10). This double liberty will be perfected when the free will of rational beings is exempt from all necessity and the human race is secure from sin and immune from suffering. Like the holy angels, there will be this blessed experience of the threefold liberty which proves all that is "good, acceptable, and the perfect will of God" (Romans 12:2).

This condition of possessing the threefold liberty is not so now, for men have only freedom of choice. Freedom of counsel they only partially possess; that is among those choice saints of God who have crucified their flesh with its passions and desires (Galatians 5:24) so that sin no longer reigns in their mortal bodies (Romans 6:12).

V. Is Freedom from Sorrow Granted in This World?

13   What shall we say about freedom from sorrow in this unhappy life (Galatians 1:4)? We especially ask this when evil seems more and more rampant (Matthew 6:34).

This world is a sphere where every creature groans (Romans 8:20-22). It is all subject in futility in its labor. It is a realm where not only men are in constant conflict, but even the godly are in constant groaning awaiting the re-

demption of their bodies (Romans 8:23). In such a context of life, do you really believe it possible to have scope
for such glorious liberty? When everything seems caught
up by such evil calamities, is freedom from sorrow really
possible?

Indeed, neither innocence nor righteousness are immune from sorrows, so the just man cries out incessantly:
"O wretched man that I am, who shall deliver me from
this body of death?" (Romans 7:24). And again: "My tears
have been my food day and night" (Psalm 42:3). When
days follow nights in one rhythm of continuous distress,
can there be any room for real enjoyment of life? Moreover, the apostle teaches that "all who will live a godly life
will suffer persecution" (2 Timothy 3:12).

If virtue is therefore not immune, perhaps vice is. In   14
the touch of pleasure can it escape for a brief respite from
sorrow?

Indeed not! Vice cannot escape sorrow. Those who rejoice in doing evil and delight in the worst forms of depravity (Proverbs 2:14) only find themselves with the wild
laughter of the mad. The false gaity of such only condemn
them to more misery. As the wise man said: "It is better to
go into the house of mourning than to go into the house of
feasting" (Ecclesiastes 7:2).

Corporal Joy Is Not without Suffering

We know the enjoyment of such bodily pleasures as   **Life involves**
food, drink, and warm clothing. But even these do not es-   **suffering.**
cape from suffering. For bread is only a relish when we are
hungry as drink is only refreshing to the thirsty. Even to be
satiated with food and drink is a burden and not a pleasure. Once hunger and thirst are no longer there, then
even the purest stream will have no more attraction.

Only those who are hot will look out for a shady spot.
Only those in the cold or in the darkness will seek the sun.
So there are no pleasures without the itch for need. Take
need away and the former pleasures are no longer attrac-
tive; instead, they become boring or even unbearable.

So in one form or another, it has to be admitted that all in this present life involves some form of suffering or another. The only thing that mitigates this is the truth of relative suffering. Lighter tasks, for example, come as a relief for heavier burdens. The interlude between the worse and the better brings some happiness when we are going through severe trials. They help to make our sufferings bearable.

Contemplatives Enjoy the Freedom of Pleasure

15   On occasion those who exercise a contemplative life can be caught up in the Spirit to savor the bliss of heavenly things. Do they really escape from sorrow on such occasions?

Yes, they do escape. They can be like Mary who chose the better part which will not be taken away (Luke 10:42). Although this joy is short-lived, it is a reminder of another realm of existence that is reserved in heaven. This is the beatific life. Yet as the beatific life and suffering occur in the same person, it is only by the Spirit the person can have the former and be released from feeling the latter. Thus only the contemplatives can enjoy the freedom of joy in this world, at least partially so (1 Corinthians 13:9-12) and on infrequent occasions.

The Just Enjoy the Freedom of Counsel

This freedom is enjoyed by the righteous man. Again, it is only partially enjoyed, but yet in more abundance.

Freedom of Choice

This belongs to everyone as we have already seen. For it belongs to all who have the use of reason. So it is enjoyed by the bad as well as by the good. It is no less in this life than in the life to come.

VI. THE NEED OF GRACE TO WILL WHAT IS GOOD

I have tried to show that this freedom of choice is always limited to some extent as long as it is unaccompanied by the other two freedoms. Paul speaks of this inability when he says, "So you cannot do what you would" (Galatians 5:17). While we have the freedom to choose, we do not have the power to do freely what we will. I am not talking about the power to will the good, but simply the power to choose. For the will to do good is perfection; to will evil is badness. The will, then, is capable of choosing good or evil.

To the one who chooses rightly, redeeming grace helps us to achieve the good. But when we fail, it is because we do so in our own impotence.

Free will enables us to choose; but it is grace that enables us to choose the good. Because we are granted the faculty of will, we are able to choose. But because of grace, we are able to choose the good. To fear is one thing, but to fear God is another thing. To love indicates we have affections. But it is only when these affections are associated with God that they become virtues. Thus to will is one thing, but to choose the good is quite another matter.

The simple affections are natural to us all. But those disciplines we acquire can only be matured through grace. Thus virtues are disciplined affections that have been regulated and matured.

17
Virtues are disciplined affections.

It is written of some people, that they were in great fear (Psalm 14:5) when there was no cause to fear. It was a fear badly controlled. But David says, "I will teach you the fear of the Lord" (Psalm 34:11). So, too, those with inordinate desires were told, "You do not know what you are asking" (Matthew 20:22). Instead, the disciples were taught how their perverse wills should be trained when He asked, "Are you able to drink the cup that I am to drink?" (Matthew 20:22). Thus He taught them in words and then also by example, how to reorient their wills. In supreme illustration, He said at the beginning of His Passion, "Nevertheless not My will, but Yours be done"

(Matthew 26:39).

Thus we have received from the Lord how we may will as well as how to fear and love. In these things we are but creatures. But how to will the good, how to fear God, and how to love God requires for us the touch of His grace that we might truly become the sons of God.

Contrast Between Good and Bad Free Will

18   To some extent we have been created with freedom of will; but it is only by good will that we have been restored to God's kingdom. He Who made the will to be free is also the One Who makes the will to be good, so that we have become the first fruits of His new creation (James 1:18). But for this provision of grace, it would have been better that we have never existed than being left on our own. For those who wish to live only to themselves, behave indeed like gods, knowing good and evil (Genesis 3:5). Yet when they are merely their own god, they find that they really belong to the devil.

So we find paradoxically that when we live to ourselves in self-will, then we belong to the devil; while when we are surrendered to "good will," we are enabled to belong to God. This perhaps is the meaning of the text: "The Lord knows them that are His" (2 Timothy 2:19). For about those who are not His, He says: "Truly I never knew you" (Matthew 25:12).

We conclude from this statement that once we belong to the devil by "bad will," we no longer belong to God's kingdom. For no man can serve two masters (Matthew 6:24). But when we pass over by "good will" to belong to God, we cease to belong any longer to the devil. Whether we belong to God or to the devil, we do not cease to have the responsibility of being ourselves. For in either situation, we do not cease to exercise free choice. If we choose wrong, we are judged accordingly; and if we choose right, we are blessed. But without our wills, we could not make such choices. So our will is vital. It is our own will that enslaves us to the devil. Yet it is by God's grace, not our wills, that we become subjects of the kingdom of God.

Truly our will has been created good by the goodness of God. But it can only be perfected by its Creator. For I do not wish to attribute its possible perfection to itself but only to God, its Creator.

To be perfected means much more than merely to exist. It would be blasphemy to attribute to ourselves what is better and to God what is worse. So the Apostle Paul acknowledges that what he was naturally, he was in contrast to what he hoped to become by grace. "For to will is present in me; but how to perform that which is good I find not" (Romans 7:18). He realized that by free choice, he could will; but to will perfectly, he needed grace. For to will what is evil is the defect of the faculty of the will. To choose what is good requires another faculty. To measure up to all we desire that is good is indeed the perfection of the will.

Thus to reach this perfection of willing that which is good—all of the time—we need a twofold gift of grace: We need true wisdom, which is to turn the will towards that which is good; and we need the full power to establish the will in that which is good.

19

Perfect Good Will

Now, perfect conversion consists of turning to the good to enjoy only that which is permissible. Perfect confirmation of choice lies in the enjoyment of only what is good.

From the beginning of its existence, the soul had two expressions of goodness. First, there is the reality of creation, meaning that since all was created by a good Creator, all that has been created is also good. "God saw everything He had made, and behold they were very good" (Genesis 1:31). Second, in a special form of goodness arising out of the freedom of choice, the soul of man was created in the image of his Creator (Genesis 1:26). Added to these two aspects of goodness has been a third, namely that of conversion freely towards the Creator once more. This may rightly be regarded as sublime.

Goodness, then, can be regarded in a threefold manner: goodness as a part of creation; goodness which is better within its own sphere of free choice; and goodness which is best in its redemptive relation to God.

The last of these implies that there is a total conversion of the will to the divine Majesty of God, freely, wholeheartedly, and devoutly so. Then such submission in perfect righteousness is linked with fullness of glory. For righteousness of this kind cannot exist without glory, for such glory cannot be without righteousness. Thus it is well stated: "Blessed are they who hunger and thirst after righteousness, for they shall be satisfied" (Matthew 5:6).

20
What true
blessedness is.

Such blessedness is the two qualities mentioned above, namely, true wisdom and fullness of power; wisdom with reference to righteousness and power with reference to glory. But the terms "true" and "fullness" are added, "true" to distinguish wisdom from that of the carnal man and "fullness" to distinguish power from those who will be "powerfully tormented" (Wisdom 6:6).

Neither true wisdom nor fullness of power can be found except in the combination of freedom of counsel and freedom of pleasure with freedom of choice. That is why I would only regard a man as truly wise and fully powerful who is not only able to will a thing from free choice, but is also able to do it by virtue of the other two freedoms. Then he would be neither capable of willing what is evil, nor lacking the power to do so.

But who is such a man? (Romans 3:21) Where are these qualities to be found in this world or in the world to come? Indeed, such a man would be better than the Apostle Paul who confessed, "I cannot do it" (Romans 7:18). If it had been Adam, then he would never have been banished from paradise.

VII. WAS ADAM ENDOWED WITH THIS THREEFOLD FREEDOM?

It is now time we faced up to this question. Did our first

parents enjoy this threefold freedom? Did they have freedom of choice, of counsel, and of pleasure? In other words, did they have freedom from necessity, from sin, and from sorrow? The first is easy to answer, for they did choose. Did they have the other two? Well, if not, they had nothing to lose. But they were expelled from paradise, so it must have made a difference. Freedom of choice was certainly retained. But beyond the mere fact of sinning, Adam was in the body neither free from sin nor sorrow. If they had once been received, could they ever have been lost? If Adam had not had these freedoms, could he have had perfect choice? Or could it be that he had them, but only imperfectly so?

Freedom of Counsel and Freedom of Pleasure Has Each Two Degrees

There is a higher and a lower degree with each freedom. In the freedom of counsel, the higher is the freedom not to be able to sin, the lower being the freedom not to sin. Likewise, in the freedom of pleasure, the higher degree is the freedom not to be able to be made sorrowful, and the lower is the freedom not to be sorrowful.

Man thus received with the full freedom of choice these two lower degrees of freedom. When he sinned, he fell from both. Losing completely the freedom of counsel, he became unable not to sin. Likewise, losing the freedom of pleasure, he could only be sorrowful. For his punishment, there only remained to him the complete freedom of choice. Yet it was through this freedom that he had lost the other freedoms. Enslaved to willing only sin (Romans 6:17f.), he deservedly lost the freedom of counsel. Through his sin, he came into bondage to death (Romans 5:12), thus forfeiting his freedom of pleasure.

Man had received three freedoms. By abusing one, he forfeited the others. He abused it by turning it to his shame instead of glorifying God. As the Scripture says, "Man cannot live in his pomp, he is like the beasts that

22
All freedoms are interrelated.

perish" (Psalm 49:12).

Among all the living creatures, man alone was given this ability to sin as part of his prerogative of free choice. He was given it not to choose sin, but rather that he might appear more glorious in rejecting it in full freedom. But this honor he lost once he had sinned. This was no failure on the part of the Giver of this gift, but on the part of its recipient. He abused the gift. He willed to sin. Just as when the devil and his cohorts willed to rebel, there were those angelic beings who preserved their freedom not to sin. They refused not because they could not do otherwise, but because they willed not to do so.

23   Likewise, the fall of the sinner was due not to the gift of will, but to the abuse of that gift. Unfortunately, in man's fall, he was not able to rise again with the same use of his will. For he now wills only to sin.

VIII. FREE CHOICE REMAINS AFTER SIN IS IN CONTROL

Sin does not remove free choice.   Does this therefore mean that because man cannot help himself from *not* sinning that he has forfeited free choice?

No, but man has lost free counsel by which he previously had the ability not to sin. Knowing he has lost this also means he has lost freedom of pleasure which once kept him from being sorrowful. Thus in spite of losing freedom from sin and freedom from sorrow, he still has freedom of choice. The loss of wisdom and of power does not incur on this other freedom of choice. He can still will even when it may not be to will what is good.

25   Although unimpaired in man's ability to will, he is both without true wisdom and real moral power.

26   Now this is where Christ comes in. In Him, man can possess the necessary "power of God, and the wisdom of God" (1 Corinthians 1:24). For as wisdom He can restore

to man true wisdom, and so restore also His free counsel. As power, He is able to renew His free pleasure to man. Yet man must wait for the next life to receive these gifts perfectly. Meanwhile "in this body of death" (Romans 7:24), we must await through "this present evil age" (Galatians 1:4) and resist the will to sin through our freedom of counsel. We must also have no fear of adversity which we accomplish through our freedom of pleasure for the sake of righteousness.

So here below we must learn from our freedom of coun-   27
sel not to abuse free choice. One day we shall enjoy fully the freedom of pleasure. Thus we are on the way to restoring the image of God in us by means of grace.

IX. THE IMAGE AND LIKENESS OF THE CREATOR ARE EXPRESSED IN THIS THREEFOLD FREEDOM

I believe that the threefold freedom of man expresses   28
the image and likeness of the Creator (Genesis 1:26). It is possible that in freedom of choice there lies the image and in the other two freedoms there lie the likeness of God. Could it be that in freedom of choice there is no lessening, because it imprints more of the substantial image of the eternal and immutable deity?

Free Choice Is Like Eternity

It knows neither end, nor diminuation. Whereas in the other two freedoms there is loss, irreparable loss.

The holy angels still enjoy the other two freedoms, of   29
being unable to sin and from being disturbed by sorrow. They live (and God has always lived) in this state. True, we cannot be completely without sin or sorrow here on earth, but we can with the aid of grace avoid being overcome by sin or sorrow. "For blessed is the man to whom the Lord imputes no guilt" (Psalm 32:1f.). The highest angels then have the highest degree of freedom and of di-

vine likeness and we the lowest. But the devils have none
at all.

30   In hell both of these freedoms disappear, namely those
which pertain unto His likeness. "Bind him hand and
foot, and cast him into utter darkness" (Matthew 22:13).
What else does this binding refer to, other than utter pri-
vation of freedom?

31   Of the likeness contained in the freedoms of counsel
and of pleasure, nothing can remain in hell. But the image
remains, even there, permanently and unchanged in free
choice.

X. IN CHRIST, THE LIKENESS OF GOD
IS RESTORED TO MAN

32   We know that when He shall appear, we shall be like
Him, for we shall see Him as He is" (1 John 3:2). Who
could better do this transformation than the Son of God,
"who reflects the glory of God and bears the very stamp of
His nature" (Hebrews 1:3), and Who upholds all things by
the word of His power? He has been able to reform what
was deformed, to strengthen what was weak, and to dispel
the shadows of sin and make men wise, lending strength
to man against the tyranny of the demonic world.

33   That very form came (Philippians 2:6) to which free
choice could be conformed unto so that it could be reformed from what it had become—and yet originally had
been. Now wisdom is to the image what form does in the
34   world. Form reaches all the world. This is likewise the way
that free choice should try to govern its body, as wisdom
does the world. It should not allow sin to reign in its mortal body (Romans 6:12), but rather as the slave of righteousness (v. 13). Man, too, should no longer be the slave
of sin, as he does not commit sin (Romans 6:18). Thus set
free from sin, he can begin to recover his freedom of counsel and vindicate his dignity by becoming a worthy like-

ness of the divine image. But this can only be in willing-ness that the offering is acceptable, for God loves a cheer-ful giver (2 Corinthians 9:7).

We cannot achieve this without the help of Him whose   35
example we are inspired to follow. It is only in Him and by Him that we are conformed, yes, and transformed into the same image from glory to glory as by the Spirit of the Lord (2 Corinthians 3:18). So let no one ever think that this is done by free choice, as if free choice could with equal fa-cility choose good or evil. We were indeed able to do so before the fall. But now we can only do so through the power of the Holy Spirit.

XI. Freedom of Choice Remains

As we have seen, the Creator endowed man with this   36
prerogative of His divine dignity—to choose. When we read in the Gospels "No one can come to me unless the Father draw him," and again, "Compel the people to come in" (John 6:44; Luke 14:23), does this mean the loss of free choice?

Other texts show that the will and its freedom are not undermined: "Each person is tempted when he is lured and enticed by his own desire" (James 1:14); and again "I find in my members another law at war with the law of my mind and making me captive to the law of sin which dwells in my members" (Romans 7:23).

So however we may be assailed by temptation, whether from within or from without, yet freedom of choice still really determines the outcome. Clearly with regard to freedom of counsel and of pleasure, the soul is less free be-cause of the strong desire of the flesh and the misery of life in its resistance. When Paul complains of being made cap-tive to the law of sin, it is because he had not full freedom of counsel.

XII. DOES FEAR OF DEATH OR OF PUNISHMENT DEPRIVE ONE OF FREE CHOICE?

37   But what of those who are forced to make a choice because of fear—the fear of death or of some other penalty? The Apostle Peter may serve as an example. He appears to have denied the truth against his own will: It was a matter of deny (His Lord) or die. Fearing death he denied.

What was really wrong was that Peter chose rather to lie than to die.

Peter's weakness of will was unmasked when Jesus told him, "Before the cock crows three times, you will deny me three times" (Matthew 26:34). Before the sudden fear of the moment, Peter had cultivated a weak will. The crisis only exposed it. Had he not loved Christ, his denial would not have been unwilling. But had he loved Christ more than he did, then there would have been no denial.

39   So what then are we saying? That our earlier insistence on the freedom of choice was mistaken? Or that we have discovered that the will can be forced?

No. We have seen that Peter was not forced. The fact is that he used the will to avoid death. How else could such a simple woman have been able to tempt such a saint to blaspheme so horribly if the will—the master of the tongue—had not already been willing? Later when Peter restored control of his excessive self-love for more love of Christ, he then did so with all his heart, soul, and strength (Mark 12:30). No longer was his tongue inclined to be an instrument of sin (Romans 6:13). Instead, he courageously asserted in response: "We must obey God rather than man" (Acts 5:29).

Passive and Active Compulsion against Free Choice

40   Indeed, there are two forms of compulsion by which we are forced to suffer against our own will.

First, there is passive compulsion, which can occur without the conscious consent of the agent. But active compulsion never can. So evil can never be imputable upon us as long as we are unwilling. But when we are prevailed upon, we must recognize that we are culpable in allowing the circumstances to lead us that way. More serious is the active compulsion that we are free to choose. Such would be the denial of Christ even if we do so with sorrow in our hearts. Thus in persecution, all that the ferocity of men can do is to show us if the will is weak or not.

Free Choice Stands between Flesh and Spirit.

Man is free to go either way. Although he is weakened **41** by carnal desire, yet he can also have God's Spirit and His constant grace (Romans 8:26). He is like a mountaineer who can fall at any time by the pull of gravity into the abyss, or he can go on climbing the steep slopes. He can go up with the promise of the psalmist—Psalm 36:6.

XIII. HUMAN MERITS ARE SOLELY THE GIFTS OF GOD

We have seen that free choice must not look for con- **42** demnation anywhere else than in itself. Nor can the soul look for salvation in any merit of its own. Mercy alone will save. For all efforts to do good are in vain, without the help of grace. Such efforts would not even begin without grace.

As Scripture observes, man's senses are prone toward evil (Genesis 8:21). Thus his merits cannot be seen to come from himself, but only as coming from above, "from the Father of lights" (James 1:17), Who alone provides the merits of eternal life, and Who gives those good and perfect gifts.

God Gives Gifts and Rewards

God, our King of Eternity, came to earth for the salva- **43** tion of mankind and divided all the graces He gave into gifts and rewards.

On the one hand, God gave gracious gifts that enable us to exercise our freedom in virtues. On the other hand, He has given us hope by gracious promises concerning the future. Paul draws our attention to both of these aspects when he says: "You have your fruit unto holiness, and the end, everlasting life" (Romans 6:22). Further on, he says, "We have the firstfruits of the Spirit, even we ourselves groan within ourselves, waiting for the adoption, to wit, the redemption of our body" (Romans 8:23). Paul calls sanctification "the firstfruits of the Spirit," that is to say, those virtues by which in our present condition we are sanctified by the Spirit to be His adopted. To those who renounce the world, the Evangelist promises, "He shall receive a hundredfold and possess eternal life" (Matthew 19:29).

Salvation is the gift of God.
Salvation, then, is not the work of free choice, but the grace of the Lord (Psalm 3:8).

Indeed, God is both our salvation and the way to it when it is said of Him, "I am the salvation of my people" (Psalm 35:3); and again, "I am the Way" (John 14:6). He Who is our salvation has also made the way to it, so that no man can boast (1 Corinthians 1:29).

If salvation and life are the character of the homeland, then the blessings of the pilgrimage are those of grace. David truly said, "There is none that does good" (Psalm 14:3), to which is added, "No one is good, except God alone" (Luke 18:19). So our works and His rewards are both His gifts. God does not stand in need of our merits, but He benefits His creatures by the ministry with which He graciously endows them to perform.

God's Threefold Action in Man.

44
God completes the salvation of those whose names are written in the book of life in three ways: without their consent; against their consent; and with their consent.

Often God's creatures benefit when they are quite un-aware of His blessings upon them, as indeed nonrational creatures benefit all the time. God also benefits many in spite of their being wicked men or in opposition to Him, such as Pharaoh (Exodus 9:16), Balaam (Numbers 22:18), or the Chaldaeans (Habakkuk 1:6). In spite of their desire to inflict harm, they inadvertently served God's purposes.

There are also those who, like the angelic messengers (through whom and with whom God operates), are willing to do whatever God wants them to do. Of such the Apostle Paul could acknowledge: "It is not I, but the grace of God, which was in me" (1 Corinthians 15:10). He admitted the deeds were his own, yet he could equally acknowledge they were also the grace of God. For he preferred to see himself simply as an instrument of God. In the exercise of his free choice, he chose to be the associate of God.

What Reward Does Each One Merit?

Of the three situations mentioned above, the first merits none; the second only demerit; and the third, true merit. Other objects like stones or other creatures like animals have no merits. One has perception, and the other has no capacity to consent. The devil or evil men merit something, for they do consent. But they only merit punishment because they have rejected the good.

45
Merit can only be with consent.

Paul speaks of the third situation when, active in his evangelism, he does not describe himself as a mere hireling (1 Corinthians 9:16), but as one who serves willingly. For such then is laid up a crown of righteousness (2 Timothy 4:8), because it is given to those who obey by consent of their will. Paul again says, referring to himself and to his followers, "We are God's fellow workers" (1 Corinthians 3:9).

God gives man the recognition as often as he wills to act through God and for God. That is why we can dare to give ourselves such titles as "God's fellow workers." Such cooperators with the Holy Spirit merit the Kingdom because we have become united with the divine will by our own voluntary consent.

XIV. Grace and Free Choice— the Work of Salvation

Yet all merit is of God's grace.

What then is the role of free choice in the work of salvation? Is it simply its free consent? Yes. Not that any merit lies in consent as such, for we have no merit in ourselves at all (2 Corinthians 3:5). All comes from God.

All Is of God

"For it is God who works in you both to will and to do of His good pleasure" (Philippians 2:13). These are not my words, but those of the apostle who attributes to God not only his free choice, but all that he can do, whether it be his thoughts, his will, or his deeds. If, then, God does all three things in us, so that God endows us with good thought, righteous will, and the accomplishment of the deed, then God must work in the first instance without us, in the second with us, and in the third by us. He anticipates us in inspiring our thoughts aright. He associates with us in our consent, in changing our perverse wills. And when he has given our consent the power to do a good work, He then reveals the goodness of all that He has done.

It is obvious that we cannot anticipate our own actions. But He who finds no one is good anticipates in grace all saving action. Thus the beginning of our salvation is found in God alone, and not in us, nor with us. Yet while the consent and the work are not in us, they are still impossible without us.

Good Will Is Needed for Both Consent and Action

Neither the first step (that of initiative) in which we have no part nor the last step (that of action, which often is corrupted in us by fear or damnable hypocrisy) can give us any merit. It is only the second (free choice).

Good will suffices at all times on its own. If it is lacking, nothing else can replace it. Intention is capable of merit. Action can give example. And good thought, preceding both, is able to arouse us from inertia.

We must be careful, therefore, to realize when these things are happening unconsciously within us and with us not to attribute them to our own will; it is weak. Nor should we attribute them to necessity on the part of God where there is none. We can attribute them only to the grace of God, of which He is full.

God's grace arouses free choice.

It is God's grace alone which arouses free choice when it sows the seeds of good thought. It heals by changing the disposition of will. It changes will to action. It saves the soul from experiencing a fall. Yet the grace of God so cooperates with free choice that it only goes ahead of the first case; and it accompanies the other cases.

Grace begins all, and grace finishes all, but in such a way that free choice works simultaneously with grace. So it is not a question of grace doing half the work and free choice the rest. Each does its own function in grace. Grace then does it all, but so also does free choice. But there is this one qualification: Whereas all is done *in* free choice, all is done *of* grace.

In all this we trust we have nowhere strayed away from the apostle's own teaching. For we keep coming back to the apostle's own words. "So then it is not of him who wills, nor of him who runs, but of God that shows mercy" (Romans 9:16). He is not using the language of one who runs in futility (Galatians 2:2). Rather he means that those who will and those who run must give themselves the credit, but only in what they have received of God, to will and to run. In a word, he asks, "What have you that you have not received?" (1 Corinthians 4:7).

The Threefold Work of God

When you received your existence and when you were sanctified, and when you received eternal salvation, which of these, O man, did you or could you perform? Which is not impossible to free choice?

You did not create yourself as you were not there to do so (Job 38:4). Nor in sin could you restore yourself to grace. Nor in death could you rise again. Nor were you capable of doing all those good things which are necessary to lay in store for those who have to be healed or saved.

God alone grants, saves, and sanctifies.

All this is obvious enough, as far as creation and salvation are concerned. No one even doubts this about justification, except the one who is being ignorant of God's righteousness and seeks to establish his own righteousness and who does not submit to the righteousness of God (Romans 10:3).

Could you be so ignorant that while acknowledging the power of the Creator and the glory of the Savior, you are ignorant of the righteousness of the Sanctifier? The prophet thus speaks, "Heal me, O Lord, and I shall be healed; save me and I shall be saved; for You are my praise" (Jeremiah 17:14). Jeremiah shows that only in God can he be provided with the double garments of sanctity and salvation.

But who can then ignore that righteousness only comes from God? Who can justify himself? For this reason David himself acknowledged, "Not to us, O Lord, not to us but to Your Name give glory" (Psalm 115:1). For it was from God that he was looking for both garments, that is to say, the robe of righteousness and the robe of glory.

The Self-Righteous Does Not Know God

Who then is unaware that righteousness comes only from God? The self-righteous man.

And who is he who justifies himself? It is the man who imagines that his merits come from some other source than grace.

The One who gives rewards is He Who made them in the first place. The one on whom He bestows His favors says, "What shall I render unto the Lord for all His benefits?" (Psalm 116:12). That is to say, to give back for what He has previously given? The psalmist proclaims that his existence and his righteousness belong solely to God, lest in denying their source, he lose them both. For then he would cut himself off from their source and so condemn himself.

The psalmist finds a third point which he needs to repay: "I will take the cup of salvation" (Psalm 116:13). Now the cup of salvation is the Savior's blood. If you lack anything you can call your own—which you think will enable you to repay—from what source can you seek to repay God? "I will call upon the name of the Lord," he says. For that name is that upon which whoever shall call shall be saved (Acts 2:21; 3:12).

We have nothing then with which to repay God other than His own Name.

That is why those who have true wisdom acknowledge a threefold operation—not of free choice, but of divine grace relating to the exercise of free choice. The first part of this operation is creation, the second is redemption, and the third is consummation.

Divine grace aids free choice in a threefold way.

First, we have been created in Jesus Christ (Ephesians 2:10) to freedom of will. Second, we have been rehabilitated by Jesus Christ in the spirit of freedom (2 Corinthians 3:17). Third, we shall reach fulfillment and be established with Jesus Christ in the eternal state. For that which had no existence should be created by One who had. That which was deformed needed to be reformed by Jesus Christ. The members of His Body can only receive their final perfection in Jesus Christ their head.

All of the above will happen "when we all come to the fullness of the measure of the stature of Christ" (Ephesians 4:13), and are made manifest with Him in glory (Colossians 3:4). The consummation will not be accomplished *by* us, but only *in* us. For the creation was not made without us and redemption only occurs with some of us who voluntarily consent. And redemption is imputed to us for righteousness.

Intentions, Memory, and Affections

Our merits are our fastings, watchings, self-discipline, works of mercy, and all other practices of virtue by which the inner man is renewed day by day (2 Corinthians 4:16).

Bent down under the weight of earthly cares, our intentions are only gradually raised heavenward. Languishing in carnal desires, our affections only rise slowly to be reinforced by spiritual love. Sullied by the shame of former deeds, our memory becomes purer and more joyful in the remembrance of our good deeds.

By these three ways the renewal of the inner man occurs. It is by the rightness of intention, the purity of affliction, and the remembrance of good deeds that this occurs. The good deeds fill the memory to shed light on the conscience.

The Holy Spirit and our merits Since these things are truly the gifts of God, it is the divine Spirit who works within us. Yet because they come about by the consent of our wills, they are also our merits. "For it is not you who speak" says our Lord, "but the Spirit of your Father which speaks in you" (Matthew 10:20). Likewise Paul asks, "Do you seek a proof of Christ's speaking in me?" (2 Corinthians 13:3). If, then, Jesus Christ or the Holy Spirit so speaks in the person of the Apostle Paul, do you think He is not also working in him? "For I will not dare to speak of any of those things which Christ has not wrought in me" (Romans 15:18), he confesses.

But what does this imply? If the words and works of the apostle are not his own, but of God who speaks through him, where then are the merits of Paul? What becomes of those confident words, "I have fought a good fight; I have finished my course; I have kept the faith; henceforth there is reserved for me a crown of righteousness which the Lord, the righteous judge, shall give me on that day" (2 Timothy 4:7-8)?

Do you think that Paul was expecting his crown because of the good works that he had performed? Not at all. For we see innumerable good works that are done by bad angels and by crippled men which certainly deserve no merit. Was it not his hope that these good works would be done in liaison with his good will? "For," he said, "if I preach the Gospel willingly, I have a reward, but if against my will, the dispensation of the Gospel is committed unto me" (1 Corinthians 9:17).

Finally, if this will upon which all merit depends did not motivate the Apostle Paul, how could he talk about his crown which he presumes is laid up for him as indeed a crown of righteousness? Can we justly demand as a debt whatever is promised without obligation and is gratis?

Paul's Crown Is God's Crown of Righteousness

He says, "I know whom I have believed, I am sure that He is able to keep that which I have committed against that day" (2 Timothy 1:12). He called the promise of God his deposit. Because he trusted in the One who promises, he repeats the promise with confidence. For he well knew that this promise was made only by grace, and never doubted that it would be fulfilled in righteousness.

Thus the crown which the Apostle Paul awaited is well described as a crown of righteousness, for it is the righteousness that comes from God and not from the apostle. It is righteous that God should give what He owes, and He owes what He promised. Now it is the promise of God which is the righteousness in which the apostle relied.

If Paul had desired to have his own righteousness, without the knowledge of God, he would never have submitted to God's righteousness (Romans 10:3). But God desired to have Paul as a partaker of His righteousness in order that he might also deserve the crown. God made him a partaker of His righteousness in the works that were deserving of a crown. But God made him a partaker when Paul was willing to be conformed to the divine will. The will was given in order to help, and this help was reckoned for a reward.

If the will comes from God, it is clear that the reward or the merit also comes from God. For it is incontestable that the will and the deed are only the results of the grace of God (Philippians 2:13).

The will and the reward are both from God.

God, then, is the Author of merit since He applied will to the good work and supplied the work to the will. If we wish to give significant names to our actions and to call them merits, they can only be but the seedbeds of our hopes, the incentives of love, the portents of a hidden predestination, the harbingers of our future blessings, the road to the divine Kingdom. But they are no cause for pretending that we can rule like kings. In a word, we conclude with the Apostle Paul again:

"It is those whom He did predestinate, them He also called; and whom He called, them He also justified; and whom He justified, them He also glorified" (Romans 8:30).

Part II

THE NATURE AND GREATNESS OF GOD'S LOVE

Treatises by William of St.-Thierry and
Bernard of Clairvaux

IV
THE NATURE AND DIGNITY
OF LOVE*

I. PROLOGUE

LOVE IS THE ART ABOVE ALL OTHER ARTS. NATURE teaches it, but God is the Author of nature. In fact, love has been given to us by the Creator even though adulterous affections have corrupted its purity. This love teaches us that we are not naturally the disciples of God, but when we are docile to God's love, we can be teachable (John 6:45). Indeed, this love in the soul is a power which, by its momentum, carries it to its purpose and its end.

All creation, whether spiritual or material, has its own sphere which attracts. It is like being influenced by the force of gravity. This law was enunciated by a certain philosopher (Aristotle). But not everything is dragged downwards. For as water falls, fire rises, and so with each thing. Man likewise obeys this law, so that while his soul ascends, his body goes downwards, and each part of him goes to its desired end.

> All things have their own tendencies.

What then is the place of the body? Scripture says, "You are dust, and to dust you shall return" (Genesis 3:19). But of the spirit, it says in the book of Wisdom, "The dust returns to the earth as it was, and *the spirit re-*

> All dust tends to dust, so man should tend to God.

*This essay was written by William of St.-Thierry in the early 1120s, possibly in the form of daily chapter homilies to the monks at St.-Thierry.

61

turns to God who gave it" (Ecclesiastes 12:7).

So we see that man is expressive of the nature which he has. The spirit returns to God Who has created it; and the body returns to the earth, not only into the earth, but returning to the elements out of which it had been fashioned. Thus earth, fire, water, and air each reclaim something of the body. We call this natural disintegration or putrefaction. When this is completed, then all elements are back in their place.

Yet the sinful soul does not tend to God.

Now while none of these natural elements deviates from its course, only the miserable soul and degenerate spirit that are corrupted by the vice of sin do not know (or else learn with difficulty) how to return to their proper origin. True, the soul will be driven by its desire for blessedness and to seek nothing else but blessing. Yet "happy is that man, whose God is the Lord" (Psalm 144:15). To seek such blessing in any other way or from any other source than the Creator of all goodness is to wander in futility. But having wandered from such teaching, the soul has need of a proper teacher, one who can teach about that blessedness which the soul seeks through love. Thus the soul will be taught by admonition where, how, in what sphere, and by what path it may seek to go.

Lust is not love.

Tragically, carnal love has had its teachers of vice. They are persons who are so skillful and effective in having been corrupted and in corrupting others that even their master of love—Ovid—was forced by the lovers and companions of such foulness to recant what he had so passionately praised. Thus Ovid, who had written passionately about the fire of carnal love, was also forced to write about a cure for love. He had lavished all his skills on incentives to produce love either by arousing all passions or by inventing new ones.

Out of this depravity of the Graeco-Roman world came a licentious madness of uncontrolled and superfluous incentives to lust. The entire structuring of nature was disarranged and destroyed by the depravity and wicked perversions of men who had only the uncontrolled vice of unrelenting desire. These destroy the natural order of things.

According to the natural order that God ordained in creation, the spirits of these men should have led upward by their own momentum and by their own love to the God who created them. But the person who is humiliated and corrupted by the allurements of the flesh does not do so. Rather he becomes like the animals. Thus the psalmist says, man "is like the beasts that perish" (Psalm 49:12, 20). Again, the Lord declares: "My Spirit shall not abide in man forever, for he is flesh" (Genesis 6:3). Again, the psalmist says, on behalf of his fellow men: "My heart has become like wax, melting away within my viscera" (Psalm 22:14).

Lust is animal.

The heart has been placed by the Creator in the narrow and central part of the body where it may govern and regulate both the fortress of the higher senses as well as the general government of the lower body. Its role, therefore, is to govern the whole territory of thought and action around it. But under the corrupting influence of carnal desire, the heart's sentiment is turned into a bestial appetite which not only dishonors man's senses and rules him with ignoble passions, but it makes him forget his original dignity that was created exclusively for God.

The heart should rule and not be tyrannized by lust.

Created for God alone, the heart is considered by corrupt persons and corruptors of others to be a dwelling more natural to lust and a house of prostitution for all vices. How unblessed, therefore, are those who so defile themselves by the clamorings of their lusts. They have made the place of their soul which belongs to God the Creator, and which is communicable to no creature, the seat of Satan (Revelation 2:13). The heart has become the seat of filth and of an innumerable series of vices.

II. THE ORIGIN AND PROGRESS OF LOVE

We want rather to speak of love—not in its corruption—but in the measure to which God Himself will in-

3

spire us to do so, for He is the source of love.

First, let us see the origin of love, and how love through its successive stages of growth reaches a ripe old age. This elder age is not full of senile melancholia; it is full of rich mercy. For as the various stages of life increase or decrease (depending how you view them), so that the child becomes a young man, a youth becomes a mature man, and a mature man becomes an old man. There are changes in quality at each stage. It is so with love. The world develops its virtue, virtue grows into love, love leads into charity, and charity develops wisdom.

The origin of love We need to know the noble lineage of the love we are speaking about now. For it comes from a noble family. Indeed, its birth is of God. There it is born, there it is nourished, and there it grows in its development. There it is a true citizen and not a foreigner (Ephesians 2:19). For love is given by God alone, and love continues to exist in Him. Love is due to no one else but to God and for God.

As we discuss the birth of love we are reminded of the triune God. God created man in His own image. God formed man in His own likeness so that the triune character of the Creator should shine through and in man also. He desired that by this image, this new inhabitant of His creation, man, should adhere indissolubly to God, his Creator. Otherwise, let us stray and become alienated, distracted by the many differing varieties of creatures. Man in this lesser, created trinity would separate himself from the unity of the supreme, triune Creator.

Man's trinity of existence When God then breathed into man the breath of life (Genesis 2:7), man was granted a spiritual or intellectual power. This is the meaning of inspiration—breathing into man. He was also granted an animal power, a biological vitality, which made him a living creature. God established in man's superior faculty the power of memory so that he might ever be mindful of the power and goodness of the Creator. And God saw that the memory should beget reason, and that memory and reason should then also beget the will.

For memory knows and guides towards the goal for which it must strive. Reason tells us that for which we must strive. Will strives. It is the power to strive. These three—memory, reason, and will—are one; yet they work effectively as three. Likewise in the Holy Trinity, there is one substance and yet three Persons. As in that Trinity, the Father is the One Who begets, the Son is begotten, and the Holy Spirit proceeds from both. So likewise memory begets reason, and will proceeds from both memory and reason.

In order that the soul created in man may adhere to God, the Father claims the memory to Himself; the Son claims reason; and the Holy Spirit, who proceeds from both, would claim the will proceeding from memory and reason.

Man's need of the Triune God

This, then, is the origin of will: its birth, its adoption, its dignity, and its nobility. When grace anticipates and cooperates, the will begins to cleave freely to the Holy Spirit, Who is the Love and Will of the Father and the Son. The will begins to desire spontaneously and to will ardently what God wills and to will what memory and reason suggest that it should will. This ardent will is love, and love is nothing else than ardent desire for the good. By itself the will is a simple attitude that desires good (i.e., *affectus*).[1] It is rooted in the rational soul and is capable of good as well as evil.

4

This *affectus* is good when it is aided by grace. It is evil when it is left to itself, for it is lacking in itself. From the viewpoint of the Creator, the human soul should lack nothing, and so the soul is given free will in two ways.

First, with the aid of grace, will progresses toward virtue. It then takes the name of—and becomes—love. Second, when it is left to itself, the will chooses to enjoy itself selfishly, and so it suffers lack within itself. Thus there are assigned to it the names of many vices: cupidity, avarice, lust, and so on.

Grace is the true gravity of the soul.

5   From the very beginning, the will is created free much like the Pythagorean letter Y. If, in accordance with the dignity of its origin, the will is raised into love, then according to the structure ordained by God, it will progress from love to charity and from charity to wisdom.

Without grace the will is destructive. On the contrary, without this self-ordering, the will by the just ordinance of God will rush headlong into destruction. It will be overwhelmed by the darkness of confusion and buried in the hell of vices, unless help comes to it promptly in the grace of God. Only when it truly forsakes this way to hell, will it begin to lift its steps once more and follow the grace that leads and nourishes it (Psalm 31:3). Only then will it mature into love.

Filled with the powers of youth, the will is inspired by the fear of the Lord, so that it is not frightened by the childish fear of punishment. It is inspired by the true reverence and love of God. This is true piety. As Job says, "Behold the fear of the Lord, that is wisdom" (Job 28:28).

True youth is not found in the expression of a man's natural strength and power according to his age. So let him not dissipate his youth's natural incentives; reason would forbid him to corrupt them. For those who corrupt youth's ideals do so in superficial wandering. Their spirit is like that of the animals themselves (Psalm 49:12), and their flesh is like that of wild asses; that flesh drives them insane by its mad incentives (Ezekiel 23:20).

If this is what happens to those who misuse their will, how much more does it benefit those who direct their wills rightly, in a fervor of spiritual youthfulness. But it is tragic when we see how the corrupt make so much more progress in their corruption than the true lovers make toward the things that are good.

III. HOLY FOLLY IN TRUE LOVE

Listen to the holy insanity of the apostle! He says, "If we are out of our mind, it is for God; if we are sober, it is for your sakes" (2 Corinthians 5:13).

Do you still want to listen to this holy folly? Moses says, "If you forgive their sins, forgive; and if not, blot me, I pray you, out of Thy book which you have written" (Exodus 32:32).

Do you want a third example? "I chose to be anathema and separated from Christ for the sake of my brothers" (Romans 9:3).

Is it not, then, a holy sanity in this disposition of a resolute soul which produces the apparent insanity? How can the heart so set in *affectus* toward Christ, be ever anathema and separated from Christ?

This was the apostles' drunkenness at the coming of the Holy Spirit (Acts 2). This was Paul's insanity when before Festus he said to him, "Paul, you are insane!" (Acts 26:24). No wonder Paul was pronounced mad. At the point when he was about to be sentenced to death for following Christ, Paul was seeking to convert those very judges to Christ.

Holy order is divinely inspired.

It was *not* the great learning of Paul which produced this insanity in him as Festus said (Acts 26:24). For the king knew the truth and had concealed it. No, it was the drunkenness of the Holy Spirit, so that the apostle longed to make those who were judging him like himself in small and great matters, except for the chains (Acts 26:29).

Let us cite one more example. What greater and more unexpected folly can we conceive than for a man who has abandoned all things for Christ to return again to the world for the sake of Christ, to return in obedience and love for his brothers? Reaching out for heaven, does he plunge himself into such filth? Yet such was the case of Benjamin who, in his folly, was not aware of his own interests or anything else. He was aware only of Him to Whom he aspired so completely (Psalm 68:27).

This insanity was also the madness of the martyrs who rejoiced in their torments. It may even be permissible to quote the poet Virgil, who said in the fervor of his sensuousness: "A folly is well permitted."

Holy order is
unfettered by
reason.

It becomes youthful ardor to be conspicuous in love, in the way of the heart before God, and in the fervency of one's piety. At this stage, ardor does not yet have—nor ought it to have—the bridle of reason. Indulgent self-interest, lenient possessiveness, and soft living are not compatible with the order of the true novice. So this spirit should not be discouraged in others. For oneself, stringent and uncompromising discipline should be imposed. But toward others there should be paternal and fraternal love.

Piety which guides and counsels the novice should be humble, gentle, and obedient in all things. If any of these is lacking, there will not be much hope for perseverance when there is such a slothful and lukewarm spirit. Or indeed one may fear youthful ardor's ruin in rashness. That is why the whole life of a novice should be to make himself a fool in all things for Christ's sake (1 Corinthians 4:10).

Holy order
needs spiritual
direction.

At the same time, the novice should be guided by one who is wiser and older, one who is known for teaching what he has learned of God. For one who is still youthful in learning the ways of God cannot persevere to have the freedom and to make judgments until he has had long and patient experience in the things that he has heard. Instead, therefore, let him strive above all else to discipline himself in the obedience of God. As it is written: "Purify your hearts in the obedience of charity" (1 Peter 1:22). For this is God's will, that which is good, pleasing, and perfect (Romans 12:2).

8
Holy order
needs prayer.

In order to obtain and keep these dispositions, it is necessary to seek the aid continually of attentive and persevering prayer. It is prayer in which faith is such that it hopes for all things (1 Corinthians 13:7). It is devotion such that one seems to constrain God. It is love such that everything it seeks, it feels that it obtains through prayer itself. It is humility which is so gracious that in all things it prefers that God's will and not one's own be done (John 6:38).

Thus enabled, let the youthful devotee seek at this stage to have purity of heart, cleanness of body, silence or prudence in speech, modesty of eyes, ears that do not itch, a calm and gentle manner, and discipline and self-control so that all the good works he does are not hindered. May he not bring further lust from a deceitful heart by laughter but grace by a gentle smile. May he cultivate spiritual meditations assiduously and read well-chosen books that do not make him idly curious. Let him be subject to his superiors, reverent to his seniors, and loving to his juniors so that, instead of being desirous of authority, he is loving and helpful to those in whose company he is. May he not be overwhelmed by severity nor overcome by leniency. Let him have serenity in his face, kindness for everyone in his heart, and generosity in all his works.

Holy order needs cleansing.

This stage of love, then, is the time and place to cut out indulgent pleasures, to root out all vices, and to crush all false desires. He will be able to deal with other artificial desires which need to be cut off as adulterous and as false branches that grow spontaneously. These are not so much desires as false appetites of the soul, the lust of the eye, and the ambitions of the world (which the apostle describes in 1 John 2:16). He can then hope to make spiritual and true progress.

IV. THE DELIGHT AND EFFORTS TO PROGRESS IN LOVE

This is the stage when the one who loves pushes forward and labors in hard work (1 Corinthians 9:24-26). This is labor with much sweat and the work of many efforts. Since love is still blind, let it do what it desires. But let not love know where it comes from or where it goes (John 3:8). In this way it will work with the affections rather like a blind man who "sees" with his hands. True, a blind man will work with his hands, but he does not see what he is working on nor does he see the work which is performed. This stage is like the training of a blind man so

9
Holy order is assiduous.

that the teacher bends over him and guides him, teaching him how to undertake his work more for utility than for artistry.

Blind love is shaped from the outside by a kind of honesty of life and of its standards. But when the inner man has been made tender by the long practice of discipline, he will be able to be impressed and formed inwardly by its form. Then the one being molded will bring forth the peaceful fruit of salvation (Hebrews 12:11). And then he will understand the utility of all these and other observances in their intrinsic, and not merely external, appearances.

Holy order is conscientious.

We have not yet outlined *affectus;*[2] but we have dealt with the desire and tutelage of reason. It is of these the Psalmist can sing with humility: "I have desired to desire your commands" (Psalm 119:20). I have spoken of the blind man who does not see with his eyes; yet his hands are still working. So is he who desires to progress in great things. He must be faithful also in small things (Luke 16:10). In those areas, one already has the privilege of power from the Creator, namely over his own body.

Let the young man show also the service of a good will. Let him do what the apostle says: "I speak after the manner of men because of the weakness of your flesh. For as you have yielded your member servants to uncleanness and to iniquity, even so now, yield your member servants to righteousness and to holiness" (Romans 6:19). It is as if the apostle were saying: When love will have matured into charity, and when the soul will have perfect purity, then I shall tell you or indicate to you something completely different, something that is divine.

Holy order is righteous.

In the meanwhile, receive what is human. Formerly you were freed from the judgment of your negligence and sins. You then yielded the service of your members to sin in everything, even in iniquity. Nothing was given to righteousness.

Now, however, you have yielded all your members to serve righteousness for the sake of sanctification. Faithful in this, the soul will now begin to experience in itself what David said: "I will lift up my hands in your name. My soul shall be satisfied as with marrow and fatness" (Psalm 63:4-5). If this growth is by the Spirit, a person will put to death the deeds of the flesh (Romans 8:13); and if he will glorify God in his body, then the result will be that his soul is filled with the marrow and fatness of the Holy Spirit. Then he will begin to be renewed in the spirit of his mind. Then he will put on the new man, created according to God in righteousness and true holiness (Ephesians 4:22-24).

By these spiritual experiences, things will begin to have a new look for a person. The spiritual gifts that he had labored until now to emulate will begin to take on a more familiar appearance. The body, humbled by holy discipline, will begin to pass from habit, however good, to a more spontaneous service of the spirit. The inner frame of the new man will begin to be renewed day by day (2 Corinthians 4:16) until it is illuminated in the contemplation of the goodness of God (2 Corinthians 3:18).

10
Holy order needs to become habitual.

Now also frequent and unexpected visions of the splendor of the saints will begin to revive and illumine the soul and strive with continual spiritual desires. For wisdom runs joyously through the streets. As Job says, wisdom "hides the light in his hands and commands it to appear again to him who loves the light that He makes known. It is his possession and he is able to ascend into it" (Job 36:32-33).

From this time on, the soul now agitated for a long time begins to gather some unaccounted and sweet, precious affections whose presence is for the soul a sweet repose. When the affections are taken away and do not return even as the soul longs for them, a person suffers intensely. For the soul is like a person that is raised in the country and is used to country cooking and has begun to taste the raw diet of the palace. When it is ignominiously chased away from the court and thrown out violently, it can hardly adjust again to the house of poverty. So the soul re-

Holy order is persistent.

turns time after time at the door, importunate, persistent, and eager as one who is in great need. As a beggar, the soul looks to see if anything will be offered to it whenever the door is opened.

Sometimes by shamelessness and importunity, the soul has so overcome all obstacles that, leaping along in the desire to be at wisdom's innermost table, it takes its seat impudently. It longs to hear the words: "Eat friends; drink freely, my dearest friends!" (Song of Solomon 5:1). From this there is now born within the soul a love of holy poverty, the desire to be unknown, the horror of worldly distractions, the practice of prayer, and frequent psalmody.

V. THE DANGERS AND DAMAGES OF NEGLECTED GRACE

11   It is at this stage, unless one is on one's guard, that the temptations of hindrance will begin. Hindrances will tend to slow down those who, until now, have been prosperous and blessed in their souls. Sometimes they will be turned back by *accidie* into lethargy and lukewarmness. Whatever has been received for the journey from their dutiful Father (Matthew 15:32) will begin to be thought of as adequate. Then they will set up a milestone in their journey and pause, failing to advance any further.

Carnal languor is morally careless. More serious still, they will trample on the grace of God. From God's openheartedness they forge an empty self-confidence. Boasting with their mouths and with their hearts, they presume God will never abandon them. So they eat and drink damnation to themselves (1 Corinthians 11:29) every time they perceive the grace of a visit or consolation from God. Hence they put their trust in the exercise of self-will but not in the will of God.

The psalmist said, "The enemies of the Lord lied to Him and their time shall be forever. And He fed them with the finest wheat and satisfied them with honey from the rock" (Psalm 81:15-16). Notice that they are fed. Yet notice that they are enemies! Notice that they are satisfied. Yet notice that they are liars! Notice that not only with wheat but with the finest wheat they are fed. And they are not just given the rock, but honey from the rock. With these they are satisfied yet they are convicted of being enemies! For if they had not been enemies, they would have never been so quickly satisfied.

Anyone who is satisfied seeks no longer what he has been given, for he is full. What he has is enough for him. This is precisely what the apostle says: "For it is impossible for those who were once enlightened, and have tasted of the heavenly gift, and were made partakers of the Holy Ghost, and have tasted the good word of God, and the powers of the world to come, if they shall fall away, to renew them again unto repentance; seeing they crucify to themselves the Son of God afresh, and put Him to an open shame" (Hebrews 6:4-6). Such abuse is to crucify again for themselves the Son of God (Hebrews 10:29).

To so abuse God's grace in doing evil that good may come of it (Romans 3:8) is to sin boldly and to attribute any inner sin that is committed to the cross of Christ. What is this but to crucify the Son of God all over again for themselves?

Carnal languor abuses the grace of God.

Oh, if we would only listen to the consequences! Often the earth, drinking in the rain falling on it, and bringing forth seasonal herbs for those by whom it is tilled, receives blessing from God. "But that which beareth thorns and briars is rejected, and is nigh unto cursings; whose end is to be burned" (Hebrews 6:7-8).

So let us return to the better things which, as the apostle himself says, are nearer to salvation. "Beloved, we are persuaded better things of you, and things that accompany salvation, though we thus speak" (Hebrews 6:9).

Already, then, the young lover who is full of good hope and whose youth God blesses (Psalm 43:4) begins to grow into the fullness of the measure of the stature of Christ (Ephesians 4:13). For now, love begins to be strengthened and illumined and to pass into the *affectus* with the name of a stronger virtue and a greater dignity.

Love enlightened is called charity. Yes, love comes

from God, for John says, "God is love" (1 John 4:16). Brief praise though this is, yet it says everything. Whatever can be said to be of God is said also of charity. Thus charity considered according to the nature of the gift and of the giver is the name of the substance in the giver and a quality in the gift. But for emphasis, God is called the gift of charity. The virtue of charity is over all other virtues for it unites and is made like God.

What can we say about charity?

We have not seen charity, we have not known it, but we have heard of it (Jeremiah 6:24). The apostle knew it. He outdid himself in his praise, extolling charity as a more excellent way, saying, "I show you a more excellent way" (1 Corinthians 12:31).

Paul's hymn of love

"Though I speak with the tongues of men and of angels, and have not charity, I am become as sounding brass, or a tinkling cymbal. And though I have the gift of prophecy, and understand all mysteries, and all knowledge; and though I have all faith, so that I could remove mountains, and have not charity, I am nothing. And though I bestow all my goods to feed the poor, and though I give my body to be burned, and have not charity, it profits me nothing. Charity suffers long, and is kind; charity envies not; charity vaunts not itself, is not puffed up. It does not behave itself unseemly, seeks not its own, is not easily provoked, thinks no evil; rejoices not in iniquity, but rejoices in the truth; bears all things, believes all things, hopes all things, endures all things. Charity never fails; whether there be prophecies, they shall fail; whether there be tongues, they shall cease; whether there be knowledge, it shall vanish away. For we know in part, and we prophesy in part. But when that which is perfect is come, then that which is in part shall be done away. When I was a child, I spake as a child, I understood as a child, I thought as a child; but when I became a man, I put away childish things. For now we see through a glass darkly; but then face to face: now I know in part; but then shall I know even as also I am known. And now abideth faith, hope, charity, these three; but the greatest of these is charity" (1 Corinthians 13:1-13).

This is the Lord's sweet yoke and light burden (Matthew 11:30). This burden bears and lightens the bearer. This light burden of the gospel is sweet to those to whom the Lord declares: "I will call you no longer servants but my friends" (John 15:15). The person who has not formerly been able to bear the precepts of the law now finds the precepts of the gospel light by reason of enabling grace. The person who could not fulfill the command "you shall not kill" (Luke 18:20) now finds it easy to lay down his life for his brothers (1 John 3:16). And so the same principle works for the rest of the commands.

If a heavy burden is laid upon a mule, and it refuses it as unbearable to carry, a four-wheeled wagon is brought up. This is like the gospel, which traverses the whole world (Psalm 19:5). It takes the burden which the mule balked at as too heavy to carry. Now it carries double the load without any effort.

Or like a little bird which cannot fly away without wings and feathers, it adds the weight of the wings and the feathers in order that it will soar away without effort. So also it is like hard crusts which cannot go down the throat but need to be soaked in milk or in another liquid. Then it will be capable of being swallowed.

Love involves efforts and also *affectus* which both lead to charity. And the hand of charity operates with a likeness more easily as the enlightened eye helps it. For we operate at first with the hand, and then we rub our eye with our hand to clear it. This is what David declares: "For by your commandments, I have been given understanding" (Psalm 119:104).

The soul begins to understand his works by discerning

13
Love requires effort.

his own affections. Then the virtues begin to penetrate his being so that just as God is good, so now the heart is just and holy and begins to live a holy, righteous, and pious life. In the sanctity of one's own life, in justice to all men, and in devotion to God, the soul now lives in such relationships.

Love is righteous.   By the growth of such grace, the *affectus* of righteousness so penetrates the righteous soul that in all its ways—of thought, of affections, and of actions—the soul is wholly righteous. For the soul is affected completely and indissolubly in its whole being in all that pertains to righteousness. That is why the apostle says, "Charity never fails" (1 Corinthians 13:8). Sometimes it is true that our affections or our works may deviate and diminish in their effect as long as we see dimly as in a mirror, or as an enigma. But the sentiment of *affectus* of charity always remains whole and steady in its power.

VI. STABLE AND UNSTABLE LOVE

14
Having sustained
affections   *Affectus* (as a steady movement toward God) is one thing, while affections (as spasmodic movements toward created things) are another.

The *affectus* is what possesses the mind with a pervasive power and perpetual virtue; it is maintained by grace, firm and stable. Affections, however, vary according to the variety of times and objects. Because of original sin, the weakness of the flesh offends, fails, and often seriously wounds. The mind is wounded when it remains more passive than active, and then it suffers interiorly and wrongly. The mind does not wholly lose charity, but it sighs and cries out to God: "Oh wretched man that I am! Who shall deliver me from the body of this death?" (Romans 7:24).

For this reason, the apostle also says: "With the mind I myself serve the Lord God; but with the flesh the law of sin" (Romans 7:25). Again, he says, "It is no more I that do it, but sin that dwells in me" (Romans 7:17). There-

fore, anyone who is born of God according to the reckoning of the inner man "does not sin" (1 John 3:9), insofar as
he hates rather than approves of the sin which the body
does externally. Inwardly, he is kept by the spiritual re-
birth by which he is born of God. Even while he is occasionally wounded and weakened by the attacks of sin,
nevertheless he is not destroyed when the roots of charity
rest deep within him. Instead, he rises up again and recov-
ers. He becomes more fruitful and alive in the hope of
good fruit.

That is why the Apostle John says: "Whosoever is born
of God does not commit sin; for his seed remains in him;
and he cannot sin because he is born of God" (1 John 3:9).
The force of these words needs to be considered. "He cannot sin," that is to say, he cannot persevere in sin, because
anyone who is born of God endures rather than deliberately wants to sin. He wants to subject even his flesh to
the law of God, whom he serves in his mind, even though
he may seem to serve the law of sin and endure an attack of
sin and temptation.

Peter did not forfeit love when he sinned (Matthew
26:6). He sinned more against truth than against charity
when he lied by saying with his mouth that he did not belong to Him. Actually, he belonged to Him wholly with
all his heart. Therefore, the truth of charity washed away
the tears of falsehood's denial.

Love overcomes sin.

David, too, when he sinned did not lose charity
(2 Samuel 11-12). It is truer to say of him, that the charity
in him was stunned by this vehement blow of temptation.
Charity was never destroyed in him, but merely dazed by
it. Aroused by the voice of the prophet who accused him,
it woke him up. Immediately he broke down in confession
of a very ardent love: "I have sinned against the Lord." So
he deserved to hear at once the words of forgiveness: "The
Lord has taken away your sin. You shall not die"
(2 Samuel 12:13).

15
Love holds faith and hope in its embrace.

We see that love is in faith and hope. But charity is in itself and of itself. It is possible to think of faith and hope existing without charity, but charity cannot be conceived of without faith and hope. For faith establishes the reality of what is love. Hope promises love to us.

He who loves in faith and hope loves in believing in—and in hoping for—what can be loved. Love possesses the object of faith and of hope. It holds them both in its embrace. As a result, love desires to see the God of faith and hope because it loves. Charity loves because it sees. It is itself the eye by which God is seen.

The soul, in fact, has its senses. It possesses its own sight or eye by which it sees God. As the body has five senses by which it is joined to the soul by the instrumentality of life, so also the soul has its five senses by which it is joined to God by the instrumentality of love. This is why the apostle says: "Be not conformed to this world, but be transformed by the renewing of your mind, that you may prove what is that good, and acceptable, and perfect will of God" (Romans 12:2). We have the proof here that the bodily senses involve us in a kind of senility and render us worldly. With the aid of the Spirit, we are renewed in the knowledge of God (Colossians 3:10) into a new life (Romans 8:4) that is according to the will and goodness of God (Ephesians 1:9).

VII. THE FIVE SENSES OF LOVE

16
Love's sense of touch

There are five animal or physical senses by which the soul communicates with the body. From the lowest, I begin with touch, then taste, smell, hearing, and sight. Likewise, there are five spiritual senses by which love enlivens the soul. These are: physical love, such as the love of parents; social love; natural love; spiritual love; and the love of God. By the five senses of the body and the instrumentality of life, the body is united to the soul. By the five spiritual senses and the instrumentality of love, the soul is united to God.

First, the love of parents is comparable to touch. This *affectus* is spontaneous to all and it is ordinary and palpable. For it is offered naturally to all, and it is so natural that none can avoid its encounter even if one wanted to do so. A sense of touch encompasses all one's physical being and is activated by contact with other physical objects; the only condition is that one or the other of the bodies in contact must be alive. No matter where you go, your body cannot be without the sense of touch.

Likewise, your soul cannot be without the sense of love. But on account of love's omnipresence, Scripture does not highly recommend it. Rather, love is restrained lest it become excessive. As the Lord says, "if anyone does not hate his father and mother, he cannot be my disciple" (Luke 14:26).

Second, social love is comparable to the taste. It is the love of brothers and the love of the holy church. Of the latter, it is said: "Behold how good and how pleasant it is for brothers to dwell together in unity" (Psalm 133:1). Just as life is administered to the body through taste, so the Lord has given love the blessing of life. For although taste is exercised physically, nevertheless it generates an inner savor which affects the soul. Because of this, the sense of love is particularly physical in the sense of being biologically life-giving.

17
Love's sense of taste

Social love is linked and nourished by mutual duties through physically living together, through like professions, and through like tastes; it feeds upon mutual services. That is why we say that it is mostly physical in character. Yet it is also to a marked degree spiritual, because just as there is a savor to taste, so the *affectus* of brotherly love burns in that *affectus*. Of this it is written: "It is like the precious ointment on the head, that ran down upon the beard, even the beard of Aaron, which ran down to the hem of his garment; and it is like the dew of Hermon on the Mountain of Zion" (Psalm 133:2-3).

Third, the sense of smell can be compared to natural love which naturally loves every man because of sharing

18
Love's sense of smell

the same nature. We carry love to all men without thought of return. This love comes from the hidden recesses of our being and penetrates into the soul so that it allows nothing human to be alien to itself.

But this sense—I speak of it as smell—seems to belong more to the soul than to the body. It penetrates into the interior of the body with the perception of the nostrils. This inhalation is through the body and affects the soul, not just the body. So, too, natural love appears to be more spiritual than merely biological because it goes beyond the natural bounds that unite all humanity in one blood by society and by similar ties.

19
Love's sense
of healing

Fourth, hearing is to be compared with spiritual love, that is, the love of one's enemies. Hearing does not affect our interior sensation; it is outside us as a vibration is on the eardrum. It calls the soul to come and to listen.

So likewise no power of nature in the heart, no *affectus* of any need whatever, arouses us to love our enemies. It is obedience alone which can do this; this is signified through hearing. Yet this love is said to be spiritual because it promotes likeness to the Son of God. It also expresses the dignity of the sons of God as the Lord says: "Do good to those who hate you, that you may be the children of your Father in heaven" (Matthew 5:44-45).

20
Love's sense
of sight

Fifth, vision is like divine love. For as vision is the principal bodily sense, so divine love has the first place in our affections. All the other senses are said to see through the vision of the eyes although only the eye can see. We say touch and see, taste and see, and so on (Psalm 34:8; 45:10).

Thus all the objects which are loved by a good affection are said to be loved by divine love since it is clearer than light that nothing should be loved except for God's sake. An object is loved not so much for its own sake, but more on account of *why* it should be loved. From this it follows: "from Him all fatherhood in heaven and on earth is named" (Ephesians 3:15).

Sight is indeed a kind of force of the soul: untainted,

powerful, and pure. Likewise, divine love is powerful because it operates with great things; yet it is pure. For as
someone has said: "Nothing that defiles will enter in"
(Revelation 21:27). God does not deign to be loved along
with any other thing which is not loved on account of
Him.

Sight is placed in the foremost part of the body, in the
chief and prominent spot on the head. It has placed beneath it organs of all the other senses according to order,
dignity, and their capacity for good. And as I have argued,
the closer these senses are to sight, the more vital they are;
the further away from sight they are, the more physical
they are. Touch, then, is the least of all and more undis-
tinguished than the rest. While it belongs to all the body,
it belongs properly to the hand.

The mind (as the intellectual soul peculiar to man) is   **The mind of love**
the summit of the soul. It should be viewed as the seat of
God's love so that it may have under its rule all other
loves. Nor should there be in any of the other senses anything which hides them from the heat and light of the
mind. The mind (or *mens*) is nearer the more spiritual
loves and more remote from the vital and physical loves.
That is when we "love the Lord our God with all our heart
and with all our soul, and with all our strength, and our
neighbor as ourselves" (Luke 10:27).

Sight having the more special place in the body, it also
appears to have something over and above the principle of
vitality in the body. For it tends to imitate the power of
the mind of memory. One moment it will dart over half
the sky, and the next instance it will flash to the uttermost
part of the earth. Thus also the revealed love of God ac-
quires its own throne in the soul of the believer to move it
toward some likeness of the divine power.

At the same time, the soul is shown to be so finite and
creaturely that it is as nothing before God. Yet it is made
to realize that "all things work together for good" (Romans
8:28) when love trusts all that is in the Father's hands
(John 16:15). For whether it be Paul or Cephas, life or
death, things present or things to come, all things belong

to love (1 Corinthians 3:22). Indeed, the whole world of blessings belongs to the faithful.

VIII. REASON AND LOVE GIVE FORTITUDE TO THE SOUL

21   The vision for seeing God—the natural light of the soul created by the Author of nature—is love. Now for this vision there are two eyes whose focus ceaselessly seeks the light which is God. This function may be likened to love and reason. The efforts of the one depend also upon the other, so they are very effective when they are united. But they are not much use when they are separated from each other. Then they are like the situation described in the Canticle: "You have wounded my heart, O my friend, with one of your eyes" (Song of Solomon 4:9).

The soul's two sources of vision

Both sources of vision suffer much in their own way. The one—reason—cannot see God except in what He is not. While the other—love—cannot have rest except in what God is. In fact, with all its efforts, all that reason can apprehend or discover in all its efforts is to say: Is this my God? Reason can only find out what it discovers is not God.

Reason has its limits and set ways which circumscribe it. But love advances more by its shortcomings and apprehends more by its ignorance. Reason appears, therefore, to move forward through what God is not toward what God is. Love, in setting aside what God is not, rejoices to be lost in what God is. For from God love has come forth, and it naturally longs to return to its beginning. Reason has the greatest sobriety, love the greater happiness.

How reason and love help each other.

However, as I have said, when both of them help each other, such as when reason teaches love, and love enlightens reason, then reason merges into the *affectus* of love, and love lets itself be confined within the limits of reason. Then they can do great things for each other.

But what is the power that they can achieve? Just as the ardent soul only makes progress in learning the art of experience, nevertheless, it "cannot communicate to those who have not so experienced." As it is said by the wise man: "A stranger does not meddle with his joy" (Proverbs 14:10).

From this moment, then, the soul sweetly nourished by a gentleness and the delight of love is also sometimes bruised by the disciplines of God's fatherly care. But from all this, the soul is strengthened to prevail. The sword of love cuts the soul off and snatches it away from the love and desires of the world. This is like Enoch, who was taken by God so that he was no longer found in the worldly affairs (Genesis 5:24).

*22
The discipline
of love*

By death, the body is deadened to all the senses. And the soul by its death progresses and is quickened and strengthened in all its faculties. Now it advances determinately, steadily, and wisely in all its steps and ways (Psalm 17:5). For until now, the soul was held back by ignorance, doubt, and wavering, so that it could scarcely dare go forward to seek after good. But the fortitude of the simple is the way of the Lord (Proverbs 10:29).

Now the soul is insensitive to the world, deadened to the many worldly activities and desires. As the Apostle Paul says: "The world is crucified to me and I to the world" (Galatians 6:14). Separated by their contrasted desires, the one does not care for the other. They could not, nor did they care to, approach one another. Paul and the world have been crucified to each other.

*The soul's
indifference
to the world*

Nevertheless, Paul's whole life was in heaven (Philippians 3:20), yet he was with man on earth when needed. He longed, saying, "I desire to depart and to be with Christ" (Philippians 1:23). Yet Paul knew that Christ would be always with him, even to the end of the world (Matthew 28:20). What assurance this gave Paul, to have Christ always with him! To have Christ here on earth in contemplation, and to have Christ there in glory: what a blessed and glorious state for Paul to enjoy! Thus did the love of God lift him up on high while the love of his neighbor pressed him down like a weight around his neck. So he adds, "But to abide still in the flesh is needful, for your sakes" (Philippians 1:24).

23
The soul's
delight in God

The vitality of love's desires for God adheres indissolubly together. They see judgment in the light of His countenance (Psalm 17:2) so that the soul acts only in pleasing the good will of God (Romans 12:2) which speaks inwardly to it. The soul finds delight only in living beneath God's countenance, reading and understanding there the Word of life (Revelation 22:19). This is the law by which the soul must live: to illumine faith, to strengthen hope, and to kindle love.

In fact, the Holy Spirit is the Spirit of knowledge which teaches openly the saintly soul what to do and how to do it. The Spirit of power equips the soul with strength and virtues to accomplish this. And when the soul is free to be free in God—to hold on to God—it is made like God, through the piety of devotion and by the unity of will. But when the soul is forced to return to men and to human affairs, the soul radiates glory and serenity, in speech and conduct, and in all the traits of that oil of God's love. The soul's kindness and grace conquers mankind and obtains from them respect and their obedience in what it wills.

Sometimes when the soul returns from its hiding place to rebuke the vices of the delinquent and the corrupt manners of the sinners, it may appear awesome and terrifying because of the seriousness and truth of the judgment before God's countenance. When the soul stands before those who need to be corrected according to the unchangeable law of God's truth, when the soul is ready to accomplish, and when the soul strives to do everything with gravity and with justice, it gives way to love. For its anger is understood now as a discipline of love.

The soul's
docility in God

Like the wheels which Ezekiel saw in his vision (Ezekiel 1:21) which moved with the Spirit of life, the soul is moved along to accomplish God's will. They do not spin backwards to do their own thing. If they are commanded

to go forward, they lead with solicitude. If they are ordered to stop, they do so with humility. If they are obliged
to cooperate with others, they do so in love. If they are
prelates, they act like fathers to their sons. If they are subjects, they are like children to their parents. If they are living among their peers, they become the servants of all
(1 Corinthians 9:19).

Thus the affections of the godly are reverent to everyone. For their desire to do good is pleasant. Their meeting
with others is in cheerfulness. Their dwelling together is
in grace. Their going out to reach others is an evidence of
love. To those under them, they are tender in affection.
To their elders, they love in subjection. To those above
them, they serve reverently.

The godly soul's
relationship with
others

In all things, the affections do not look after their own
interests but for those of everyone else. If possible, they
make everybody's concern their own. So they readily
adapt to others, living submissively to whatever the law
has ordained. For they have received the seal of pledge of
the Holy Spirit to do this service (2 Corinthians 1:22).
They also realize that they will soon be transformed into
the adoption of sonship and their revelation as sons of
God (Romans 8:15, 19).

IX. THE SCHOOL OF CHARITY

Let us now come to consider what the apostle calls the
fellowship of the Spirit (Philippians 2:1) in praise of this
disciplined life which is united in goodness and joyful
brotherliness. For it is there where the Lord gives life and
blessing (Psalm 133:3). Of it, the Lord says: "Fear not
little flock, for it has pleased the Father to give you a kingdom" (Luke 12:32). This disciplined life takes its origin
from the apostles who, when they had learned from the
Holy Spirit and were endowed from on high (Luke 24:69),
established a way of living together. This would enable a
multitude to live as one heart and one soul, having all
things in common, and always be in the temple together

24

(Acts 2:44-47; 4:32).

The disciplined life modeled on the apostles

People have imitated this way of apostolic life—being without the possession of homes and livelihoods and in other than the house of the Lord as the house of prayer (Isaiah 56:7; Luke 19:46). All that they do, they do in the name of the Lord (Psalm 124:8). They share the same way of life, they live under one rule, they have nothing of their own; not even their bodies or their wills are their own.

These people retire at night, they rise up in the morning together, pray, sing psalms, and read together. Their fixed resolve is to obey their superiors and to be subject to their discipline. Yet their superiors realize also that they will be accountable for them. They preach to them what Gedaliah preached to Israel: "I will answer for you to the Chaldeans, who are coming to us. You, however, gather the harvest, the wine and oil in your vessels, and dwell secure in your cities" (Jeremiah 40:9-10).

On behalf of others they offer to God daily the laughter of their heart and their joyfulness as the Isaac of the free woman who is the son of promise (Genesis 21:6). For themselves, they keep Ishmael, whom they serve as the son of bondage (Genesis 21:6) when they neglect the fruits of the Spirit (Galatians 5:22) and get absorbed in service for its own sake. Preaching a sabbath rest to the people of God, they encourage their people to be strangers to the world and so freed from all anxieties that are caused by avarice.

A simple life

Once their wants are reduced to minimum, they live on very little. Their clothing is simple, their diet is plain, and all else is determined by the rule that they follow. So no one is permitted to have more than he should, and so there is sufficient for all. Nor is there anyone to encourage to seek more if everyone has what is permitted to him to keep.

25   Does this sound like a utopian rather than an earthly paradise? No, because in this paradise only the superiors are permitted to eat steadily of the tree of the knowledge

of good and evil. They are permitted to dispense with discretion. But as for the community itself, it is their duty to
obey and not to discriminate for their own benefit.

All the time, they strive to maintain silence, so that instead they can communicate with the desires of the heart
instead of with the mouth. While their superiors may
stimulate them with frequent exhortations, they encourage each other much more by mutual example. In honor
and service to each other, they outdo one another (Romans 12:10). As the apostle says, "considering one
another to provoke unto love and to good works" (Hebrews 10:24). They do not allow anyone to remain on his
own, lest the Preacher say to him: "woe to him that is
alone when he falls" (Ecclesiastes 4:10). They consider
that person as solitary who does not choose a companion
to whom he can unburden his conscience, or who upsets
his brethren by always keeping to himself.

When the circumstances demand it, there is permitted
a quiet conversation about matters necessary for the affairs
of body and soul. Otherwise, silence prevails.

But everywhere there is the continuous and intense devotion to the study of prayer, "in all places" (Psalm
103:22) under the provident rule of God. There is also the
dutiful, melodious, and fervent melody of the Psalter, the
songs of life that deepen the desires of the heart for God.
Well composed, they are sung not so much on the basis of
musical harmony, but from the upwelling of love.

In the common exercises of devotion are to be seen that
serenity of disposition in faces, that quiet deportment of
bodies which, like the Seraphim (Isaiah 6:2-3), surround
the presence of the Lord with holy desires. One worshiper
catches more of the love of God from the other so that no
one can give as he would ardently seek to give.

This is the unique school of love. Here its exercises are
practiced, its themes are rehearsed, and its solutions are
reached, based not only on reasoning, but on the fruits of
reason and experience and by the very nature of the truth
of things. Here the weary traveler can sit down upon his

baggage which he had carried with him because of his needs and those of others living with him. He will not die, nor need he turn back whence he came, nor need he feel compelled to proceed further. For if he will remain faithfully guarding his baggage, he will hardly differ from those who have marched ahead of him. He too will triumph in victory (Isaiah 30:21-24).

For is not the place of our baggage all those things that oppressed us? Are they not like the blows to the heart—those to the back (Psalm 129:3)—the family loyalties that we cling to? Are they not fights without and fears within (2 Corinthians 7:5), daily so, and yes, even the continual cares of all we serve (2 Corinthians 11:28)? Yes, there is still a long way to ascend to the mountain of the Lord and to the house of Jacob (Isaiah 2:3). But beyond this point, no one with baggage is allowed to pass. See pp. 108-109.

But old age begins when there is no longer strength for the baggage. Then reverence is due to old age. Yet one is reputed to be venerable not by the years that one has but by the virtues that one exercises. So one aspires to the maturity of wisdom where one can rest from one's labors. It is as the reward for the completion of military service.

27   Wisdom in making such progress on the pilgrimage does not jettison love. Instead of being abandoned, love is rather developed further. Yet wisdom is tired of carrying love's baggage as we have seen because wisdom is preparing for other things in view. Indeed, it prepares and gets ready to enter into the joy of the Lord (Matthew 25:21, 23).

Therefore, wisdom detests to be preoccupied with any cares. Even though it goes on laboring, it does not wish to be obsessed with them. It does not lack the necessary strength. It is just that it flees from any impediment between the soul and the presence of God. Thus in order to encourage the saintly soul in the progress of the journey, and to incite it to enter into the rest of the Lord, the word of the Lord is given. "You shall love the Lord your God, with all your soul, with all your heart, with all your strength and with all your mind" (Deuteronomy 6:5).

X. THE TASTE FOR HOLY THINGS

Here we are called upon to exercise four affections. For **28** these words "with all your heart" imply that God claims for Himself the whole will. "With all your soul" means He claims all your love. "With all your strength" describes the virtue of charity. "With all your mind" claims the enjoyment of wisdom.

First, the will moves the soul toward God; then love carries it forward; charity then contemplates and wisdom enjoys.

Wisdom is well placed in the mind. As the mind is called such because it reflects or is the most eminent faculty of the soul, it is well to ascribe to it that superior virtue among the soul's other qualities. For the mind is a distinctive power of the soul by which we are united to God to enjoy God. Now this enjoyment consists of a certain kind of divine savor, and wisdom comes from this savor of divine things. This savor results from a certain kind of taste, which no one is capable of describing unless he is merited with it. As Scripture says: "Taste and see that the Lord is good" (Psalm 34:8). By this tasting, according to the apostle, one tastes "the good Word of God and the powers of the world to come" (Hebrews 6:5). But we need to inquire more subtly about this taste which wisdom savors.

First, it should be said that the soul which ascends only **The lover of** does so by degrees to the palace of wisdom. However, at **wisdom** every step taken, wisdom herself seeks out those who look for her as it is said in the book of her name. Wisdom goes out into the streets seeking those who seek her, and joyfully reveals herself to them (Proverbs 1:20-21). Without her initiative, the will would not be moved, nor would love come forward, nor would contemplation lead to charity, nor enjoyment to wisdom. That is why we need to investigate further what this taste signifies.

The body of Jesus Christ is the church universal in both **29** the Old and the New Testaments. Under the headship of **The sense of Christ** this body in the primitive or early church, there are four senses: sight, hearing, smell, and touch. The eyes are as the angels, because of their loftiness of contemplation. The ears are the patriarchs because of the virtue of obedience. The nose or smell is as the prophets because of their awareness of absent reality. Touch is a sense common to all.

All of these senses were in the head before the advent of the Mediator, but they languished because the lower body was quite dead due to the absence of one sense, namely that of taste. Without it, the body was unable to live and the senses were unable to obtain the powers to vivify themselves.

In fact, take any function of the body that depends upon the nourishment of the whole body and place it before, under, and around the whole body with all its senses. If taste alone is lacking, what good is there in the other senses? Shout the nourishment into the ears, introduce it into the nostrils or into any other part of the body, but it will not be nourished. It will remain useless.

But a certain sweetness of savor will follow from taste which the soul feeds upon with its inner being in a remarkable way that is incommunicable to all the other senses. When received, it discerns and judges all else. It invigorates and affirms itself as well as all the other senses. Placed in the throat, between head and body, it connects both.

Christ our suffering   Thus it symbolizes Him who took our flesh and became a little lower than the angels (Psalm 8:5; Hebrews 2:7). By showing patience and humility, He made Himself somehow still less and more humble. For while the saintly patriarchs and prophets could cast down their enemies to the ground by their powerful virtues, He taught the disciples very differently. "But whosoever shall smite you on your right cheek, turn to him the other also" (Matthew 5:39).

30   Coming after the patriarchs and the prophets and placed at the boundary between law and grace, between the head and the body, He was the savor which brought out through the mystery of His humanity, passion, and

resurrection whatever in the law, the prophets, and the psalms was needed for vitally nourishing the body. The Christ-Man did this as taste is to the mouth of the body. By a certain inward savor of divinity, Christ, the Wisdom of God, was made wisdom for us (1 Corinthians 1:30). He found the things that are savory and has made them savory and useful for us also.

In fact, having life in Himself, He has invigorated life **Christ our joy** and given comfort to the whole body. He gives joy to Himself and He gives joy to the angels by the consummation of His body (Luke 15:7, 10). He rejoices also the patriarchs and the prophets in revealing to them that Day of the Lord. He said about Abraham, "Your father, Abraham, rejoiced to see my day: he saw it and was glad" (John 8:56). Joy and life, common to all the body, are given! By such transports of delight and influenced by this universal and spiritual attachment, we proclaim aloud: "that which we have seen with our eyes, which we have looked upon, and our hands have handled, of the Word of life . . . declare we unto you" (1 John 1:1, 3).

That is why in all our prayers we add, "through Jesus **Christ our prayer** Christ our Lord." For it is through Him, as our Mediator, that we address God as our Father with our prayers and our sacrifices of praise. That is why also we hope for the best gift of all from the Father of Lights, who gives every perfect gift (James 1:17). The gifts we ask for do not come then through our ears or our nostrils. They come from Him who is our mouth, our taste, our wisdom, so that there is nourishment to all who receive Him.

This, then, is the taste which is created for us by Jesus **31** Christ, the Spirit of understanding, namely the under- **Christ our** standing of the Scriptures and of the mysteries of God **understanding** (Isaiah 11:2). This was how Jesus Christ appeared to His disciples after the Resurrection, for "He opened their understanding that they might understand the Scriptures" (Luke 24:45).

We begin now not only to understand but to penetrate

even into the interior sense of the Scriptures, into the virtues of God's mysteries and the divine sacraments. Then we begin to touch with the conscience and to handle with the hand of experience what can only come by some special savoring of the things of God. It is this which goes inwardly within itself and senses the goodness and merits of God which the work of grace itself accomplishes within us by its powerful goodness and its effective virtue. It is then that wisdom really accomplishes what is its proper role. Then the soul can judge those things which are worthy. By its anointing, the soul can then teach all things (1 John 2:27).

Christ our anointing

Having been sealed by the affixing of God's goodness upon our lives, He then imprints upon us and confirms us. He anoints us to be calm in everything and gentle within our spirits. But if He finds any hardness or rigidity, His Spirit will pound and crush, cleanse and purify until the saintly soul has received the wholesome joy of the Lord (Psalm 51:7-8). Then renewed and strengthened by the spirit of wisdom, the saintly soul will cry out in His joyfulness: "Lord, lift up the light of your countenance upon us. You have put gladness in my heart" (Psalm 4:6-7). For this also we have the Word of our Lord: "This is life eternal, that they may know You, the only true God, and Jesus Christ whom you have sent" (John 17:3). How blessed is this knowledge which contains eternal life!

This life then—eternal life—comes from such tasting, because to taste spiritually in this way is to really understand the things of God. The apostle who described himself as the least of the apostles was nevertheless so filled, exhilarated, and strengthened in this wisdom that through this tasting he could say:

> "Unto me, who am less than the least of all saints, is this grace given, that I should preach among the Gentiles the unsearchable riches of Christ; and to make all men see what is the fellowship of the mystery, which from the beginning of the world has been hidden, in God who

created all things by Jesus Christ" (Ephesians 3:8-9).

A little further on he says: "for this cause I bow my knees unto the Father of our Lord Jesus Christ, of whom the whole family in heaven and earth is named, that He would grant you, according to the riches of His glory, to be strengthened with might by His Spirit in the inner man; that Christ may dwell in your hearts by faith; that you, being rooted and grounded in love, may be able to comprehend with all saints what is the breadth, and length, and depth, and height of this love" (Ephesians 3:14-18). Let us then endeavor, if possible, to penetrate a little way into the meaning of the apostle's wisdom.

XI. OUR NEED OF CHRIST OUR MEDIATOR

There are four attributes of God: power, wisdom, charity, and truth/eternity (which are one). For nothing is true unless it is immutable.

32

To these attributes we need to make two responses. To the power which can punish us and to the wisdom from which we can never hide, we need to exercise true fear. That is to say, a fear which false confidence does not eliminate, nor pretense can undermine. Pretense occurs when we pretend to keep the commandments (Psalm 93:20) or when we assume God gives "cheap grace."

To charity and to truth we owe true love, a love which is not frustrated by lukewarmness nor the scruples of mistrust. For what is indebted to charity but charity itself? Indeed, the truth of charity and the character of truth remove every scruple of mistrust (2 Thessalonians 2:10). I call mistrust that fear which does not love charity, which does not believe truth is reliable, and which does not believe eternity will never fail. It is for this reason that Paul says: "that you may be able to apprehend with all saints what is the breadth and length and height and depth" (Ephesians 3:18). Its height is its power; its depth is its

The reality of true love

wisdom; its breadth is its love; and its length is eternity. Truly this is the cross of Christ.

Elsewhere the same apostle expresses more clearly the virtue of supreme wisdom within us. He says:

> "Wherefore, I also, after I heard of your faith in the Lord Jesus, and love unto all the saints, cease not to give thanks for you, making mention of you in my prayers; that the God of our Lord Jesus Christ, the Father of glory, may give unto you the Spirit of wisdom and revelation in the knowledge of Him; the eyes of your understanding being enlightened; that you may know what is the hope of His calling, and what are the riches of the glory of His inheritance in the saints, and what is the exceeding greatness of His power to us-ward who believe, according to the working of His mighty power, which He wrought in Christ when He raised Him from the dead and set Him at His own right hand in the heavenly places" (Ephesians 1:15-20).

33
Christ, the
savor of God

Thus, the prayer of the apostle and the exercise of God within us gives us the spirit of this wisdom and the gracious revelation of the knowledge of who He is; then we have within us a savor of God. For it is He Himself who is the savor. Then when our eyes are opened by showing us of His bounty, then we can communicate the intelligence of this world being, which is the hope of our calling. This is what it means to know the glorious riches of that eternity destined for the saints. In all of this we see the goodness and the bounty of God who has illuminated and called us.

But when grace is bestowed upon us so that we can respond to this heavenly calling, the experience of the spirit of wisdom reveals to us the nature and the grandeur of His truth within us. Then the soul so armed with this disposition as possessing the divine palate can enjoy divine contemplation and discern all things. For in Christ, the source of all blessings, the soul can taste—primarily by his conversion to God, then by the forgiveness of sins, then by a multiple sequence of experiences of the grace of God instead of anger—that we are the children of God. All of the favors the soul possesses uniquely from our Lord Jesus Christ. For He is our Mediator, our Wisdom, and without Him, the wisest of human beings is a fool (1 Corinthians 1:25).

The bounty of God is so rich and offers His treasures to all. But no one can receive as much as He offers. No one can, therefore, teach how it can be so received. Nor is anyone able to ascend to where these gifts are distributed. No one is able to descend to bring them down (Romans 10:6-7). That is why we need a mediator between us and God, through whom we can receive and be given (1 Timothy 2:5).

34

In like manner the whole Triune God counsels about what the prophet says: "The counsel of the Lord stands forever, the thoughts of His heart to all generations" (Psalm 33:11). For God, having seen the total confusion of mankind, his trouble, instability, and disorder, also saw how estranged man was from God in the realm of delusion and incapable of either knowing or resolving his needs. God saw that the angel of light, the devil, in his presumptuous usurpation of the divine likeness, had said: "I will ascend into heaven, I will exalt my throne above the stars of God—I will be like the most High" (Isaiah 14:13-14). Man, likewise, pretended to be God at the suggestion of the serpent who said to him: "You will be as God" (Genesis 3:5). Thus God the Father replied, "My Son, the true splendor of my glory, the express image of My person" (Hebrews 1:3), will have many rivals who, jealous to be equal, will desire to be companions of the Godhead.

Christ our humiliation

Thus God has cast down both demonic angel and rebellious man.

God the Son, the Image of the invisible God (Colossians 1:15), is so contrasted with both fallen angel and man who were made as God's image (Genesis 1:26-27). They perished because of their inordinate desire to be like

God in image and likeness. Instead, the Son alone could say: "Humiliation alone lacks envy! Therefore, I shall show myself to man, as a man despised, the least of all men, a man of sorrows and acquainted with grief" (Isaiah 53:3). In that way man may in turn be zealous to imitate My humility, so that he comes to the true glory, from which he would fly. Then he can hear from Me my words: "Learn of me, for I am meek and lowly of heart, and you will find rest to your souls" (Matthew 11:29).

XII. THE CHARACTER OF OUR REDEMPTION

35   Thus the Son of God set His course, drawing near to reclaim man to save the perishing in his pride by the humility of His mission. He intervened between God and man, man who coming from God was enslaved by Satan. In this way, He acted and fulfilled the role of a good Mediator.

> "And there shall come forth a rod out of the stem of Jesse, and a branch shall grow out of his roots: and the Spirit of the Lord shall rest upon Him, the spirit of wisdom and understanding, the spirit of counsel and might, the spirit of knowledge and of the fear of the Lord" (Isaiah 11:1-2).

Imagine in this context a most powerful athlete, being entered into the stadium of the world and anointed by the oil of the Holy Spirit for the contest. How he casts himself joyfully into the race of this human dispensation (Psalm 19:6)! Note also how the prophet began with the higher and moved towards the lower when announcing the descent of the Mediator. We, on the contrary, in our efforts to rise to the higher with the aid of the Holy Spirit and of the Mediator, begin with the law, that is to say, out of fear.

Christ our obedience   Christ did have fear for the Father, but it was a chaste and filial fear (1 Peter 3:2), in which He offered Him glory in all things, saying:

"My meat is to do the will of Him who sent me and to finish His work" (John 4:34). Or as the Psalm exclaims: "Let my heart rejoice that it may fear your Name" (Psalm 86:11).

And there are many other passages like these. Christ was seen to humble Himself through this fear, to abase Himself, to disregard His own interest, that He might restore to the Father, redeemed and renovated, the work which God had done through Christ but which had been corrupted.

In this manner then, our Mediator had fear towards the Father from His exaltation, and in His bounty He made the downstoop to reconcile miserable man to God. Of both relationships, He had knowledge, knowing how to relate to both God and to man. To fulfill His mission of mediation, He had the good will of His Father from above; but He had nothing from the wretched sinners here below. Since His mediation required that He had something from man, He demanded faith. He demanded faith first by exercising grace to man. Yet nothing could have been more appropriate to ask for, since miserable man, receiving such grace, could only trust in Him who had so overwhelmed him with such goodness. **36**

Yet since no one can believe in Christ without hope—for who can believe in someone in whom there is no hope—He brought hope with faith. With hope, He added fear, for without fear there could be no real hope. This was the hope that no one would ever be abandoned by such a gracious Mediator. The Mediator, having then received such a pledge of salvation on behalf of man, returned to the Father. So He went back alone to the mountain to pray (Matthew 14:23).

Being in an agony, He continued to pray in a bloody sweat (Luke 22:43-44). "Father," He cried, "glorify Your Son!" (John 17:1). **Christ our mediator**

"Here is what I shall offer You," said Christ. "Here is what I shall offer man. Here is what I have from You. Here is what I have from man. I am the Mediator, and the bases for my mediation are the fulfillment of man's salvation.

"Man has been taken captive and bound. A strong enemy has captured him, and unless one stronger comes to overcome the tyrant, this enemy will steal his goods (Matthew 12:29).

"But send your Son from above (Psalm 144:7), and I will save the captive from his strongest enemies (Psalm 18:7) in the spirit of strength, Your strength and Your virtue (Revelation 7:12). For I well know what I am doing. Innocent, I shall die for the guilty. My goodness will do incomparably more than what the malice of the enemy can ever do. The punishment of my innocence will do far more than the punishment inflicted on the disobedience of man."

37   In answer to these words, the Father says, "I have both glorified You and will glorify You again" (John 12:28).

Now the most powerful mediation needs a spirit of counsel because "if the prince of this world had known it, he would not have crucified the Lord of glory" (1 Corinthians 2:8). But the Son of God hid His glory of divinity, revealing only the weakness of the flesh without sin. Thereby He took away the envy of the hostile wickedness by the holiness of His life. Through His weakness the enemy hoped to be victorious over Him.

Christ also aroused Satan's envy by His accompanying miracles which He used to strengthen man's faith in Him as reconciler. Satan, the deceiver, having been deceived, inflicted on Christ, who was unworthy of punishment for sin, the penalty of sin; that is, a very cruel death. Yet the righteous—so struck unjustly for righteousness' sake—obtained a new righteousness from the enemy of death which was unjustly inflicted upon Him.

Since this death was not incumbent upon Him—for He was without sin—by sharing this victory with sinful man, He absolved the accused through the punishment of His innocence. Taking His own body and blood in His hand, He said: "Eat this! Drink this! And live by it!" (John 6:57). Then presenting it before His Father, He said: "My

Father, here is the price of my blood" (Matthew 27:6). "Lord and Father, You have bestowed liberality, and My Body has also produced its fruit" (Psalm 85:13). "And to save all justly who were lost justly, You, Lord, will walk in righteousness in the path before You" (Psalm 85:13). "You have given the directives, You have established justice, and the judgment in Jacob" (Psalm 99:4).

XIII. THE WISDOM OF GOD'S CHILDREN

Thus has man been satiated with the fruit of such mediation wrought by divine wisdom. For not only has he been reconciled, he is also made wise. For he can now savor what he eats. He eats and drinks the body and blood of His Redeemer as heavenly manna (Hebrews 9:4), the bread of angels (Psalm 78:24-25), the bread of wisdom (Ecclesiastes 9:11). While eating it, he is found transformed into the nature of what he eats. For to eat the body of Jesus Christ is nothing other than to be made like Christ and to be the temple of the Holy Spirit (1 Corinthians 6:19). And when this temple has been embellished by the graces received and the devotion consecrated to God, it can no longer receive other extraneous inceptions. For now it is that dwelling place of God Himself who created and fashioned it.

38

Such a soul is no longer, therefore, concerned or in love with earthly things that are material and corruptible, now that the baggage room of life has been surrendered and left behind. Although, on occasion, the soul will use the baggage once more; it is only in passing, with no desire for possessiveness. If the soul is blessed with prosperity, it still passes on. If adversity strikes, it is untroubled. The reason is that the soul savors fully all things, for the loving soul cannot taste anything without the heavenly saliva of Christ, the Head.

Christ our satisfaction

All, then, that affects the body, whether good or evil, is external and cannot affect what lies within the spirit of man.

It is for this reason that the apostle in the depth and squalor of miseries and bound by prison chains, writes to his disciples: "I will send Timothy shortly to you, as soon as I see how it will go with me" (Philippians 2:23). He speaks of what is around him, what will go with the exterior man, affecting perhaps the exterior garment of flesh, but which does not penetrate into the interior man of whom he really is.

**39
Christ our
wisdom**

This is the wisdom about which the apostle speaks: "We speak wisdom among the perfect" (1 Corinthians 2:6). Concerning this, we speak as those who have heard it said but have not experienced it as we might describe a city that we have never visited, but merely have hearsay about many things. Yet once one has visited it for oneself, then one will speak very differently and much more realistically.

Over against this spiritual wisdom, Paul speaks of a very different wisdom, "the wisdom of the princes of this world" (1 Corinthians 2:6). The contrast is like day and night, white and black. Of one, it is said, "wisdom triumphs over malice" (Wisdom 7:30). Malice is the savor of evil, and wisdom coming from another savor confronts it.

Thus the wisdom of the princes of this age is opposed to the wisdom that is from above (James 3:15-17). This malicious wisdom that is from below hates divine wisdom. In the incompatibility of the two wisdoms lies their intrinsic savors of good and of evil, respectively. Yet the unlimited craftiness of the evil destroys such (Job 5:13; 1 Corinthians 3:19), while the prudence of the good saves.

**Prudential
wisdom**

But between these two principles (of divine wisdom and earthly malice) their is an intermediary wisdom, like a middle shade of color between white and black. It is so balanced between them that its motive is what raises or lowers it between heaven and earth. This is the wisdom that the apostle speaks of as being of this world which he places between the wisdom which is of God and the wisdom of the princes of this world (1 Corinthians 2:6-7). It deals with honest and useful things and so it is determined by calculated prudence. It consists very largely of knowing with prudential discernment, so that it judges what is useful and impractical, what is honest or dishonest, although it may not necessarily follow its own judgment. So many use this knowledge as knowledge which puffs up (1 Corinthians 8:1), because the motive is only to satisfy curiosity, or to be recognized as "an authority" which is only vanity. But in all these efforts to be knowledgeable, none of these studies truly elevate to that sphere where reason finds it is incapable of existing without love.

XIV. CONTRAST BETWEEN FALSE AND TRUE WISDOM

Now this human wisdom or philosophy is divided into the knowledge of human affairs and of the divine. As long as it is concerned with human things, it is at home with the familiar. But when it is raised to deal with the divine, the higher it ascends the more its fall is harsher and the clearer becomes the word of the psalmist: "for You have lifted me up, and cast me down" (Psalm 102:10).

41

Sometimes the efforts of natural genius carry one so far that, according to the apostle, one knows something of God, that is whatever reason is able to grasp about God (Romans 1:19). This is apprehensible by the wise. For God has revealed it to them, creating within them the faculty to know. They rise above their own ethical norms to a certain knowledge, from the creatures of this world to the invisible things of God, through those things which have been made (Romans 1:20).

Failure of man's wisdom

Having understood them, they catch a sight of both His eternal power and Godhead. And so they are without excuse (Romans 1:20), because they do not choose to go further nor to advance to where they could go to have the true theology. "Knowing God, they do not glorify Him as God, but become vain in their imaginations and their foolish hearts are darkened" (Romans 1:21). "Professing themselves to be wise, they become fools" (Romans 1:22). Having foolishly destroyed theology, they have failed in their natural knowlege also, for "they have changed the glory of the uncorruptible God into an image made like to corruptible man, to birds, and four-footed beasts, and creeping things" (Romans 1:23).

Because of this, they are not permitted to hold onto their ethics either. Instead, God gave them over to the desires of their hearts, to uncleanness, to dishonor their own bodies with each other (Romans 1:24). God therefore gave them up to uncleanness, to a depravity which does those things which are not natural (Romans 1:28).

Victory of God's wisdom

Instead, true wisdom always overcomes evil. Dwelling always with God (Proverbs 8:3), wisdom knows how to move forward and never slacken. It reaches therefore from one extremity to the other, and disposes all things gently (Proverbs 8:1). It conducts itself wisely in regard to the things of God, cautiously with natural knowledge, and prudently in moral questions.

42   The wise sage, as has been expressed above, once cleansed from all false affection and savoring only the things of God, exposes man before man. Fully under the influence of God in all things, the soul sees all creatures as under God as God sees them, disposing and ordering all in the light of efficacy of true wisdom. The soul acts in the same way, and judges in the same way about them as its own being and living. For the wisdom of God, as it declares itself, is "the radiance of the eternal light, the mirror of God's majesty" (Wisdom 7:26). It is a pure emanation of the untarnished brightness of Almighty God and the breath of His virtue.

That is why the saintly soul bears within itself the radiance of eternal life and the mirror of the divine majesty. When wisdom expresses itself to a creature, it communicates and shows forth the image of the goodness and righteousness of God. And just as it is breathed upon inwardly by the virtue of God, so it flows forth outwardly an emanation of the brightness and charity of God. That is why Solomon says in another place: "The wisdom of a man shines in his countenance" (Ecclesiastes 8:1). Elsewhere he says: "the eyes of a wise man are in his head" (Wisdom 2:14), because it is only through his natural ability of the mind that wisdom can look out and dwell there.

Solomon also says, "the multitude of the wise is the health of the earth" (Wisdom 6:26). Happy, then, are the affairs of mankind, if fools were always under the direction of the wise! How blessed would human affairs become, said a certain philosopher (Plato, *Republic*, 473, 487), if only the wise were kings or if all kings were philosophers. But as the wise flee away wisely from governing, so the fools on their part have horror of ever being under the authority of the wise. So there is total folly, total confusion, and universal disturbance. The wise hide and sulk, and the mere children reign and govern. They become princes who dine in the morning. "And woe to their land" (Ecclesiastes 10:16). But let us now return to our proper subject.

The soul, then, who is enlightened by the spirit of wisdom, loves justice and hates iniquity; because of this God has anointed it with the oil of gladness, which is so rich in Jesus Christ (Psalm 45:7; Hebrews 1:9). Absorbed in the grace of God, the soul pleases all and is loved by all. Even its enemies, seeing this, are full of fear and have to respect it. For even though hardened wickedness does not choose to imitate the good in the righteous, yet the nature of reality cannot be gainsaid.

43
Godly wisdom
enlightens.

For wise men have among themselves a certain particular grace, an angelic language, to help them understand the heart, and even their form aids them in expressing a spiritual grace. This is language known only to the Ruler of the angels, and to His angel, and to those who are of the tribe of Israel, who are the citizens of Jerusalem. No Egyptian or Chaldean knows it. For, they seem to have a foretaste of this in this present life, and are initiated into the blessedness of the life to come in their holiness of present existence. The glorification of their inner life is in contemplation and enjoyment of the divine life. Thus while still on earth, their existing bodies are given some glorification which they will fully receive later after death.

Godly wisdom empowers

Having had experience of that grace of which we have spoken which enables them to live in unity together, they are also bound to God and enjoy God for themselves. For they realize that all the contradictions of the flesh are only instrumental to enable them to good works. For although they suffer miseries, and infirmities consume them, yet they are renewed in their inner man (2 Corinthians 4:16). For as the apostle says: "When I am weak, then am I made strong" (2 Corinthians 12:10). Their senses perceive the advent already of some new spiritual grace. Their eyes are single-minded, and their ears are disciplined.

Often in the fervor of prayer, they are fragrant of an unfamiliar scent, for they enjoy a gentleness that is so penetrating and yet inaccessible to the sense of ordinary taste. It is found through mutual touch as an incentive to charity. They seem to bring forth out of themselves a paradise of spiritual delight. Their countenance, their whole demeanor, the decorum of their life, their conduct, the devoted services that they render, their mutual acceptance, their intimacy, their unity—all so bind them together that they appear as one heart and one soul. Thus by the purity of conscience, and by the grace of their mutual manner of life, they anticipate today the corporeal glory whose future life in all its fullness is reserved for them.

XV. The Blessed Consummation of the Wise

44

Just as all forms of life are bathed by the sunshine and appear to be penetrated by their interrelatedness, so too we live mutually interdependent without actually seeing the life that is the principle of our existence.

Godly wisdom integrates

Likewise, in the life to come, God will be seen by each person to be all and in each one. Not that the divine life is visible to the natural eye, but the glorification of the body will manifest the presence of God in each one.

Since we scarcely understand anything except in material and tangible ways as long as we live in this sphere of images, the material sacraments will lead us to God and keep us from being alienated from each other. That is why religion is said to derive from *religare*, "to bind back." But to the faithful soul the sacraments are only instruments to aid by these means so that the physical should lead toward the spiritual, and the spiritual should lead toward the Creator of both spiritual and physical beings. Truly, then, the soul will lead behind all that creates handicaps.

For having left behind in the body all earthly cares and bodily obstacles, the soul will forget everything except God and attend to nothing else but God. "My beloved is mine, and I am his" (Song of Solomon 2:16). "Whom have I in heaven, but Thee? and there is none upon earth that I desire beside Thee. My flesh and my heart fails: but God is the strength of my heart and my portion forever" (Psalm 73:25-26).

Then comes death. For this entrance to life unbelievers call "death." But for believers is it not a passover? By bodily death, one dies completely to this world to live completely in God. One enters into the perfect tabernacle, one enters into the house of blessing (Psalm 42:4). As we said at the beginning of this treatise, each one of the elements of man proceeds according to its own order. So, the body returns to the earth from whence it came. And the spirit will be raised up and glorified in its due time and return to God who created it.

But what is this transition of life to God?

After all obligations have been severed, and all hindrances have been overcome in perfect blessing and eternal love, the saintly soul is fully linked with God much more so than it ever experienced on earth. The soul will then become one of those of whom it is said: "I have said, you divine ones, you who are sons of the Most High" (Psalm 82:6). This is the destination of those who seek for Jerusalem as the basis for their joy (Psalm 137:6), and to

Godly wisdom is eternal.

45

whom the unction of the Holy Spirit teaches all things (1 John 2:27). They are those who are disposed wisely in their hearts to ascend to the mount, virtue by virtue (see Matthew 5:3-12), until at last the God of gods is seen visibly in Zion (Psalm 84:7). For He is the God of gods, the Beatitude of the blessed, the Joy of those who are filled with joy, the unique and beneficent sovereign Lord.

Godly wisdom is fulfilled.   From the goal of good aspiration at the beginning of the ascent, until the goal of the ultimate consummation, Wisdom deploys its force and guards the energy of those who climb to keep them from falling. Wisdom disposes all things in gentleness, both the adversities as well as the prosperities, turning all things to good (Romans 8:28). Then the soul is redirected to the source of all things and hidden in the secret of the presence of God (Psalm 31:20).

However, everyone who would ascend wisely has to learn that the ascension can only take place in stages like those of a stairway. So each *affectus* in fact does have its own ordering and timing in the scheme of things to fulfill a specific role. All, however, work together in mutual support, anticipating and following one another. Often the first becomes the last, and the last of all becomes first (Matthew 20:16).

---

[1]The Latin is preserved for this untranslatable word. As "the *affectus* of love," it means that basic tendency which thrusts a gravity upon the soul that should be *explained* in good, noble, and generous desires.

[2]For *affectus* toward God nurtures the reality of God.

V

ON CONTEMPLATING GOD
–A PRELUDE*

PLUNGED INTO AN   1
OCEAN OF MISERY WHERE MY
feet do not touch bottom, I cry out, O God.
Lord, hear my cry. For it is to vindicate Your
image and likeness that You have implanted within us
that I cry out to You. I cry, because You cannot leave me
disfigured by the misery of my present state. It is because of
my iniquity that Your hand is heavy upon me. Yet Your
hand is just as restrained in judgment. For in the sea, in
this depth, on this earth, You allow nothing to happen
that will drive us to despair.

O my God, deep calls unto deep (Psalm 42:7). The   2
deep of my profound misery calls to the deep of Your infinite mercy. I look around in vain for any hope and realize
that only You can give that solid assurance and the support that I need. There can be no existence without You. I
find that there is only one reality, and that is that You are
always dependable. I look to find what my heart can love;
and it is only *love*. I look up and down the streets of the
city, and throughout the countryside. But I find that they
who live to themselves, are "strangers from the life before
God" (Ephesians 4:18).

*This essay was written by William of St.-Thierry before he wrote *On the
Nature and Dignity of Love*, about 1119 or 1120. It consists of oral meditations he
shared with his monks.

I search everywhere, in all the wide realms of the world, in all that is inside me, as well as all that is outside me, including all the crises of my life, but they only highlight the reality that I need You. They also attest the truth that the kingdom of God is within me, for I find You in my heart. You are not outside. Thus You are within the most intimate faculties of my being, for are You not what my soul longs for?

My memory also responds to what I most desire within me. You, O God, are like an immense ocean, an ocean of love. There I can repose and find sanctuary. Love is natural to You, O God. So if You seek love, then You seek it in Yourself. But what You seek, You would not find, if You did not love. You possess, then, what You seek, for it is in You.

Guard me then, O God, from seeking strange gods that keep me from You. Receive me in Yourself, give me of Your mercies, and raise me in the delight of Your justice. Help me to dwell entirely in God, in my affections, in my remembrance, and in my entire being. For You are the source of all my being, and of my well-being, O God.

It is given to me, then, to love You. In conscience and in certitude, I am given this blessing, to love You with increasing ardor and desire. In order to enable us to be loving, effective, adoring, soft, tender, and infinitely merciful, honor us with Your love. Unite my nature with yours, O God. Your embrace is as the revelation of Your grace. The left hand of Your consolation lacks nothing. By it You uphold my head and sustain it. But with Your right hand, You embrace me with Your spiritual and eternal consolations, filling me with joy (Psalm 4:7). In all the kisses of Your sweetness, my soul is quieted and reposes in peace. For You, O Savior, You have established me in hope (Psalm 4:8).

I. THE FLIGHT TO GOD

1   "Come, let us ascend to the mount of the Lord, to the house of the God of Jacob. There, He will teach you His

ways" (Isaiah 2:3).

Intentions, thoughts, longings, affections, all that are within me—let us go up to the place where God sees or is seen. Cares, worries, anxieties, toils, concerns, and all efforts involved in the conditions of bondage, all must be left behind with the ass (that is, my body) while I and the lad (I mean my intellectual faculties) will hasten to go up the mountain (Genesis 22:14). When we have worshiped, we will return again (Genesis 22:5). See page 88.

Yes, we shall return again, and that, unfortunately, all too quickly. Love of the truth does separate us; indeed the love of our brethren does not permit us to abandon you completely. But while your needs will bring us back, that sweet experience must not be forfeited for your sakes.

"Lord, God of Hosts, change us, show us Your face, and we shall be saved" (Psalm 80:19).

But, alas, O my God. Alas! What false pretenses, temerity, rash presumption, out of order and against the rule of the word of truth and of wisdom, is my desire to see God when my heart is so unclean. O bounteous Sovereign! O, Supreme Good! Life of the hearts of men, in Your beneficence, have pity upon me! For it is in beholding You that I have my cleansing, my confidence, and my justice. Have Your way with me, O God, and speak to my soul, in the language that is known to You: "I am your salvation" (Psalm 34:4, 5).

In response, I exclaim, "Master, Absolute Lord, uniquely our Sovereign, You alone are able to teach me how to see the things that I long to see." You say to Your blind beggar, "Do you want Me?" (Luke 18:41). You know I do, since it is by Your grace I am so prompted. You know my heart, so You know my inmost being. You know that I have put away all strivings after worldly delights and pleasures that so often have tempted, all ambitions for earthly honors, all else that would seduce me, including the lust of the flesh, the lust of the eyes, and the pride of life (1 John 2:16). You know how my heart cries out for You: "Your face, Lord, do I seek. Do not turn away in anger from Your servant" (Psalm 27:8, 9).

2 You see how outrageously I behave, yet it is for love of You that I act like this. For it is in fact the gift of Your grace that I have turned away from carnal things. So anything that pleases You is Your own gift to me. You can see this for Yourself, although I cannot see You. So the only desire I have is to see You face to face.

Being so close to You, what is it then that separates us? Why am I so naked before You? Do You regard me as an enemy? Will You consume me in the sins of my youth? Am I not really converted and restored to You? Why are You so far from me? You said to Israel, "Return to me, says the Lord of hosts, and I will return unto you" (Zechariah 1:3).

You know that Your grace has calmed my poor heart. My heart is ready, my God, yes it is ready. Command what You will. Give me knowledge of Your precepts. Give me the power, after You have given the will; then I shall do what You will.

3 But as for me, I shall respond with all my being to the powerful voice of Your testimony, a voice that penetrates to the depths of my being. My inward eyes are dazzled by the brightness of Your truth that declares: "No man shall see God and live" (Exodus 33:20). Since I am yet in my sins, I have not learned how to die to myself in order to live in You (2 Corinthians 5:15). And yet it is by Your Word and by Your grace that I stand upon the rock of faith in You, the Christian faith, and the place where You are truly present. There I wait with endurance, kissing and embracing Your right hand that covers and protects me.

Sometimes in my contemplation, filled with longing for You, I get a glimpse of Your "back," You who see me (cf. Exodus 33:23). I see the way of the incarnation of Christ, Your Son, passing by me. But when in my eagerness, like the woman with the issue of blood, I would approach Him, I am ready to steal the healing of my poor sick soul by touching the hem of His garment (Matthew 9:20f.). Or like Thomas, that man of desires, I want to see and to touch Him entirely (John 20:25). Even more, he wanted to put his hand into that sacred wound; it was like the ark of the covenant, the golden urn, the soul of our humanity, that contained the manna of the Godhead. Alas, I am then comanded, "Touch me not!" (John 20:17). Then I further hear the words of the Apocalypse: "Dogs outside!" (Revelation 22:15).

Then my conscience justly condemns me and plagues me, and forces me to pay the penalty for my presumption and wickedness. Then I return to the rock, that is refuge for badgers[1] like me (Psalm 104:18), furry with sin, and once again kiss and embrace Your hand that protects me; this only intensifies my impatient desires. For I long to see the day when Your protecting hand will become the illuminating hand that opens out to me Your illuminating grace. Then, at last, dead to myself, and living in You, according to Your truth, I shall with unveiled face behold Your face (2 Corinthians 3:16). By such a vision, I shall then be united with you.

O visage, O blessed visage, that in seeing You I am enabled to be united to Yourself! It provides for the heart to become a tabernacle for the God of Jacob. It reveals all that was given on the mount (Exodus 25:40). Then it can sing rightly, "My heart has said to You, 'My face has sought You, Your face, Lord, will I seek' " (Psalm 27:8). That is why, as I have examined all the nooks of my conscience with the aid of Your grace, I find there only one desire, which is to see God. It is also my desire that all the ends of the earth may also see You, as their salvation (Isaiah 52:10). My desire is to see Him so that I may love Him, whom to love is life indeed. For faint with such longing I ask myself: "Who can love whom he cannot see? (1 John 4:20). How can anything be loved when it is invisible?"

4

II. THE LONGING SOUL

Here then, is the assiduous exercise of my heart! It is to examine my heart unceasingly. For Your blessings and

5

love are like hands and feet to help me gently move toward You and Your absolute and sovereign love. But alas! Such an experience is not to be enjoyed with unmitigated pleasure. Instead, it is one of yearnings, struggles, and frustrations, mixed with bitter sweetness. For just as You are pleased with my offering, unless also I bring myself, so our contemplation of You gives delight, yet not fully so, unless You present Yourself also in the act.

Into this contemplation my soul pours out all its energies, yet like a flint it also needs a steel to produce the flame. So using those qualities of Yours that make it possible to love You just as Your hands and feet would aid me, so I use all my powers to reach up to You, You who are Love supreme, and sovereign Good. But the more I reach up, the more relentlessly I seem to be thrust back and down into myself, and even below myself.

And so, as I look at myself, and examine myself, and pass judgment upon myself, I become one big troublesome and vexing question.

Yet Lord, I am assured by Your grace that I do have in my heart, and in all of my heart, the desire to desire You, and the love to love You. For it is by Your aid that I am able to desire You, and to love You.

But when I love like that, can I know what love that is? What does it mean to desire desire, and to love love?

If we desire anything, it is by desire we do so, and it is by love that we love. Yet perhaps when I love love, it is not love which I want to love, and by which I love everything that I do love at all. But it is I myself whom I love in the process of loving. Yet when I am loving the Lord, Whom I praise and love with all my soul, I should loathe and detest myself if I were to find in it anything else but in the Lord Himself and in His love.

What then of desire? If I say I desire desire, I already find the desire is in myself. But is it, then, the desire that should come from your desiring? Where, then, can I have the desire of desiring You, that is Your desire? For where else can come such a great and vital desire?

6　　So when my eyes of introspection get confused, dim,

and even blind, I pray that You will open them quickly; yet opened not in shame as Adam's eyes were opened (Genesis 3:7). Rather may they be opened to behold Your glory (Exodus 33:18). Then, forgetting all about my own poverty and insignificance, my whole being may be able to stand up, to run into Your embrace of love, and see You Whom I love, and love You Whom I have yet to see. In this way, dying to myself, I shall begin to live in You, I who am so sinful in myself. For the grace of Your wisdom, Lord, or the wisdom of Your grace has its compensations. For neither rational arguments nor discussions will lead one on and upward to the torrents of Your delights and the full joy of Your love. Only he will receive it, as by surprise, who seeks diligently and knocks persistently (Matthew 7:7).

But Lord, all too seldom that happens. When it does so, I shout out: "Lord, it is good for us to be here! Let us make three tabernacles," one for faith, one for hope, and one for love! (Matthew 17:4). But do I know what I am saying when I say, "It is good for us to be here?" For immediately I fall down to the ground as if I were dead, and when I look around I see nothing (Matthew 17:4; Revelation 1:17). Then I find myself back to my old ways, full of sorrow of heart and affliction of soul. Then I cry out: "How long, O Lord? Will You forget me forever? How long will You hide Your face from me? How long must I bear pain in my soul, and have sorrow in my heart all the day?" (Psalm 13:1-2). How long then will Your Spirit come and go in mortal men, but never remain with them? (Genesis 6:3; John 3:8).

But when the Lord leads back the captives of Zion, then we shall be comforted. Then will our mouth be filled with joy, and our tongue with gladness (Psalm 126:1, 2). But until now, I have been an exile too long. How wretched this has made me! I have dwelt among the inhabitants of Kedar, very alienated in my soul (Psalm 120:5-6). But deep within my heart the truth of your consolations and the consolations of Your truth speak to me.

III. Is There Inequality in the Love of the Blessed?

7   The truth is, there is love of possession and also love of desire. Desiring love is sometimes rewarded with vision. The reward of vision is possession, and the reward of possession is perfect love.

I thank You with such insights, that Your grace has spoken to my heart with comfort, I who am Your servant (Ruth 2:13). I accept and embrace this token of Your Spirit, and with it I look forward with joy to the fulfillment of Your promise. For I desire to love, and I love to desire You. So I look forward to the day when I shall love You perfectly. For You Who loved first, You are so worthy of love, You who are love (1 John 4:8).

But does this blessed state of loving You in this state really exist? If so, where and when? Is the soul that so thirsts for God as for the fount of life ever so satisfied and so filled that it cries "Enough"?

I would be very surprised if someone could say that. It might rather suggest that there must be something lacking in him. But if we suppose there is indeed insufficiency within us to enjoy this bounty, how then can we reach the perfect state? Is it nowhere and never to be reached? Then what about the unrighteous? Will they possess Your kingdom?

Now an unrighteous man is one who has no desire, no awareness of his indebtedness, no understanding of Your love and of his need to return that love as much as a creature can do. It is certain, however, that the seraphim's love—they whose blessed nearness to God and clarity of vision of God have earned them the name of "the burning ones"—is a love for God which is greater than those who are least in the kingdom of heaven (Matthew 5:19).

Now here is someone who, being in the kingdom of heaven, may not be able to say he is the least, yet he is one who desires to love You as much as he possibly can. This may be something the angels desire to witness (Ephesians 1:18). So, without a spirit of rivalry, he desires to love you, though others may do so more. Yet he does so, with devotion and godly imitation. If he makes progress in love, then his inward eyes will be enlightened (Ephesians 1:18). Then the more he grows with these inward realities, provided he is not ungrateful, nor unrighteous, he will learn to see that he can love God with increasing delight. As a debtor he may even learn to love as the angels do. But he who desires what he cannot get is in a pitiable condition. Frustration like that is far removed from the kingdom of bliss. But up there, all who desire get what they want.

What shall we say to this? (Romans 8:31). I pray, Lord, **8** that You will speak, "for Your servant hears" (1 Samuel 3:10). Those who are in the kingdom of God, whether great or small, all desire to love You, each according to his own order. Is it not the unity of love that permits them to have their own diversity? He who has been given more to love does so, while he who may be his "lesser" brother loves also, without envy, for he, too, desires that which he sees. Does he not also have, to his full capacity, the love that he desires?

For the truth is that it is Love Who is loved. For it is out of the abundance and the nature of His goodness that He fills with the same grace those who love and love together, those who rejoice and rejoice together. For the more He pours His love into their souls, the more capacity they are given to go on loving. He satisfies, but He never surfeits. The satisfaction always increases the desire instead of diminishing it, but it does remove worry and anxiety. For this love, as I have said, who is loved fills him with delight. He relieves him of all distress in desiring and all jealously in zeal. As the apostle says, He enlightens them, "from glory to glory" (2 Corinthians 3:18), so that in that light they will see light (Psalm 36:9). Likewise, they will understand love in love.

Here, then, is the source of life that flows inexhaustibly. Here is the glory, whose riches fill the home of Your beloved (Psalm 112:3). Here he who desires finds what he wants, and he who loves always finds whom he loves, O Lord. Also, he who desires loves always to desire more, and he who loves, desires to love always. And for him, O Lord, who desires and loves, You make what he desires to so abound that he is never frustrated, nor never smug with what he has.

Is it not in this connection that the psalmist prays: "See if there be any wicked way in me, and lead me in the way everlasting" (Psalm 139:24). Perfection is this relationship. To travel always like this is to be there. Of this the apostle says: "Not as though I have already arrived, but I press on, towards the mark of the high calling of God" (Philippians 3:12, 14). Then he adds, "Let all of us who are mature be like minded" (v. 15).

IV. WE MUST LOVE GOD FOR HIS OWN SAKE AND ALL ELSE FOR GOD

Your love, O kind Creator, with which You love those who love You comes from Your bounty toward Your creature. It inspires Your lovers, both to desire and to love You. For You are quite independent of our love; You simply are what You are. You are unchangingly the same, always good, good in Yourself, for Yourself, and in Yourself also for all Your creatures. When we love You—and we wretched creatures can in evil exist without loving You—when we love, we are affected by You, toward You, and in You (Philippians 3:15).

But You are always the same (Psalm 102:27). Your love is unaffected by us. Nothing is added to it when we love, and nothing is taken away when we do not do so. However, when You love us, You do so for Your own sake, for in ultimate justice You desire we should love You and You alone.

Is it possible, then, that when a great gift of grace is granted it is granted not to love You or himself for his own benefit, but to love You and himself only for Your own sake? For in doing so he is reformed into Your image after Whom he was created (Genesis 1:26). For by the reality of Who You are as God, You can only love Yourself as God does alone. You can neither love angel nor man other than for Your own sake.

Blessed then, incurably so, is the soul that is so loved by   10
God. Blessed, too, is the soul who is so acted on by God in
the unity of His Spirit, that he is not only able to love
God, but does so for God's own sake. Loving and approv-
ing as God Himself does, the soul loves in God. Or to put
it in another way, it loves only what is loved by the
Creator and His creature.

Thus love is not the private property of any creature as
a personal right, but as Yours alone. You are so worthy of
love, for You are true love; this we know is the will of Your
Son in us in His prayer to You on our behalf; "Father, I will
that they also may be one in us" (John 17:21f.). This is the
goal, consummation, and the perfection. This is the
peace, the joy in the Holy Ghost (Romans 14:17), and
the silence in heaven (Revelation 8:1).

Here below we are sometimes given this love to enjoy
like the silence of ineffable peace that is like the silence of
heaven. It comes to the righteous soul who is like the seat
of wisdom. But this peace remains briefly, for perhaps an
hour or two (Revelation 8:1). But the thoughts of it are
enough to provide a perennial feasting. But in that blessed
and eternal life, it shall be said: "Enter into the joy of the
Lord" (Matthew 25:21). Then, there alone, we shall find
perfect and perpetual enjoyment. The bliss, then, will be
proportionately greater to all the obstacles and hindrances
we now suffer, for they will all be done away. Then the security of the soul's love will be eternally assured with inviolable perfection and incorruptible bliss.

V. PRAYER IS THE NATURE OF LOVE

O Love, as smoke is driven away, so take away from   11
Your presence all those obnoxious infections which the
lust of the flesh, the lust of the eyes, and the pride of life
(Psalm 68:2; 1 John 2:16) have infected within us. Our affections have been like those of bastard children. For this
sentiment we call our love is only that which has not been

corrupted in the soul that You have formed and which should be for You. For You alone it was created so when it resists You, it is rightly called by such names as gluttony, lust, avarice, and the like (Galatians 5:19). But as long as it remains uncorrupted, and is obedient to the purpose of its being, it will be directed to You to whom only such love is worthy.

Indeed, as one of Your servants, the love of the reasonable soul is a quiet abiding motion in which the will neither seeks anything beyond it nor considers anything else as worth having. For anyone who is looking for something else beyond You is looking for something that cannot exist nor never has existed alone. For there cannot be anything or anyone lovelier than You are.

So when a person flies beyond You in his desires, he only makes himself a non-being in such indulgence as fornication and other lusts, aliens to the authentic love that You alone are. For I must repeat it, love can only be directed to You, and it is alone in You. For no one truly exists without You. There in You, in You alone, is the quiet hiding place, for "to fear the Lord," with a chaste and loving fear, and "to keep all the commandments, this is the whole duty of man" (Ecclesiastes 12:13).

VI. GOD'S INITIAL LOVE FOR US IN THE SON PROVOKES US TO LOVE

12   Remove far from my soul all unrighteousness so that I may love You with all my heart, my Master and my God, with all my heart, soul, and strength! Let all other rivals depart from me, lest I should love anything else alongside of You and fail to love for Your sake alone, for You are truly my Lord and my Love. When I love anything for Your sake, then I love it not for its own sake, but for You for whose sake I love it. For truly You are alone the Lord (Psalm 86:8-10). To be ruled by You is to be saved by You.

What does this salvation mean, O Lord, from whom it comes and whose blessing is upon your people, if it is not in the gift of loving You and being loved by You? That is why You desired that the Son of Your Right Hand (Psalm 80:17), the Man affirmed by You, should be called Jesus, for "He would save His people from their sins" (Matthew 1:21). Outside of Christ, there is no salvation (Acts 4:12). He alone has taught us to love Himself, when He first loved us (1 John 4:19), even to the death of the Cross. In loving us, He has purified us. In loving us, He has incited us to love Himself. With infinite tenderness, this is the purpose of His love (John 13:1).

Among the children of men, there is this basic principle: "Love Me, for I love You." Rarely do we find those who can say: "I love you that you may love me!" [That is disinterested love.] But as the disciple of such loving delight who proclaims and preaches this loving delight, "You who first loved us, did just this." Lord, You first loved us so that we might love You. That is not because You needed our love, but because we could not be authentically what You created us to be except by loving You. That is why after a thousand occasions, and an infinite number of ways, You have spoken to the fathers by the prophets. But now, in these last days, You have spoken to us by your Son (Hebrews 1:1f.), that is by your Word. It was by your Word that the heavens were established, and by the breath of your Mouth all their host was given (Psalm 33:6). Thus in speaking of your Son on Your behalf, You proclaim in the rising of the sun and in the circuit of life (Psalm 19:5-6), how much You loved us.

Such is the degree, and such is the way in which You have loved us. For You spared not your Son, but delivered Him up for us all (Romans 8:32). And the Son, in turn, how He has loved us and given up Himself for us (Galatians 2:20). This, Lord, is your Word to us, this is the all-powerful message that has resounded through the silence of the cosmos, when darkness brooded over the world (Genesis 1:2). It was, then, that You descended from your royal throne, stern opponent of our errors, and the gentle eulogist of love. All that He did, and all that He said on earth, even amidst the insults, the spitting, the buffeting, the cross, and the grave, all that was nothing else but Your speech in the Son. This was Your appeal to us by Your love, to stir up our love for You.

You know, O God, Creator of all souls, that the love of the human heart cannot be coerced. It has to be evoked. You know that compulsion eliminates freedom, and that the absence of freedom is the absence of righteousness. But You, O righteous God, You desire to save us. You never save nor condemn anyone otherwise than in righteousness. You are the Author both of our judgment and of our cause. Sitting upon Your throne You judge in righteous judgment. For You judge by the righteousness that You Yourself have created (Psalm 9:4). So every mouth is shut, and all the world is made subject to God (Romans 3:19), when You have mercy on whom You will have mercy, and extend Your compassion to whom You will be a compassionate God (Exodus 33:19; Romans 9:15). Righteously, we could not have been saved had we not loved You. But we could not have loved You without Your gift of love to us. So You willed that we should love You. As the apostle of Your love reminds us, "first You loved us" (1 John 4:10), for You love all lovers first.

VII. How God Loves Us

We love you Lord, with the love *(affectus)*[2] that You have implanted within our hearts. For You are the source of all good affections. But how is it with You? Are You "affected" in the same way and by the same principle so that Your love for others is excited by some other extraneous, incidental action? No indeed! Such a corollary is absurd, for it is contrary to the reality that You are the Creator of all things! So how, then, do You love us when You are not loved by love?

Ah, Lord God, You who are supremely good and ultimate Goodness, love is your bounty, as the Holy Spirit which proceeds from the Father and from the Son! From the beginning of creation He has brooded over the waters of chaos (Genesis 1:2), as He has over the hearts of men (2 Corinthians 4:6), offering Himself to all, as He also draws all to Himself (John 12:32). By breathing upon them and in them (John 20:22), He expels the bad and supplies the good so that God is united to us and we to God. Thus, it is Your Holy Spirit that is also called the love between the Father and the Son. For He is Their Union, He is Their Will. Yet by His grace (Romans 8:11), He also dwells within us, He also implants within us the affection of God's love (Romans 5:8). It is this that makes us acceptable to God and unites us to His good will. It is this that inspires us! The power of this good desiring is what we call love, love by which we ought to love, yes indeed to love You! Love then, is only another name for that overwhelming and well-ordered will of God.

You love then, O love-worthy God, You love yourself when the Holy Spirit, love of the Father for the Son, love of the Son for the Father, proceeds from the Father and from the Son (John 15:26). The greatness of that love is in its union, and the union is such that it is one in substance *(homousion)*, for the Father and the Son are the same being. You also love Yourself in us, when You send the Spirit of Your Son into our hearts crying, "Abba Father!" (Romans 8:15; Galatians 4:6). This is the sweetness of love, and the power of the desire that You have inspired. This then, is how You enable us to love You in return, for it is really how You love Yourself in and through us. When we first hoped in You it was because we knew your name of Savior and so we were inspired by Your grace (Psalm 5:11). But now, through Your Spirit of adoption, we are assured that all the Father possesses has now become ours also (Romans 8:15). Now we can invoke the same name as Your only Son, invoked by the right of His unique nature.

O Sovereign Father of Light (James 1:17), since all this blessing derives wholly from You, so that to love is to do good, good that is all Your endowment to us, love Yourself in us that we may love You through us! Then are we made one with You, and only made worthy of Your love when we participate in that union. As we have already said, we then become partakers of the prayer of Christ Your Son: "I will that they all may be one even as You, Father, are one in Me, and I in You" (John 17:21). For we are Your people, Lord, the people of God as the apostle says (Acts 17:28f.). Thus are the words of the pagan poet made into a perfume jar of fragrance so that only the scent of that good thought is inhaled. Yes, we are indeed God's "offspring" (Aratus *Phaen.* 5), sons of the Most High (Psalm 82:6). In such a spiritual kinship we are promoted, however, to claim a closer relationship with You, because by the Spirit of adoption (Romans 8:15) Your Son does not disdain to take our name (Hebrews 2:11). Because of Him, and by Him we are taught in a divine school, so that we can be bold to say: "Our Father who art in Heaven" (Matthew 6:9).

Thus, You love us by making us lovers of Yourself. We love You, as we receive Your Spirit, Who is Your Love. You let Him penetrate and wholly possess all the most intimate affections of our hearts. You change them into the perfect purity of Your Truth and bond them into full accord with Your love. From such a wonderful union and such an adherence, there is such enjoyment of Your sweetness, that it is expressed in the words of Your Son our Savior: "that they may be one in us" (John 17:21). Great then, is the dignity of this union! Great is its glory that He should add: "as You and I are one" (John 17:11). O the joy, the glory, and the exaltation of it! For even wisdom has its sorts of pride, and it can say: "riches and glory are with me, glorious opulence and righteousness" (Proverbs 8:18).

VIII. How We Love God

But what can be more incongruous than to think that we can be united to God by love, and yet not be blessed also by God? For it is those who love You truly and fully, who are also truly and fully blessed. "Blessed are the people who possess these blessings," they said, but they lied! For he alone is blessed who acknowledges God as Lord (Psalm 144:15). For what in fact is blessing? Does it not consist in seeking only good and to possess it fully? So to want You, to want You intensely is to love You, and to love You exclusively. For You will not tolerate being loved along with any other creature whatever, carnal or spiritual, earthly or heavenly, that is not loved for Your own sake. To want You in this way is the only way to have what is good. That is tantamount to saying we can love anything we want. For every person possesses You as he loves You.

By the help of the Holy Spirit who dwells within us, all these things He permits us to believe and understand. For this Spirit, as it has been said, in affirming and uniting with our spirit, turns us towards the breath that He breathes, whenever, however, and wherever He pleases. We are His workmanship (Ephesians 2:10). Created for good works, He is our sanctification, and our righteousness, and our love. Yes, He himself is our love by which we reach out to You, O God. We embrace You, O inaccessible Majesty, but in love You are accessible. For although no human faculties, nor spirit, can ever comprehend You, nevertheless the one who loves You understands You wholly in loving You wholly, even in all Your greatness. Yes, even when such totality has no parts, or when quantity is immeasurable, or when understanding is ineffable. But when we love You, Your Holy Spirit acts truly upon our spirit. Through His indwelling love we possess the love of God that is shed abroad in our hearts (Romans 5:5).

When You love, it is as the love of the Father for the Son, and the love of the Son for the Father. When the Holy Spirit then dwells within us, He is our love to You for He is love. He turns toward Himself and sanctifies all "the captives of Zion" (Psalm 126:1), that is to say all the affections of the soul. It is then, when He has done all that, that we can love You, or rather, You love Yourself in us— we affectively so and You effectively so—making us one with You. For it is only through Your own triune unity, through the Holy Spirit given to us, that this is possible. So it is all reduced to this one essential. For the Father to know the Son is nothing else but to be what the Son is. For the Son to know the Father is only to be what the Father is. That is why the Scripture says: "No one knows

the Father except the Son, and no one knows the Son except the Father" (Matthew 11:27).

So for the Holy Spirit to know and to understand the
Father and the Son is simply to be what the Father and
Son are. So likewise is this principle true of us. We were
created in Your image (Genesis 1:26). But through Adam
we have grown old in unlikeness. Now through Christ we
are being renewed in that image day by day (2 Corinthians
4:16). So then, for us who love God, I tell you that to love
and fear God is nothing else than to be of one spirit with
Him (1 Corinthians 6:17). For to fear God and to keep
His commandments is the whole duty of man (Ecclesiastes
12:13).

O God, so that we can truly adore, worship, and bless
You, give us then this Holy Spirit. "Send forth your Spirit
and all shall be created and You will renew the face of the
earth!" (Psalm 104:30). For it is not in the deluge of
waters, nor in the flux and confusion of our emotions,
which are as numerous in their number as in their kind,
that we shall draw near to God (Psalm 32:6). Lord, that
catalytic fall of Adam's seed has lasted long enough in all
its consequences. So bring Your Holy Spirit to this earth.
Let the sea withdraw its bounds to those that You have
prescribed (Genesis 1:9). Let the parched earth be transformed by the water of life (Revelation 21:6). Come,
Holy Spirit, as the dove, bringing the olive branch in his
beak, after the raven has been driven back (Genesis 8:7-
8), to proclaim peace. May Your holiness sanctify us. May
Your unity unite us. So that like a blood-bond relationship, we may be united to the God who is love in virtue of
the name that is Love (1 John 4:8).

But it is important, Lord, that we should know how to
love You. As one of your enlightened saints has said,
many people "only love the truth when it shines upon
them, but when it rebukes them then they no longer love
it" (Augustine, *Confessions*, 9:23, 24). Many people cultivate righteous feelings, yet they do not behave in this
way. They approve and love the idea of truth for themselves, but they do not put it into practice. Do they then
truly love You, O God of true righteousness? Do such love

You in truth?

The philosophers of this world have earnestly sought in the past for the truth. They have sought it effectively through love, and effectively through deeds, so that it can justly be said of them "the love of virtue makes good men to hate sin" (Horace, *Letters* 16:52). But the fountain and spring of true righteousness is in You alone. It returns to You, as to its end. Without You, all human righteousness is as filthy rags (Isaiah 64:6). So those who have not loved You are also convicted of not loving righteousness. For while they had love of a sort and they had honest actions to their credit, yet they lacked the faith that alone works by love (Galatians 5:6). Because their love—such as it was—and their good deeds, did not spring from the fountain of true righteousness, nor did they lead to that end, such have gone astray so that the faster they run the more lost they become. For the Way, O Father, is your Christ who said, "I am the Way, the Truth, and the Life" (John 14:6).

IX. Love Consists in Obedience to God's Commandments

Your truth is also the Life and the Way towards which You lead us. This is the true and divine Philosophy in its real and simple form:

> As the Father has loved Me, even so have I loved you. Abide in My love. If you keep My commandments, you will abide in My love even as I also have kept the commandments of My Father and abide in His love (John 15:9f.).

Here is the "beloved of the Beloved" when we read that the Father loves the Son and the Son abides in the love of the Father (John 3:35; 5:20), fulfilling His commandments perfectly. Again, "the beloved of the Beloved" is when the disciple loves Christ, his Master, and fulfills all His commandments, remaining steadfast even unto death. Illumined by His truth and love, He sees that all things work together for good (Romans 8:28), and in good account he makes good use of all things, whether they be bad or indifferent or good as Christian love does. For, as we have already seen, this is the good use of freedom. For good deeds are the transformation of what we could misuse as bad.

In order that love may not be misused, we are, therefore, commanded to love our neighbor according to the law of perfect love. But just as God loves only Himself within us, and we have learned to love ourselves only in God, so we are to begin also now to love our neighbor "as ourselves" (Matthew 22:39). For in our neighbor, we love God alone, even as we love Him also in ourselves.

Why then, O Savior, do You give us such words? My poor soul is naked, cold, and benumbed. It longs to warm itself at the fire of Your love. I have no raiment to put on to cover my nakedness (Revelation 3:17, 18). I am forced to gather these poor rags anywhere I can, and sew them together (Genesis 3:7). Unlike the wise widow of Sarepta, who collected a couple of sticks, I am in my own desert of the spacious vanity of my own heart, where I have only collected these few tiny twigs. I have done so, that in coming to the tabernacle of my house (Psalm 132:3), I may have a handful of flour and a vessel of oil to eat before I die (1 Kings 17:9).

Yet perhaps, Lord, I may not die as quickly as that! Rather, it could be that I shall not die, but live to declare the works of the Lord (Psalm 118:17). Thus I stand in the house of solitude, like the lone wild ass that has its dwelling place in the wilderness of salt (Jeremiah 2:24; Job 39:6). I breathe the breath of love, I open my mouth in your direction, and I breathe the breath of the Spirit (Psalm 119:131). Then sometimes, Lord, when I gasp with closed eyes, gasping for You like this, You put something in my mouth, although You do not let me know what it is! But I sense a savor so sweet and gracious that it comforts and fulfills me so much that I do not need to look for anything else. When I receive this, I realize that I cannot discern it with my understanding nor with the senses. But I know that I want to keep it, to contemplate over it, and to taste its flavor. Then, it is gone! Whatever it is, I believe I have swallowed it down in the hope of eternal life.

Long have I pondered its effect upon me. In doing so, I have longed to absorb within the veins and marrow of my soul this vital sap. I want to get rid of the taste of every other affection, so that I taste this savor alone and forever. But it has quickly passed. Seeking to retrieve and re-experience it, I try to make my memory retain the most specific impressions of it. Or else, as my memory is poor, I help it in writing something down. But all these efforts only remind me of what You said concerning the Holy Spirit in the Gospel: "You do not know whence He comes nor whither He goes" (John 3:8). Whatever the particular features of this experience may have been, I have wanted to commit them to memory, so that I could retrace the way back to the initial experience, whenever I was so minded. Also, I wanted to control this power whenever I wanted. But every time this occurs, I hear again the Lord saying to me: "the Spirit blows whither He wills." As I know He does not breathe within me, whenever I want, but when *He wills*, I find everything else is tasteless and dead. Then I realize once again that it is You alone, O Fountain of Life, to whom I must lift up my eyes (Psalm 123:1), so that only in Your light do I see light (Psalm 36:9).

My eyes I have turned towards You, O Lord, so that they remain upon You. May my soul only make progress in the things that relate to You, that are in You, and that are turned towards You. And when my feeble strength fails (Psalm 71:9), may my very weaknesses still pant after You! (Psalm 42:1). But for now, at this time, how long, O Lord, are You going to put me off? How often must my wretched, perplexed, and hungering soul tread after You? I beseech You to hide me in the secret place of your countenance, and remove me from the tumult of the world, hiding me in your tabernacle from the strife of tongues! (Psalm 31:20).

But already the ass is braying again and the lads are clamoring for attention! (See page 109.)

X. A Closing Prayer of Love

In absolute trust then, O Lord, I worship You. For I acknowledge You to be God, the One Cause of all that is, the sole Wisdom from whom all the wisdom of the wise is derived, and the unique Gift with which the blessed man can only be blessed. It is You, the only God, whom I adore, bless, and revere. It is You whom I love—or rather am loved to love—You, whom I long for with all my heart, and all my soul, and all my strength (Deuteronomy 6:5).

All of the angels and good spirits who love You also love me. Yes, even me, who can thus love myself in Your love! This I realize. I also know that all who abide in You (John 15:4), and thus can understand the prayers and thoughts of other men, can hear me in You. So for them also, I give thanks for their witness. For everyone who has You for his treasure helps me to grow in You, and it is impossible to envy their share of You. Only the apostate spirit takes satisfaction in our misery, and counts our benefits his curse, for he has fallen away from the commonwealth and true happiness; he is no longer subject to the truth. Hating the common good, he can only rejoice in his own isolation and hug to himself a joy that belongs only to his alienated self.

You, therefore, God the Father,
    by whom as Creator we live;
You, Wisdom of the Father,
    by whom we have been redeemed and guided
    to live wisely;
You, Holy Spirit, object of our love,
    source of our affections,
We so dwell and yet look forward to
    live more so.

Eternal Trinity, One in Substance,
the One God,
    from Whom we are,
    by Whom we are,
    in Whom we are,

Sin has taken us far from You,
Sin has deformed our image of You,
Yet You do not wish us to perish.

To You we return, as the Beginning,
To You, the Pattern, that we are following,
To You, the Grace by which we are reconciled,
   we adore You!
   we bless You!
To You be the glory for ever and ever, Amen.

---

[1]Hedgehog was the term used by William, but modern translations use badger.

[2]See p. 106, note 1.

VI

ON LOVING GOD[*]

Dedicated to the Illustrious Lord Haimeric, Cardinal-Deacon and Chancellor of the See of Rome, from Bernard, called Abbot of Clairvaux, who wishes he may live and die in the Lord.

 NTIL NOW, YOU HAVE BEEN ACCUSTOMED TO ASK me to pray, but not to seek answers to theological problems. I have to confess, I am not adequate to do either of these things. True, my profession supposedly implies that I pray, but I have to confess that my actual practice falls far short of what I should be doing in diligence and ability. However, I appreciate that you still seek for spiritual direction, instead of being preoccupied only with secular affairs. I just wish I could be better able to help you than I am. Still, both the educated and the uneducated tend to give the same excuse. So it is not easy to determine whether it is given from modesty or from ignorance, unless it can be proved by deeds. So accept my poverty, lest I appear to be the diffident philosopher.

I do not promise to be able to answer all your questions, but only what you have specifically asked for concerning the love of God. Even so, the answer could only be what God Himself has already given me. Keep all other questions for other, wiser men to answer. But to me, this theme of the love of God is the sweetest to the taste, and

---

[*] It is uncertain when Bernard of Clairvaux wrote this important theological work. Lord Haimeric, to whom it was addressed, died in 1141. It is supposed Bernard wrote it some time after 1125. It is written as a devotional tract.

can be treated with most certainty, as well as listened to with the most profit.

I. Why Should We Love God?

1   You want me to tell you why and how God is to be loved?

I answer that the reason for loving God is God Himself. As to how He is to be loved, there is only one measure: It is immeasurable!

Is this a sufficient answer? Perhaps, but only so to a wise man. Now, as I am indebted (Romans 1:14) to deal with the unwise as well, perhaps I need to answer for them also. So while a word is enough for the wise, I need to elaborate the answer for the simple folk as well. Therefore, I do not find it irksome to treat the subject more fully, if not more deeply so.

There are two reasons, I insist, why we should love God for His own sake. Righteously so, God is love for His own sake. Profitably so, God is to be loved with the highest benefit. So when we ask again, "Why is God to be loved?" there are two possible meanings to the question. But the answer is the same, for God is the sufficient cause of love, because of who God is.

So let us see how God deserves to be loved.

God Is to Be Loved for His Own Sake

God deserves to be loved because He gave Himself for us, unworthy of it as we are. Yet being God, what greater gift could He give than to give Himself? Hence this is surely the greatest claim that God has upon us, "because He first loved us" (1 John 4:19). He thus deserves the response of our love in return.

Who is so worthy to be loved? Surely it is He of whom the Spirit confesses (1 John 4:2), saying, "you are my Lord, for You do not need anything from me" (Psalm 16:2). This then is the true love of the Majestic God, who does not seek His own advantage (1 Corinthians 13:5).

And to whom did God direct such a pure love? "When we were still sinners, we were reconciled to God" (Romans 5:10). Thus did God love us, freely so.

To what measure did God love? John tells us: "God so loved the world that He gave His only begotten Son" (John 3:16). Paul adds: "He did not spare His own Son, but delivered Him up for us all" (Romans 8:32). The Son declared of Himself: "No one has greater love than he who lays down his life for his friend" (John 15:13).

This, then, is the claim which the Holy One has upon the guilty, and the Supreme Being has upon all miserable mankind. Some may argue that this is true of mankind but not of the angels. It is true that it is not necessary for the angelic beings. He who succoured men in their needs preserved angels from such need. They did not need it. So the same God who loves in equal measure did not leave man to remain in his sin, while he likewise kept the angels from sinning. In both ways, God's was love revealed.

II. HOW MUCH THEN GOD DESERVES MAN'S LOVE

Those who acknowledge this truth see clearly why God should be so loved. If unbelievers would conceal this reality, this very ingratitude is only shown up by God by the innumerable gifts which He reveals by the senses to be at man's disposal. Who is it who gives food to all flesh, light to every eye, air to all who breathe? It would be foolish to go on in such an enumeration, for they are infinite in examples. It is enough to point out the chief ones—bread, sun, and air. I cite them as the chief gifts, not because they are better than the others, but because they are essential for bodily life.

But man's nobler gifts are found in the higher part of his being, within his soul. These are: dignity, wisdom, and virtue.

The dignity of man is his free will by which he is superior to the animals over whom he has dominion. His wisdom is in his acknowledgment that he has this dignity and yet recognizes that it is not of his own accomplish-

2
Why man should
be grateful to God

ment. Virtue impels man to seek continuously and eagerly for his Maker, so that when man has found Him, he will hold fast upon God.

3   Now these three prerogatives or gifts of man have a double aspect.

The proof of human dignity is not only in the excellence of our nature. It is also the authority of dominion (Genesis 1:26) which man can exercise. For the fear and dread of man is possessed by all animals. Wisdom perceives this distinction, that though man has this authority, yet it is not of man's own making.

Finally, virtue in its turn also has two aspects. It realizes that man seeks continuously and eagerly for his Maker, and when he has found Him, he clings to Him with all his might.

How love through gifts reinforces gratitude
Consider that dignity without wisdom is worthless, and wisdom without virtue is harmful.

The following reasoning may help to establish these statements. There is no glory in having a gift if you are unaware you have it. But if you know you have the gift, but think it is of your own making, that is to have only self-glory (Romans 4:2). It is no true glory to God unless you acknowledge that it comes from God. As the apostle writes of him who glories in himself: "What have you that you did not receive? Now if you have received it, why do you glory in yourself, as if you did not receive it? (1 Corinthians 4:7). He does not say simply, "how can you really boast about it?" He adds, "as if you had not received it," to show that the guilt lies not in its possession but in the refusal to acknowledge that it came from God. This is what is rightly called vainglory; it has no basis of truth. So the apostle distinguishes clearly between true and false glory: "He who boasts, let him boast in the Lord" (1 Corinthians 1:31; 2 Corinthians 10:7; cf. Jeremiah 9:23-24). To boast in the Lord is to be in the truth, for our Lord is Truth (John 14:6).

It is necessary, then, to know, two things. We must know what we are, and we must know also that we are not what we are in ourselves. Without this we shall glory in vanity, and not truly so. For it is written, "If you know not . . . go your way forth by the footsteps of the flock" (Song of Solomon 1:8). This is actually what happens.

4
Man lies not
in himself.

When a man is promoted to a high honor, but does not appreciate it as an honor conferred upon him by others, he will become like the brute beast. He will be corrupted by his power and become captive to his lusts. Thus it happens that when a man does not appreciate what he has been endowed with by others, he will mingle like the animals, living on his senses instead of by his wisdom. Led captive by curiosity, he will become like any other animal since he does not perceive that he has been given more than they have. We need to fear, therefore, that ignorance which gives us too low an estimate of our true worth.

But worse than ignorance is arrogance which makes us think not less of ourselves than we should but more than we should. This occurs when we deceive ourselves into thinking that we have some good inherently within ourselves. Worst of all is presumption, which deliberately seeks its own glory and assumes with certainty that one is self-achieving and self-fulfilled. Actually, it steals the glory from God, so that while the first ignorance has no sense of glory at all, the second kind has glory, but not in God's sight.

But the third kind of evil is sheer presumption, which ignores God wholly and even despises Him. So if ignorance makes beasts of us, then presumption makes devils of us. This is pride, the worst of all sins, which uses gifts as if they were one's natural rights and does so to usurp the Benefactor of His due glory.

For this reason, virtue is as necessary as dignity and wisdom, being their common fruit. It is by virtue that the Creator and Dispenser of all is to be sought and rightly glorified in all things.

5
Man needs to
be virtuous.

On the other hand, the one who knows what is good but does not acknowledge it, will be punished severely. Why? Because he "set himself in a way that is not good" (Psalm 36:4). Worse still, "he devises mischief in his bed" (v. 4). In fact, he is a wicked servant who grabs hold of, and even steals, the glory of God which he knows perfectly well does not belong to himself.

Thus dignity without wisdom is quite useless, and wisdom without virtue is damnable.

Man therefore needs to ascribe all to God.

But righteous man, for whom such wisdom is not harmful, and whose dignity remains fruitful, lifts up his voice to the Lord, and he confesses: "Not to us, O Lord, not to us, but to your name give glory" (Psalm 115:1). That is to say, the righteous can claim no knowledge and no distinction for himself. Rather, he ascribes it all and only to God's own character from whence all goodness comes.

6   But we have digressed too far from our subject in our desire to show that those who do not know Jesus Christ are sufficiently instructed by natural law (Romans 1:19ff.; 2:14-15) and by their own endowments of body and soul to love God for God's own sake.

Self-fulfillment is therefore inexcusable.

To sum up what we have said, we repeat briefly these considerations.

Is there a nonbeliever who does not realize that he has received all the bodily necessities of life itself by which he exists, sees, and breathes, from no other source that the One who gives food to all flesh (Psalm 136:25)? Is it not He who makes His sun to rise on the evil and the good alike, and His rain on the just and the unjust (Matthew 5:45)? Who is so impious as to attribute the distinctive status of humility to any other, except to Him who says in Genesis, "Let us make man in Our image, after Our likeness"? (Genesis 1:26). Who can ever think that the bestower of wisdom is somebody different from Him who teaches us wisdom? (Psalm 94:10). Who else can bestow virtue upon man except the Lord of virtue?

Therefore, even the unbeliever who does not know

Christ but does at least know himself is bound to see that God deserves to be loved for His own sake.

Everyone, then, is inexcusable—even the unbeliever—if he fails to love the Lord his God with all his heart, and with all his soul, and with all his mind (Mark 12:30). His own innate sense of justice and common sense, too, cries out within him that he ought to love with his whole being the One from whom he has received all things.

But it is hard, indeed impossible, for a man by his own strength and effort of will, to render all things to God, from whence they came. Instead, his tendency is to seek his own self-interest, as it is written, "for all seek their own" (Philippians 2:21). Again, it says, "the imagination of man's heart is evil from his youth" (Genesis 8:21).

III. CHRISTIANS SHOULD HAVE GREATER INCENTIVE TO LOVE GOD

The faithful, on the contrary, know how much they need Jesus and Him crucified (1 Corinthians 2:2). While they wonder and rejoice at the ineffable love revealed in Him, they are ashamed in giving Him such small return for so great a love and such great condescension. Readily, those who love more do so because they realize they are loved more. The converse is that those to whom little has been forgiven, the same loves little (Luke 7:47).

7
The shame of ingratitude

So neither Jew nor pagan feels the pangs of love in the way that the church does. She experiences, "I am wounded by love" (old Latin version of Song of Solomon 2:5). She cries, "stay me with flagons, comfort me with apples, for I languish with love" (Song of Solomon 2:5).

The Church sees King Solomon with "the crown placed on his head by his mother on the day of his espousals" (Song of Solomon 3:11). She sees the Father's only Son carrying His cross, the Lord of glory slapped and covered with spittle (John 19:17). She sees the Author of life (Acts 3:15) pierced by nails, wounded by a spear (John 19:34), and overwhelmed by abuse. She sees Him at last laying down His precious life for His friends (Jeremiah 12:7; John 15:13). As she witnesses all the suffering, the sword of love pierces her own soul, and so she repeats the same words: "stay me with flagons, comfort me with apples, for I languish with love" (Song of Solomon 2:5).

The fruits which the bride gathers from the tree of life (Genesis 2:9) in the midst of the garden of her Beloved are called pomegranates (Song of Solomon 4:13; 6:11). They derive their taste from the Bread of heaven (Hosea 13:16; 1 Corinthians 15:54) and their color from the blood of Christ. The Church sees death dead, and its author vanquished. She sees captivity led captive (Ephesians 4:8) from hell to heaven, from earth to heaven. For "at the name of Jesus every knee shall bow, of things in heaven, and things in earth, and things under the earth" (Philippians 2:10). She beholds the earth which produced thorns and thistles under the ancient curse (Genesis 3:18; Hebrews 6:8) blooming once more by the grace of a new benediction. In all of these realizations, the Church can say with the Psalmist: "My heart dances for joy, and in my song will I praise Him" (Psalm 28:7). She refreshes herself with the fruits of His Passion which she gathered from the tree of the cross, and with the flowers of His resurrection, whose fragrance will induce the Bridegroom to visit her frequently.

**8
The joy of dependence before God**

Then she exclaims: "You are fair, my beloved, yes handsome indeed, also our couch is covered with flowers" (Song of Solomon 1:15, 16). But speaking of the couch, the bride intends to express that all her desires are surrendered, and by reference to the flowers, she clearly indicates from whence her hopes are realized. She does not depend upon her own merits, but on the flowers of the field which have been blessed by God (Genesis 27:27, cf. Matthew 6:28-30). Jesus Christ delights in such flowers, for He willed to be conceived and raised in Nazareth (a name which means the consecrated).

The intimacy of God's fellowship

Pleased by such perfumes, the Bridegroom enters willingly and frequently into the chamber of the heart that He finds is decked with the flowers and fruits of grace. For when He sees a mind occupied with the grace of His passion and the glory of His resurrection, He enters frequently and dwells there freely. For the tokens and memories of His passion are like the fruits of the past year. After all the times spent under the domination of sin and death (Romans 5:25), they now come to fruition in the "fullness of the times" (Galatians 4:4). The signs of the resurrection are like the flowers of a new year, blossoming like the verdure of summer under the power of grace. There fruit will then come forth in the general resurrection when time shall be no more in the eternal state. And so it is written, "Winter is over, the rain is past and gone, and the flowers appear on the earth" (Song of Solomon 2:11, 12). The betrothed marvels at the arrival of summer in her companionship with the One who passed through the winter cold of death into the spring of a newness of life saying, "Behold, I make all things new" (Revelation 21:5). His flesh was sown in death and rose again in resurrection (1 Corinthians 15:42). By His fragrance, the dried-up grasses revive in the valley fields, the frozen plants are warmed once more by the sun, and all the deadness is restored to life.

The renewal of these flowers and fruits, and the beauty 9 of the field, all giving off a sweet perfume, enchant the Father Himself, So He speaks of His Son who has made all things new (Revelation 21:5). "The smell of my Son is as the smell of a field which the Lord has blessed" (Genesis 27:27). Yes, indeed, it is a full field, "of whose fullness we have all received" (John 1:16). But the spouse enjoys greater intimacy by the knowledge that she may gather flowers where she is so inclined, and strew them over the depth of her conscience, so that the couch of her heart will be redolent with sweet perfume for the Bridegroom as He enters.

For it behooves us, if we would have Christ as a frequent visitor, to fill our hearts with faithful meditations, fortified by the reality of our faith (Ephesians 3:16, 17) in

Privilege of
divine meditation

the mercy that Christ showed us in dying for us, and by the mighty power that He showed in rising again from the dead (Ephesians 1:19, 20). To this David testified, when he sang, "God has spoken once; twice have I heard this; that power belongs unto God. Also unto Thee, O Lord, belongs mercy" (Psalm 62:11, 12). Surely the testimonies of these truths are more than enough (Psalm 93:5) to rest in the realty that Christ died for our sins, rose again for our justification (Romans 4:25), and ascended on high that He might protect us (Mark 16:19) by sending His Holy Spirit as our Comforter (John 16:7; Acts 9:31).

Hence, He shall come again for the consummation of our salvation (Acts 1:11). In His death He displayed His mercy, and in the resurrection His power. Both are combined to reveal the glory of all His deeds.

10
Love sustained by divine contemplation

These then are the flowers and fruits which the Betrothed asks to sustain us, because she knows how easily the warmth of her own love can languish and grow cold. But such helps are only needed until she enters the bridal chamber (Song of Solomon 2:5; 3:4). For inside there, she will receive the longed for caresses (Proverbs 7:18) and say: "His left hand is under my head and His right hand does embrace me" (Song of Solomon 2:6). Then she will enjoy all the tokens of His affection, seeing how the right hand excels all the sweetness she received from the left hand when He first caressed her. Then she will understand the reality more fully that "It is the spirit that quickens; the flesh profits nothing" (John 6:63). She will then also prove what she once read: "My memorial is sweeter than honey, and my inheritance than the honeycomb" (cf. Sirach 24:27). What is added, "my remembrance will last for ages to come" (Sirach 24:28) means that as long as the present era lasts, in which one generation follows another, the elect will not be deprived of memory's consolation until they can banquet at the eternal feast of God's presence. As it is written, "they shall abundantly utter the memory of Thy great goodness" (Psalm 145:7). No doubt the psalmist is referring to "they" as those who as "one generation shall praise Thy works to another and shall declare Thy mighty acts" (Psalm 145:4).

Thus His memory is for the succession of generations down the centuries, but His presence is for the Kingdom of heaven. That presence is the joy of all those who have reached that state of ultimate bliss. But the memory is that present comfort of those of us who are still wayfarers, journeying toward the end of our pilgrimage here on earth.

IV. WHO ARE THOSE WHO TAKE COMFORT IN GOD OR WHO ARE CAPABLE TO RECEIVE HIS LOVE?

We need to know, then, which generation can find comfort in the love of God. It is not this stubborn and perverse generation (Psalm 78:8) ultimately to which He says: "Woe unto you that are rich; for you have received your consolation" (Luke 6:24). Rather it is of those who can truly say, "my soul refused to be comforted" (Psalm 77:2). For it is meet that those who cannot be satisfied by present things should be satisfied by future blessings. It is the contemplation of eternal happiness that is the solace of those who scorn to drink the waters of transitory joys. That is the true generation of the Lord, those who seek not their own advantage (1 Corinthians 13:5), but the Lord Himself, even as the face of the God of Jacob (Psalm 24:6).

The true contemplative must be detached from the world.

To those who seek thus for the presence of the living God, the thought of Him will be joy itself. But there is no satiety in such desire, for instead there is an ever increasing appetite for such nourishment of the Lord Himself. As it is said, "they that eat me shall still be hungry" (Ecclesiasticus 24:21). And those who enjoy this nourishment also say: "I shall be satisfied, when I awake with Thy likeness" (Psalm 17:15). Yes, blessed now are they who hunger and thirst after righteousness, for one day they only will be satisfied (Matthew 5:6).

Woe to you, wicked and perverse generation; woe to you foolish and stupid people (Jeremiah 4:22; 5:21), who hate Christ's memory and yet dread His presence! You have good reason to fear, for you will not be able to escape from the hunter's net since "they who will be rich fall into temptation and a snare, and into many foolish and hurtful lusts" (1 Timothy 6:9). But in that day, you shall not escape the dreadful sentence of condemnation, "Depart from Me, ye cursed, into everlasting fire" (Matthew 25:41). In the light of such a threatened condemnation, less harsh to bear is the exhortation that is brought to us by the memorial of the passion of our Lord: "Whoso eats My flesh and drinks My blood has eternal life" (John 6:54). This signifies that he who meditates on Christ's death and mortifies his members on earth after His example (Colossians 3:5) shall have eternal life. Thus the apostle says, "If we suffer, we shall also reign with Him" (2 Timothy 2:12).

Yet many today recoil from such words, and go away saying, by their actions if not by their words, "This is a hard saying, who can hear it?" (John 6:60). "A generation which has not set their heart aright, and whose spirit cleaves not steadfastly unto God" (Psalm 78:8), is one that chooses rather to "trust in uncertain riches" (1 Timothy 6:17). It is oppressed by the message of the cross (1 Corinthians 1:18). It finds the memory of the passion an oppression.

If such a generation experiences this now, how much worse it will be in God's presence. How will he bear such words: "Depart from me, ye cursed, into everlasting fire, prepared for the devil and his angels"? (Matthew 25:41). "On whomsoever that stone shall fall, it will grind him to powder" (Luke 20:18).

However, "the generation of the faithful shall be blessed" (Psalm 112:2). Like the apostle, they labor whether present or absent to be accepted of the Lord (2 Corinthians 5:9). They will hear their award: "Come, you blessed of My Father, inherit the Kingdom prepared for you from the foundations of the world" (Matthew 25:34).

Then the generation which did not set their hearts right before God (Psalm 78:8) will feel—too late—how easy is Christ's yoke, in comparison to their sorrow, and how light is submission to God's will (Matthew 11:30) compared with that now about their stiff necks (Deuteronomy 9:13; 31:27).

Oh wretched slaves of Mammon, you cannot glory in the cross of our Lord Jesus Christ while you still trust in the treasures laid up on earth (Matthew 6:24; Galatians 6:14). You cannot enjoy the sweetness of the Savior while you are still hungering after gold (1 Timothy 6:17; Psalm 34:9). So if you have not sweetly remembered Him in His absence, you will only be desolate before His actual presence.

In contrast, the faithful soul longs deeply for His presence now, resting sweetly in His contemplation, and putting its own honors under the shame of the cross (Galatians 6:14) until it is able to contemplate without a veil the glory of God (2 Corinthians 3:18). As the bride and dove of Christ (Song of Solomon 5:1-2), the soul pauses to rest itself in the inheritance it has received (Psalm 68:14) and in the mercy of Christ's abundant kindness (Psalm 145:7). Covered with silver wings (Psalm 68:13), white in purity and innocence, the soul longs for that day when above all else, it will join this joyful splendor of all the saints. There, it will be enlightened with the rays of wisdom.

12
The true contemplative is pure in heart.

Then the soul can glory and say, "His left hand is under my head, and His right hand does embrace me" (Song of Solomon 2:6). The left hand signifies the remembrance of this immense love which Jesus Christ revealed in giving His life for His friends (John 15:13). The right hand signifies the beatific vision which He has promised to them and the joy which they have in the presence of His Majesty. As the psalmist sings rapturously: "At Thy right hand there is pleasure forevermore" (Psalm 16:11). So we are justified in explaining the right hand as that divine joy of His presence. While in the left hand there is placed that admirable love, so well remembered and always memorable, when the soul can recline and rest until all evil has been done away (Psalm 57:1).

In this way, the left hand of the Bridegroom is rightly

Intimacies of divine contemplation

placed under the bride's head. Thus as she leans back, her head is supported, that means to say, her attentions are held lest her mind be turned aside toward earthly and fleshly desires (Galatians 5:16; Titus 2:12). For the flesh wars against the sprit: "the corruptible body presses down the soul and the earthly dwelling preoccupies the mind busy with many thoughts."

What else is achieved from meditating upon such great mercy, such gratuitous and so often tested love, such unexpected condescension, such unhoped for goodness, such indefatigible gentleness, and such amazing kindness? What else, I emphasize, are the consequences of such considerations but to captivate the soul, and to free it completely from all unworthy love. Deeply attracted to God's love, the soul despises whatever else would be a substitute. Nothing else will do, that is inconsistent with God's love.

Responsive ardor of the soul for God

Suffused by the perfumes of such reflection (Song of Solomon 1:3), the spouse runs swiftly, on fire with loving ardor, and yet aware that she is much more loved than she can love. As the object of such affection, she feels her love is too small, even when her heart is full of love. She has recently experienced this. For what can requite so deep a love by such a holy lover? It is as if a tiny grain of sand were to gather all its energies together to match the divine love of God's Majesty Who has first loved, and Who is revealed as wholly engaged in the work of salvation.

"For God so loved the world that He gave His only begotten Son, that whosoever believes in Him should not perish but have everlasting life" (John 3:16). These words were spoken of the Father's love. "He poured out His soul unto death" (Isaiah 53:12) are words meant for the Son. And He also says of the Holy Spirit: "The Comforter which is the Holy Ghost whom the Father will send in My name, He shall teach you all things, and bring all things to your remembrance, whatsoever I have said unto you" (John 14:26).

It is clear, then, that God really loves us, and loves us with all His being. For the entire Trinity wholly loves us. Thus the word "whole" here implies the infinite, the incomprehensible, and yet the essential being of God.

V. THE CHRISTIAN'S INDEBTEDNESS
TO SUCH LOVE

The meditations show us plainly why we should love God and why He is entitled to our love. But the unbeliever does not acknowledge the Son of God, and so he can neither know the Father nor the Holy Spirit (1 John 5:12). "He who honors not the Son, honors not the Father who sent Him" (John 5:23), nor does he honor the Holy Spirit whom the Son has sent (John 15:26; 16:7). It is not surprising, then, that he knows less of God than we, and no wonder that he loves God less. Nevertheless, even he is aware that he owes all he is to his Creator. What should then He be to me, who knows my God to be not only the bounteous Bestower of my life, the generous Giver who provides for all my needs, the kindest Comforter in all my sorrows, the wise Guide of my way? Beyond and above all else, He is my Redeemer, my Guardian, the source of all my wealth and of all my glory.

14
Unbelievers cannot understand the need for gratitude.

As it is written, "With Him is plentiful redemption" (Psalm 130:7). He also says, "He entered in once into the holy place, having obtained eternal redemption for us" (Hebrews 9:12). The Psalmist says of our salvation, "He forsakes not His that are godly, but they are preserved forever" (Psalm 37:28). Of God's bounty, it is said, "good measure, pressed down and shaken together and running over, shall men give into your bosom" (Luke 6:38). Again the Scripture says, "Eye has not seen, nor ear heard, neither has it entered into the heart of man, those things which God has prepared for those that love Him" (1 Corinthians 2:9).

The apostle witnesses to our glorification, saying: "We look for the Savior, the Lord Jesus Christ, who shall change our vile body that it may be fashioned like unto His glorious body" (Philippians 3:20f.). And again, he says, "I reckon that the sufferings of this present time are

The redeemed do know their indebtedness to God.

not worthy to be compared with the glory which shall be revealed in us" (Romans 8:18). Once more he says, "Our light affliction, which is but for a moment, worketh for us a far more exceeding and eternal weight of glory; while we look not at the things which are seen, but at the things which are not seen" (2 Corinthians 4:17-18).

15 "What shall I render unto the Lord for all His benefits?" (Psalm 116:12). Reason and natural justice alike move us to give ourselves entirely to loving Him, to whom we owe all that we have and are. Faith certainly bids me to love Him far more than I love myself, as I come to realize He has not only created me, but I also owe my existence to Him. In addition, God has actually given Himself to me.

God's claim on us to love Him Yet before the time of faith had ever come, when He entered the world in the flesh, died on the cross, rose again from the grave, and returned to the Father, God had already shown us how much He loved us. This He did when God commanded out of all the plentitude of His grace, "You shall love the Lord your God with all your heart, with all your soul, and with all your might" (Deuteronomy 6:5). That is to say, God desired of us to love Him with all our being, with all our knowledge, and with all our power.

It was not unreasonable of God to claim this from His own work and gifts (Hebrews 6:10). Why should man not love God with all his being, since it is by the gifts of God alone that man can do anything that is good? In addition, man was created out of nothing, freely so, and with such high dignity. Does this not cause man to see his indebtedness to God the more clearly, and show how just is the claim to that love?

Moreover, has not God added to His benefits in saving men and beasts? (Psalm 36:6-7). I am speaking now of how we exchanged our divine image for the likeness of the calf that eats grass (Psalm 106:20) and who became like irrational beasts because of sin (Psalm 49:12, 20). If I owe all to Him for my creation, what can I repay to Him who also redeemed my soul and did so in such a wonderful way?

For it cost God more to redeem than to create. For it is written not only about me, but about every created being: "He spake the word, and they were made" (Psalm 148:5). But to redeem that creation which sprang into being by His single word, how much more did He have to speak, what further wonders did He have to perform, what hardships did He have to suffer, and what shame did He have to endure!

"What shall I render unto the Lord for all His benefits toward me?" (Psalm 116:12). In His first work of creation, He gave me myself. But in His new creation He gave me Himself. By that gift of redemption, He also gave me back myself, restoring me to the self that I had lost. Given and regiven, I owe myself to Him twice over. What then can I give to the Lord in return for Himself? Even if I multiplied myself a thousandfold and then gave Him all, what would that be to God? (Job 9:3).

God's claim by creation and redemption

VI. A Brief Summary of What Has Been Said

To recapitulate briefly what has been said already, we admit that God deserves to be loved exceedingly. Indeed, He deserves to be loved without limit, for He loved us first (1 John 4:10). Although He is infinite and we are insignificant, yet He loved us miserable sinners with a love so great and free. That is why I said at the beginning of this treatise, you will recall, we must love God without measure. Moreover, as the love offered to God has as its object One who is immeasureable and infinite, and God is both of these, what should be the measure of our love?

16 God should be loved exceedingly.

Also, what about the fact that our love is not given gratuitously, but it is owing to God as a debt? It is thus with immensity we should love, for it is an eternal love (Ephesians 3:19), it is an infinite love, it is a God whose greatness is boundless (Psalm 145:3), who has loved us first. His is a wisdom without measure (Psalm 147:5), and whose "peace passes all understanding" (Philippians 4:7).

God should be loved indebtedly.

God should be
loved with His
empowering.

Do we think then that we can pay God back with any significant measure of love?

Ah, says the psalmist, "I will love You, O Lord, my strength, fortress, and my deliverer. The Lord is my rock and my deliverer" (Psalm 18:1-2). You are my all in all, so none less can be deserved and adored like You. My God, my help, I shall love you as much as I am enabled for your gift. Yet my love is far less than is due and less than I am able to do. But even if I cannot love you as much as I should, I still cannot love you more than I can. I shall only be able to love you with greater capacity when you give me more, although I can never be found worthy to receive it. "Your eyes did see my substance, yet being imperfect; and in your book all my members were written" (Psalm 139:16).

So all that is done, and should be done, and cannot be done, is recorded by You. Surely then, I have said enough to show how God should be loved and why. But who has ever felt, or who has ever known, or who can fully express how much we really should love God?

VII. LOVING GOD IS NOT WITHOUT FRUITFULNESS OR REWARD. FOR THE HUMAN HEART CANNOT BE SATISFIED BY EARTHLY THINGS

17
How we are
profited in
loving God

Let us now consider what it profits us to love God.

Yet can our appreciation of this love be other than remote from its reality? But even this glimpse is better than to keep silent about what we have seen, even though it falls far short of the truth. When we asked about why and how God was to be loved, we noted that there was a double reason constraining us: There is His right of our love, and there is our advantage of His love. Both questions need to be asked. So while we have dealt with the first question, though doubtless in a manner that is unworthy of God, it still remains to ask the second question, the recompense that love brings.

God is not loved without being rewarded for it, but He must be loved without concern for reward. True love is not left destitute, even though it is unselfish and "it seeks not its own" (1 Corinthians 13:5). True love then, does not seek a recompense, although it may deserve one. It is a sentiment, not a contract. It is spontaneous in its origin and action. It finds true reward in the object of its love.

Love cannot evolve from a mere contractual agreement together, for it is an affection of the soul. It cannot be gained in this way. Love is spontaneous in origin and impulse, and so it frees us to recognize that true love is its own satisfication.

Yet God must be loved spontaneously.

Whatever you seem to love ostensibly so, but it is really something else, then it will be the latter which really draws you, not the apparent object of your desire. Thus Paul did not preach the gospel in order to earn a living. He supported himself in order to preach. It was the gospel he loved, not his food (1 Corinthians 9:18). True love, then, does not seek a recompense, although it may deserve one.

Rather, recompense is offered to those who still cannot love enough. On this lower level of behavior, it is the reluctant who is given promises and is offered rewards as incentives to persist.

But who would ever dream of offering a reward to someone who longs and does so spontaneously? Thus, for example, no one will hire a hungry man to eat, or a thirsty man to drink or a mother to nurse her own child. Who could ever bribe a farmer to cultivate his own vineyard, or to dig around his orchard, or to rebuild his house? How much more then, the soul that truly loves God asks for no other reward than to go on loving God. If the soul were to demand anything else, then it would certainly love that other thing and not really love God.

True love seeks no recompense.

Every rational person naturally desires to be always satisfied with what it esteems to be preferable. It is never satisfied with something which lacks the qualities it desires to have. So if a man has chosen a wife because of her

18
Our motive in loving determines the quality of our love.

beauty, then he will look out with a roving eye for more beautiful women. Or if he is desirous of being well dressed, he will look out for even more expensive clothes. No matter how rich he is, if wealth is his desire, he will envy those who are richer than he is.

So you can see every day people who are already endowed with farms and other possessions, still busy, day after day, adding one field to another (Isaiah 5:8). With frenetic desire, they are kept hectically busy, adding to their properties (Exodus 34:24; Amos 1:13). You can see those dwelling in palaces who are always adding more and more or tearing down and continually rebuilding, or remodeling and changing according to the fashions simply because of the itch to have more, or to have better. Likewise, men in high places are drawn on by insatiable ambitions to climb higher and higher still. Indeed, there is no end to all this, because unsatisfied desires have no final satisfaction if they cannot be defined as absolutely the best or the highest.

Contentment requires the highest level of loving.

Need we wonder then that a man cannot find contentment with what is less or worse since he seeks peace and satisfaction in what is highest and best? So how stupid and mad it is to seek to find peace or satisfaction in that which cannot fulfill these needs. So no matter how many things one may possess, he will always be lusting for what is perceived to be still missing. Discontented, he will spend himself in restlessness and futility. Thus the restless heart runs to and fro looking for the pleasures of this life in weariness of the evanescent and the unreal. He is like a starving man who thinks anything he can stuff down his throat is not enough, for his eyes are still looking at what he has not eaten. Thus man craves continually for what is still lacking, with more anxiety in his preoccupation with what he lacks rather than having any joy or contentment in what he has already got.

No man can ever hope to possess everything. Even the little that one has acquired after much effort may cause one to be constantly afraid of even losing that (1 Timothy 6:7; Job 1:21). Likewise, a perverted will constantly will desire the best, longing for direct satisfaction, even though he strive in devious ways to attain it. But he is led astray by vantiy and deceived by wickedness (Psalm 27:12).

Ah, but if you desire to consummate all desiring, so that nothing is left unfulfilled, why waste and weary your efforts with nonessentials? You are like one who is running on the right path, but you will die long before you attain your goal.

It is in these ways that the ungodly behave, naturally longing for whatever their desires immediately dictate. Yet foolishly they reject what would lead them to their true goal which is not found in consumption, but in consummation. So they wear themselves out in futility without reaching their blessed consummation because they stake their happiness on earthly things, instead of upon their Creator. They seek to try each one in turn rather than to think of coming to Him who is Lord of all the universe.

Suppose, even if they could succeed in the realization of their longings, so that they possessed the whole world (Matthew 16:26), yet without having God who is the Author of all being, then the same principle that makes them restless for more would still leave them dissatisfied.

Only God can give them that ultimate satisfaction.

Rest is in God alone. Man experiences no real peace in this world, but he has no restlessness to disturb him in the eternal state with God. Thus the soul can say with confidence, "It is good for me to draw near to God . . . whom have I in heaven but Thee; and there is none upon earth tht I desire beside Thee . . . God is the strength of my heart and my portion forever (Psalm 73:28, 25, 26). Therefore, as I have said, even coming by this way of trying out all lesser goods one after the other, this eventually may drive us to realize that it is God alone who can truly satisfy.

19

True contentment lies only in God.

20
How can we be
content in God?

But this is impossible to try out, for life is too short, strength is too weak, competitors are too many, for such a course of action. One could never reach this end, though he were to exhaust himself with trying to test out everything that he conceived to be desirable. It would be far easier if they could experiment with all their desires, only by the imagination, and not having to actually experience everything! Since the mind is swifter and keener in discernment than the bodily senses are, it would be much more sensible to allow the mind to censor the desires before proving that they are worthless by bodily experiment.

We must have the right priorities.

That is why it is written, "Prove all things; hold fast that which is good" (1 Thessalonians 5:21). The spirit must govern the senses, which must in their turn submit their desires to its judgment. Otherwise, you shall not be able "to ascend the hill of the Lord, nor stand in His holy place" (Psalm 24:3).

It would be to no profit to possess a rational mind if we were to follow the impulses of the senses like brute beasts, having no regard to the guidance of reason. Those whom reason does not guide in this way may run indeed, but not in the appointed track set before them. Thus they neglect the apostle's counsel, "So run that you may obtain" (1 Corinthians 9:24). How can they hope to win the prize, then, if the challenge is the lowest priority in their endeavors? Thus the desire to experience all things first is a false route, for it is a vicious cycle that goes on endlessly.

21
We must choose
God's way.

But for the righteous man it is not like that. He realizes the consequences of condemnation pronounced on the crowd who travel the broad way that leads to destruction (Matthew 7:13). The righteous man chooses the King's highway, turning aside neither to the right hand nor to the left (Numbers 20:17; 21:22). Just as the prophet says, "The way of the just is upright" (Isaiah 26:7). Warned by sound counsel, he avoids the dangerous and fruitless round-about road and takes a direct course (Romans 9:28).

This is the word that is given against all covetousness, that commands him to sell all that he has, and to give to the poor (Matthew 19:21). For it is emphatic that "blessed are the poor in spirit, for theirs is the kingdom of heaven" (Matthew 5:3). All run in the race of life, but distinction is made among the races (1 Corinthians 9:24).

"The Lord knows the way of the righteous, while the way of the ungodly shall perish" (Psalm 1:6). As a result, "the little that a righteous man has is better than the riches of many wicked" (Psalm 37:16). Even as the preacher says and the fool later discovers, "He that loves silver shall not be satisfied with silver" (Ecclesiastes 5:10). In contrast, Christ says, "Blessed are they that hunger and thirst after righteousness, for they shall be filled" (Matthew 5:6).

> *We must desire God.*

Righteousness is the vital and natural food of the soul, which can no more be satisfied by earthly treasures than bodily starvation can be fed by the wind. If you see a starving man with his mouth wide open to the wind, inhaling great gulps of air, as if he hoped his hunger would thereby be satisfied, would you not think he was crazy? Yet it is no less mad to imagine that the soul can be satisfied with worldly things, which can only inflate his appetite without feeding him.

"Bless the Lord, O my soul . . . who satisfies my mouth with good things" (Psalm 103:1, 5). Yes, he satisfies with good things; He provokes you to do good; He keeps you safe in goodness; He goes ahead of you; He sustains and fills you. He moves you to long for Him, for it is He whom you really desire.

I have said already that God is the reason for loving God. That is true, because He is both the efficient cause and the final object of our love. He gives the occasion to love, He creates the desire to love, He brings our affection to its fruition. He is such that to have Him is a natural due, for He is lovable. It is natural to trust Him, since our love by ourselves for Him would be in vain unless we had hope that one day we would love Him perfectly. Our loves

> *22*
> *God is the reason for loving God.*

are prepared and rewarded by Him. He loves us first, leading the way for our response (1 John 4:19). So we are bound to repay Him with love. We are nurtured by Him to cherish high hopes in Him. "He is rich unto all who call upon Him" (Romans 10:12). He can give us nothing better as a prize and as a reward than Himself. For He is the refreshment of holy souls. He has sold Himself in captivity for a ransom. "The Lord is good unto them that wait for Him" (Lamentations 3:25).

What God is to the seeking soul

What, then, will He be to those who seek His presence?

Here is a marvelous thing, for it is impossible to seek the Lord unless one is already found of Him. You desire to be found first, that you may be sought for and found of God? O God, You may be sought and found, but no one can forestall Thee. God in His prevenience does this. For if we say, "Early shall my prayer come before Thee" (Psalm 88:13), yet all prayer would still be lukewarm unless it were animated by Thine inspiration.

Let us now see where love begins, for we have seen where it is consummated in God.

VIII. THE FIRST DEGREE OF LOVE: MAN LOVES HIMSELF FOR HIS OWN SAKE

23

Love is one of the four natural affections of man. It is unnecessary to name them, as they are so well known. Now as love is natural, it is right to love above all the Author of nature. That is why the first and great commandment is: "You shall love the Lord your God with all your heart and with all your soul and with all your mind" (Matthew 22:37).

Loving God must be commanded.

But nature is so frail and weak that man is forced to love himself first of all. However, this is carnal love by which a man loves himself first and selfishly so. As it is written, "that was not first which is spiritual but that which is natural; and afterward that which is spiritual" (1 Corinthians

15:46). Love does not come as a precept, it comes naturally, for "no man ever yet hated his own flesh" (Ephesians
5:29). Yet it is very natural for this love to grow excessively, and, like a strong current, burst the banks of self-
control, flooding the field of self-indulgence. A commandment, like a newly-built dike, is then needed: "You
shall love your neighbor as yourself" (Matthew 22:39).
This is a just requirement. For He who shares our own nature should also share our love, which is itself the grace of
our humanity.

If then a man finds it burdensome to relieve not only a
brother's needs but also provide for a brother's pleasures,
let him restrain his own self-love if he would avoid becoming a transgressor. He can be as indulgent as he likes about
himself, provided he shows the same indulgence with his
neighbors.

O man, you need the restraint of temperance, lest you
follow your own wanton desires to distraction, or become
so enslaved by the passions which are the enemies of your
soul. It is far better to divide your enjoyment with your
neighbor than with your enemy.

If you heed the counsel of the wise, you will turn away
from your own appetites and discipline yourself (Isaiah
18:30). Then you will follow the teaching of the apostle:
"Having food and raiment let us therewith be content"
(1 Timothy 6:8). In consequence, you will be able to
"abstain from fleshly lusts, which war against the soul"
(1 Peter 2:11). Then you will not find it a burden to share
with your neighbor what you have held back from your
enemy. You then will be temperate and righteous, able to
minister to a brother's need. So what could so readily be a
selfish love can become truly social when it can extend to
include others.

But if you find that your benevolence to your neighbor
reduces your own support which you need, what do you do
then? What indeed can you do but pray to Him "that gives
to all men liberally and upbraids not; and it shall be confi-
dently given him" (James 1:5). Again, as the psalmist
says, "You open your hand, and satisfy the desires of every

24
**Trust God to
supply your
own needs.**

living being" (Psalm 145:16). There is no doubt that God will provide for our needs; indeed, He gives most people more than they need. So His promise is true: "Seek first the Kingdom of God and His righteousness, and all these things will be added unto you" (Matthew 6:33; Luke 12:31). God freely promises to give all things necessary to him who does not withhold himself from the needs of others and who thus loves his neighbor. To seek first the Kingdom of God means really to prevent sin from ruling in our lives (Romans 6:12) and to prefer the yoke of modesty and sobriety with God's help. Again, it is righteous to share our natural gifts with those who share our common nature.

25
We need God's love to love others.

However, if we are to love our neighbor with absolute righteousness, we need to acknowledge God as our motive and cause. For how can we love with pure motive if we do not love God first of all? Only then can we love our neighbor. It is impossible to love in God without first loving God (1 Thessalonians 2:1-11). So it is essential we love God first in order to love others also.

Now God, as the source of all goodness, is the source of our ability and disposition to love others. He has endowed us with the possibility to love. He Who created our natures, sustains them, and protects them. For the whole world could not have begun without Him, owing its own existence to Him. We should never forget this or foolishly be tempted to think we can do without Him. Then when our strength fails, God comes to our help, in His wisdom, saving us that we can give due recognition to Him. As it is written, "call upon me in the day of trouble; I will deliver you, and you shall glorify me" (Psalm 50:15).

In this way, man who is animal and carnal by instinct, who only knew what it means to love himself, can begin to love God for man's own blessing. For he begins to learn that he can accomplish everything by God's help. But this he can only learn when he is reduced to impotence.

IX. THE SECOND DEGREE OF LOVE: MAN LOVES GOD FOR MAN'S OWN BLESSING

Man now loves God. Yet it is still love for his own **26** benefit, not for God's own sake. Nevertheless, it is wisdom to know what you can do by yourself and what you can only do with God's help to keep you from offending God by sin. If when sufferings occur and sins gain in frequency, then we are forced to turn to God for His unfailing help. Eventually will not even the cold heart of stone in a cast-iron rib cage be tenderized by the goodness of God's grace? Will he then not be forced to love God—not selfishly—but because God is God?

X. THE THIRD DEGREE OF LOVE: MAN LOVES GOD FOR GOD'S OWN SAKE

Man's frequent needs throws him back constantly upon God. By such continual dependence, he learns to enjoy God's presence. This intimacy with God becomes sweet as he learns to discover how wonderful God is. This experience thus promotes the love of God, so that it transcends over all our needs. Like the Samaritans, we are to respond that we know His goodness, not because we were told about it, but we have experienced it for ourselves (John 4:42). So too we tell our flesh, "we love God, not because of your needs, for we have tasted and known for ourselves the sweetness of the Lord" (Psalm 34:8).

Intimacy with God is the fruit of our need of God.

The needs of the flesh are a kind of speech by which we proclaim gladly the good things experienced. So a soul who feels like this will have no difficulty in telling his neighbor (Mark 12:31). He loves God realistically in doing so, for he now loves God for what He really is. His love is pure, and he obeys out of a pure heart and in loving obedience (1 Peter 1:22). He loves justly, and he takes this command to heart. This love is also pleasing because it is spontaneous. It is true love, because it is not just wordy, but it is demonstrated by deeds (1 John 3:18). It is righteous, because it gives as it receives.

Intimacy with
God helps us to
love like God.

The man who loves like this, truly loves the things of God. He loves truly, without self-interest (1 Corinthians 13:5). So he loves those things that belong to Jesus Christ, even as Christ sought our interests, or rather sought us, and never looked after His own. So we respond: "O, give thanks to the Lord, for He is good" (Psalm 118:1). This is not a confession of being good to the Lord, but of the Lord being good to us. It is the love of God for our benefits. The psalmist describes the man who is at the second degree of love, when he says: "He will give thanks to You, when You have done him kindness" (Psalm 49:19). But the third degree of love is when the love of God is purely celebrated for God's own sake.

XI. THE FOURTH DEGREE OF LOVE: MAN LOVES HIMSELF FOR GOD'S SAKE

27
Loving like God
helps us to love
ourselves.

Blessed is the man who can attain the fourth degree of love. Then he will love himself only in God! "Your righteousness, O my God, is like the mountains of God" (Psalm 36:6). For this love is a mountain of great elevation that is fertile and rich. Who shall ascend to the mountain of the Lord?" (Psalm 24:3). "O, that I had the wings of a dove, that I may fly away to find rest" (Psalm 55:6). For this dwelling place is Salem, a place of peace (Psalm 76:2).

Alas, my exile has been prolonged. When will this body of flesh and blood (Matthew 16:17), this vessel of clay (2 Corinthians 4:7), learn to realize this? When shall I experience this kind of love, when will my soul, inebriated with divine love, learn to be unconsciously self-forgetful, and simply be a broken vessel (Psalm 31:12)? Then it will hasten to God to depend upon Him and cling only to Him. Then will one's spirit be at one with God (1 Corinthians 6:17), saying: "My flesh and my heart fail, but God is the Strength of my life, and my Portion for ever" (Psalm 73:26).

Blessed and holy is he who has been privileged, even if only momentarily in this life, to taste of this love. For to so lose yourself that you are reduced to nothing is a divine experience and not a human sentiment (Philippians 2:7). For if a poor mortal were suddenly to attain this, he would be as rapidly held back once more by the evil world around him (Galatians 1:4). Moreover, the daily cares of life would wear him down, his carnal needs would cry out for satisfaction, and the weaknesses of fallen nature would fail him. Perhaps, worst of all, his own brother's needs would discourage him to turn back. So alas, he has no option but to return to his own affairs and to himself. In his frustrated grief he will cry out, "O Lord, I am oppressed, undertake for me" (Isaiah 38:14). Again he cries, "O wretched man that I am, who shall deliver me from the body of death?" (Romans 7:24).

Such love truly sustains us through the pressures of life.

In spite of all this, we read in Scripture that God made everything for His own glory (Isaiah 43:7). So surely all His creatures ought to conform as much as possible to His will. In Him all our affections should center, so that in all things we should seek to do only His will and not to please ourselves. True blessing will come to us then, not in self-gratification, nor in transient pleasures, but in accomplishing God's will in us. So we pray daily: "Your will be done on earth, as it is in heaven" (Matthew 6:10).

28
True blessing comes in seeking God's will.

O pure and holy love! O sweet and gracious affection! O pure and cleansed motive of will, purged from the admixture of self-interest, and sweetened in its association with the divine will! To reach this condition is to be godly. For as a drop of water disappears in a barrel of wine, taking the taste and color of wine, so is this state. Or like a bar of iron that is heated red-hot and becomes like the flame itself, so is this return to divine love. Just as air becomes so radiant with the light of the sun that it appears to be the very sunlight itself, so it is with the saints whose human love is transmuted by the will of God Himself.

God must be "All in All."

Yet this must be so. For how could God otherwise be "All in All" (1 Corinthians 15:28) if anything of man remained in man? However, our human nature will remain. We shall still be ourselves, but in another form, another glory, and another power. When will this happen? Who will see it? "When shall I come to appear before the Presence of God" (Psalm 42:2)? O Lord, my God, "my heart has talked of You, my face has sought You: Your face Lord, will I seek" (Psalm 27:8). Do you think I shall actually see Your holy temple (Psalm 27:4)?

29

I myself believe that the command to love the Lord our God with all our heart and soul and strength (Luke 10:27) will not be fully possible until the heart no longer needs to think about the body, nor the soul needs to give it life and feeling as it has to do so in this existence. Only when the soul has been relieved of these incumbrances will it be fully empowered by the grace of God. For it is impossible to concentrate all love on God as long as the cares of this weak body keep one preoccupied to this point of distraction. So it will only be in a spiritual body, immortal and perfected, at peace and fully integrated, as well as subjected to the Spirit in all things, that the soul will hope to reach the fourth degree of love. Or rather, it will be possessed by such love. For it is only by the power of God that He can establish us in such a condition. It cannot be obtained by human efforts.

We only taste this in anticipation of its fulfillment.

The soul, I have said, will arrive at this state when it will no longer be held back by the seduction of the flesh, or the weaknesses of our carnal state, or upset by troubles as it reaches out with the greatest alacrity and joy towards God (Mark 12:30). This raises the question, did the saintly martyrs receive this grace, even partially so, while they were still in their triumphant but mortal bodies? Surely it was such immeasurable strength of love that possessed them to despise their pains and enabled them to endure such excruciating suffering of their bodies. Yet the feeling of such intense pain must have affected their serenity; it could not have been wholly overcome.

XII. This Perfection of Love Will Only Be Experienced at the Resurrection

But what will be the experience of the souls who have already been released from their bodies?

Such perfect love is the life of eternity.

We believe that they are absolutely enveloped in that immense ocean of eternal light and everlasting brightness. But, if, as the fact probably is, they still hope and desire to have their bodies, is this not an indication that they are not yet wholly transformed; that indeed, something of the self still remains unsurrendered? Not until death is swallowed up in victory (1 Corinthians 15:54), and eternal light overwhelms all darkness, and takes full possession so that glory alone shines in their bodies, can our souls be entirely set free to be given wholly to God. For until then, the soul is restricted in the body, bound at least to it by the natural affections, if not also still vitally connected by physical sense. So without their bodies, they cannot reach their full consummation, nor would they want to do so.

In fact, the body cannot be left behind, nor reoccupied by the soul without advantage. For if "the death of His saints is precious in His sight" (Psalm 116:15), what must their life be, and such a life that is eternal! Is it surprising then that the glorified body will contribute something to the spirit? . . . The body is a help to the soul, in sickness, in death, and all the more when it shall be raised again from the dead. In illness, the body is an aid to penitence; in death, the body lies in repose; in the third state, it is in consummation. The soul, then, would not be perfected without the body, for it benefits in every way from its good services.

The role of the body in each state

The flesh, then, is to the good soul a good and faithful companion. Even when the body burdens the soul it also helps it. When the body no longer helps, it still lifts her

The threefold banquet of the soul

load from the soul, or at least it still helps to make the load less burdensome. The first state is one of toil, but fruitfully so. The second state is restful, but by no means idle. The third state is both fruitful and reposeful; yes, and glorious also.

Listen to the Bridegroom in the Song of Solomon, speaking allegorically about this threefold gain. "Eat," He says, "O, friends, drink, yes, drink abundantly, O beloved" (Song of Solomon 5:1). First, He invites those living in the body to *eat*. To those who have laid aside their flesh, and are at rest, He bids to *drink*. To those who resume their glorified bodies, He urges them to *drink abundantly*. For those who still groan in this fleshly existence and are burdened with this body, He calls only as "friends." They are dear to God, because they have love of God. But when the bonds of the flesh are loosened, they become still dearer, because their love is readier and freer to do so. But more than the other two, those last are called "dearest" (1 John 3:1). For renewed in a sweet garment, they are now glorified bodies. They are infinitely freer and vitally borne along toward God's love. Nothing remains to impede them personally. The first two states do not have this privilege, since in the first state the body is an impediment, and in the second state it is the object of anxious desires.

32   In the first condition, the faithful soul eats its bread only by the sweat of its brow (Genesis 3:19). For while it is in the flesh, it moves by faith (2 Corinthians 5:7), and faith must exercise itself by deeds of love, or else it will die (Galatians 5:6). When the soul puts off the flesh, it no longer feeds on the bread of sorrow (Psalm 127:2), but having eaten, it is allowed to drink more deeply of the wine of love. Yet the soul mingles the divine love with the tender desire of natural affection by which it longs to have its body restored as a glorified body. But once the soul has received what is lacking, then what can hold the soul back from entering fully into the presence of God and becoming so wholly unlike its original state, that it is now perfectly the image of God?

Then, at long last, the soul is able to drink of that cup of wisdom. It is a cup of which we read: "The cup overflows, for how good it is!" (Psalm 23:5). Now the soul can drink abundantly from the pure, fresh wine with Christ in His Father's house (Matthew 26:29).

It is divine wisdom which celebrates this three-fold **33** banquet (Proverbs 9:1f.). It consists of a love which feeds those who labor, giving refreshment to those who are at rest and giving full measure to those who reign. This then is what is meant by the words: "Eat, O friends; drink, yet drink abundantly, O beloved" (Song of Solomon 5:1). Then will come forth the Son of God Himself who will serve His saints as He has promised (Luke 12:37). They shall rejoice and be glad (Psalm 68:3). Their satiety will not be in excess, for there will be insatiable desire that yet is not distressing. For this eternal and infinite longing will not suffer from any want.

There the fourth degree of love is attained forever. It consists of loving God, only and always. Then we shall not even love ourselves, except as we do so for God's own sake. For God will be the reward of them that love Him. Then God will be the everlasting reward of an eternal love.

Part III
DEVOTION TO CHRIST

Excerpts from the Sermons of Bernard of Clairvaux
On the Song of Solomon

VII

Devotion to Christ

*(Selected passages from Bernard's Sermons
on the Song of Solomon)*

Preface

THE CISTERCIAN
SCHOOL OF LOVE WAS SEEN
as having only one real purpose—to lead men
and women to God. Such a school was not
therefore only for the purpose of theological studies.
Rather it was a school of apprentices who were trained to
practice what they preached. For them, Christian scholarship was a two-fold task: the instruction and the discipline of loving Christ. For the Cistercians, learning and
living before God could not be separated.

The following excerpts from Bernard's *Sermons on the
Song of Solomon* have been collated together to illustrate
some of the rich materials they represent on the early
Cistercian devotional life. For the full text, the reader is
recommended to use the scholarly editions published by
the Cistercian Publications that are now available. These
sermons are, as we have already noted, a literary rather
than an oral tradition. They were developed and polished
with at least a second redaction during the life of Bernard.
Indeed, toward the end of his life, Bernard revised them so
that their euphony or beauty of style might be improved to
be consistent with the loving devotion to Christ that they
expressed.

But perhaps they were presented in the first instance as
a sample of devotions to Bernard's friend, Bernard of

167

Portes. In a letter to him (Letter no. 54), Bernard re-
quests: "When you have read them, I beg you to write as
soon as you can do so conveniently, and let me know
whether you think that I should continue them or not."
On a later occasion, his friend Evervin asked him about
some heresies he was being confronted with. Bernard re-
plies specifically about this in sermons 65-66. In the *First
Life of Bernard,* William of St.-Thierry recounts that
shortly after Bernard had become Abbot, he began to
teach William about the mysteries of the marriage song or
Song of Solomon. Bernard also had read such commentaries on the book as that of Origen.

Thus Bernard's *Sermons on the Song of Solomon* are the
fruit of a lifetime of study, teaching, meditation, and rewriting. As such, they are a literary masterpiece which
Leclercq thinks were written in four groups of sermons:
sermons 1-24, 24-49, 50-83, 84-86. Sermon 1 was begun
after 1135, sermon 24 is known to have been resumed in
1138, sermon 33 was composed before Lent of 1139, and
the group of sermons 24-49 was probably completed in
1145. Sermons 50-83 occupied the next years, with sermons 65-66 responded to about 1144. The last two sermons were written toward the close of his life, and sermon
86 was unfinished at his death. [1]

In the edited passages that follow, the focus is on what
Bernard himself emphasized, namely, attachment to
Christ. For Christ is the Way back to God.

Bernard sees the wounded sinner like an unfaithful
spouse—the imagery of the Old Testament—who is abandoned by her lovers. In her shame she cannot do anything
else but return to her husband. Such a return is only possible because of the strength given by the Word and in response to His faithfulness and grace. As we have already
noted, perhaps many of the novitiates whom Bernard was
addressing had known carnal love before entering the
monastic school of Christ's love. So he saw the return to
the chaste love of Christ as a slow process of progressive
experience in the Spirit of God. Thus Bernard speaks of
the threefold experience of repentance, gracious help,
and communion with Christ (pp. 170-71). He outlines

later the three-fold loving of Christ, with heart, soul, and mind (pp. 184-88).

Bernard expresses himself personally in several of the sermons. For such desire for God can only be experienced and not just talked about. Moreover, to avoid sentimentality, such devotion must always be identified with the Word of God, so Bernard urges us to relate our desire to the Scriptures (pp. 172). Such personal love for Christ requires of us also to relate with other people and associate with those who also love Christ (pp. 175). Yet all of this affection for Christ can only be the gift of the presence of the Holy Spirit within us (pp. 173-75). For Bernard, the humanity of Jesus, His humility, His earthly ministry, His sufferings and death, was the theme of constant meditation, all of which could be summarized in the sweetness of His Name (pp. 178-83). In our love and praise of His sweet Name, we will find comfort, healing, and an antidote for all our distresses. Indeed, it is this distinctive Bernardian theme that has inspired a long tradition of hymnody in the Church.

We know God, then, in a vast range of human experiences. We can only see Him in purity of heart (p. 184). We know Him inwardly by private devotions (pp. 184-88). We learn about Him in our struggles with manifold temptations (pp. 194-96). Prayer should be expressed as holy desire, so that we get to know Him in our meditations before Him. We learn so much about ourselves only by humility, and without this self-knowledge of our sinfulness and need, how can we possibly get to know God? (pp. 196-200). Yet the conclusion is always the prevenience of God in our lives. For all our desires for God have been placed within our own hearts by His prior desire for us (pp. 204-12).

THE WAY OF LOVE: A THREEFOLD PROGRESS[2]

"Let Him kiss me with the kisses of His mouth" (Song of Solomon 1:2). Today, we shall read from the book of our experience. Turn your minds inwardly upon yourselves and let each of you examine his own conscience in regard to the things that we shall talk about. For I desire you to become aware whether in the deep desires of your own heart, you have ever spoken like the words of our text? For not all men desire to be like this. He alone is able to do so who has received, if only once, the spiritual kiss from the lips of Christ. Then he will incessantly desire a renewal of such a full and sweet experience. For I am convinced strongly that no one who has not experienced this, can ever comprehend what it is like. And he who has tasted, will long for it again. . . .

The kiss of the feet

First, according the the happy penitent (Mary Magdalene) there was *the kiss of the feet*. Like the example of this penitent, do you also, O unhappy soul, prostrate yourself that you may cease to be unhappy! Prostrate yourself to the earth, embrace His feet, appease them with kisses, bedew them with your tears. Not that you may wash them away, but that you may wash yourself. And do not lift up your countenance suffused with tears of shame and grief until you hear the words also of absolution, "Your sins are forgiven you" (Luke 7:36-48).

Before I presume to approach the higher and more sacred degrees of blessedness, I do not wish to reach the highest point suddenly, but rather to proceed toward it gradually. From the kissing of the foot to the kissing of the lips, the ascent is long and difficult, and it would show even a lack of reverence to pass from one straight to the other. What! Shall you still, marked with recent dust stains, touch those sacred lips? Having but yesterday been drawn out of the mire, would you aspire today to the glory of His countenance?

The kiss of His hand

For you there must be a middle stage of preparations: and that is by the kiss of His *hand*. It shall cleanse you from your stains and then it shall lift you up. But how shall it raise you up? It will raise you by bestowing upon you that which shall be a basis for aspiring higher still: the grace of continence and the worthy fruits of penitence, which are the works of devotion. These will lift you up from the dunghill and fill you with hope of higher things. In receiving this gift, there assuredly you shall kiss the Lord's hand; you will give Him the glory rather than take it yourself. Otherwise, what reply have you to make to such reproaches as these: "What have you that you have not received? Now if you have received it, why do you glory, as if it had not been given to you?" (1 Corinthians 4:7).

Having experienced these two kinds of kisses, as a double evidence of God's condescension, you may perhaps be bold enough to reach out still higher for more sacred things. For as you grow in grace and knock at the door with more assurance, you will seek for what is still lacking. In the first place, we fall at the feet of the Lord, and lament before Him Who has made us the faults and sins which we ourselves have committed. In the second, we seek His helping hand to lift us up and to strengthen our feeble knees that we may stand upright. In the third, when we have, with many prayers and tears, obtained these two former graces, then at length we perhaps venture to lift our eyes to that countenance full of glory and majesty, for the purpose not only to adore, but (I say it with fear and trembling) to *kiss His lips,* because the Spirit before us is Christ the Lord, to whom being united in a holy kiss, we are by His marvelous condescension made to be one spirit with Him.

The kiss of His life.

Rightly so, O Lord Jesus, has my heart declared to You: "My face has sought You; Your face, Lord, will I seek" (Psalm 27:8). You enabled me to hear Your mercy in the morning when I lay prone in the dust, kissing the prints of Your sacred steps; for You did pardon the evil of my former life. Then as the day of my life went on, You have rejoiced the soul of Your servant. Since by the kiss of Your Hand, You accorded to me the grace to live well. And now what remains, O good Lord, is to admit me into the fullness of Your Light, in fervor of my spirit, to kiss Your divine lips. You have fulfilled from within me the joy of Your Countenance.

Prayer

THE ARDENT LOVE OF THE SOUL FOR CHRIST[3]

The distinctive of the bride

"Let Him kiss me with the kisses of His mouth" (Song of Solomon 1:2). Who is it who speaks these words? It is the bride. Who is the bride? It is the soul thirsting for God. But first, let me specify the dispositions of men in various relations to each other, so that those which belong properly to the bride may appear more clearly. If a man is a slave, he fears the face of his love. If he is a hireling, he looks for wages from his lord's hand. If a disciple, he gives attention to his teacher. If a son, he renders honor to his father. But she who asks this is held by the bridal bond of love to him from whom she asks it. Of all the sentiments of nature, this of love is the most excellent, especially when it is rendered back to Him who is the Principal and Fount of it, that is God.

Nor are there found any expressions equally sweet to signify the mutual affection between the Word of God and the soul as those of Bridegroom and of bride. In as much as between individuals who stand is such a relation to each other, all things are in common, and they possess nothing separate or divided. They have one inheritance, one dwelling place, one table; and they are, in fact, one flesh.

The Soul of the Bride

If then, mutual love is especially befitting to a bride and bridegroom, it is not unfitting that the name of "Bride" is given to a soul which loves God. It is a sign of love that she makes this request. She asks neither for liberty, nor for wages, nor for inheritance, nor finally for knowledge, but only for this. She does this as a chaste and modest bride, who does not deny or dissimulate the sacred affection which she feels.

Notice how abruptly she breaks into her discourse. She has a great favor to ask of one who is great, yet she does not have recourse, as is too often the case, to caresses or flatteries. She does not wind her way to her request by gradual approaches. She employs no preface, nor makes any attempt to win good will or favor. But her request bursts forth openly and abruptly out of the abundance of her heart and even as it were with a sort of effrontery.

She simply wants to say: "Whom have I in heaven but
You, and there is none upon earth that I desire in comparison to You" (Psalm 73:5). Doubtless such love is
chaste that seeks the object of its love alone, without care
for anything that he may possess. And that love is sacred
which dwells not in fleshly concupiscence, but in purity of
the spirit. That love is ardent which is so absorbed and, as
it were, inebriated with its own affection. But it loses all
thought of the greatness of its object. For consider the reality that "He looks upon the earth and it trembles"
(Psalm 104:32). Yet it is from Him that she presumes to
ask this. Is she crazy? How abundantly manifest it is, that
"perfect love casts out all fear" (1 John 4:18).

*Bridal love
should be chaste*

BRIDAL AFFECTION AS THE GIFT
OF THE HOLY SPIRIT[4]

The kiss of God is the gift of the Holy Spirit. "No man
knows the Son but the Father; neither knows any man the
Father but the Son, and he to whom the Son will reveal
Him" (Matthew 11:27). It seems to me that here is desig-
nated an ineffable kiss, unknown to any created being.
For the Father loves the Son, and embraces Him with a
love which is unlike any other love, for it is the Supreme
embracing His Equal, the Eternal His Co-Eternal, the
One Being. Now this cognition of mutual love between
Him Who begets, and Him Who is begotten, what is it
but a kiss, as deeply mysterious as it is sweet?

Then behold how the newly made bride receives a new
proof of the affection of the Bridegroom. "He breathed on
them," says John, speaking of the way the Spirit of Jesus
breathed upon his apostles, that is the primitive church,
"and said unto them, Receive you the Holy Ghost" (John
20:22). That, without a doubt, is the kiss He gave to
them. What, that physical breath? No, but the invisible
Spirit who was thus communicated by the breathing of the
Lord. So that, by this action, it might be understood that
the Spirit proceeds equally from the Father and the Son.

It is sufficient for the bride if she received the gift of grace from the Bridegroom, although it is not the highest grace of all. Let no one suppose that this is a small favor or of little value. But this signifies no less than the outpouring of the Holy Spirit. For if the Father is rightly understood in bestowing the kiss, and the Son in receiving the kiss, then it is the Holy Spirit who provides us with it also. His kiss to us is peace that is unalterable, a bond indissoluble, love indivisible, and unity inviolable, for it is that relationship between the Father and the Son.

The boldness of the Bride   It is, therefore, by the influence of the Holy Spirit that the bride has the boldness to ask trustingly under this name or sign, that the inpouring of the Holy Spirit may be granted to her. She does indeed hold, as it were, a pledge, which deprives her request of any shadow of presumption. I mean the declaration of the sign when he said, "No man knows the Son but the Father; neither knows any man the Father but the Son"; and then adds, "he to whomsoever the Son will reveal Him" (Matthew 11:27). But the bride has no doubt that if He wills to grant this knowledge to any, it will be to her. Therefore she prays boldly that this may be given to her—that is, the Holy Spirit—in Whom the Son and the Father are revealed.

The need of the Holy Spirit in knowledge   Do you also, brethren, in order that you may conduct yourselves with prudence while searching out divine mysteries, bear in mind the warning of the wise man: "seek not out the things that are too hard for thee, neither search the things that are above thy strength" (Ecclesiasticus 3:21). Walk among those exalted subjects in the Spirit, and not in thine own judgment. For the teaching of the Holy Spirit does not sharpen curiosity, but kindles love. Rightly does the bride, when seeking Him Whom her soul loves, not trust herself to the judgment of the flesh, nor follow the futile reasonings of human curiosity, but as here prays for this Gift. Then she may invoke the Holy Spirit and through Him may receive at once the love for knowledge and the seasoning of grace to accompany that love.

Well is it said that the knowledge thus given is accompanied with love, since a kiss is the sign of love. But the knowledge which puffs up, being without love, is not thus conveyed. Nor can they who have a zeal for God, but not according to knowledge, arrogate this to themselves at all. But this gift conveys both the one and the other of these graces, both the light of knowledge and the unction of piety. For He is a Spirit of wisdom and knowledge. Let not him who is understanding of the truth, but is without love, nor him who loves but is without the understanding of truth, think that he has received that gift, for in it there is no place for error or for lukewarmness.

True knowledge requires love

Blessing, therefore, is the sign by which comes not only the knowledge of God, but also the love of Him as our Father, who cannot be fully known unless He is at the same time perfectly loved. What soul among you has ever felt in the depths of his conscience "the Spirit of the Son crying Abba, Father?" (Galatians 4:6). That soul which feels itself animated by the same Spirit as the Son, that soul I say, may believe that it is the object of the affection of the Father. Trust in Him, O soul, whoever you are, that has the blessedness to be in that condition. Trust in Him, doubting nothing. But, O holy soul, retain the deepest reverence, for He is the Lord, thy God; He is not to be embraced perhaps, but rather to be adored, with the Father and the Holy Spirit, for ever and ever. Amen.

FRAGRANCES OF BRIDAL AFFECTION[5]

The perfumes of the bride differ from those of the Bridegroom, as they are different the one from the other. There is the perfume of contrition, the perfume of devotion, and the perfume of piety. The first is pungent, and causes pain; the second is soothing, and relieves pain; the third is curative, and removes disease. Now we shall speak of these separately.

There is the perfume which the soul, when it has been ensnared and entangled with many sins, compounds for itself. When it begins to reflect upon its ways, it collects and heaps together, pounding them in the mortar of conscience. Putting them into a cauldron, the heart, as it were, heaves and boils with distress, and cooks them together over a kind of fire of grief and repentance. So that the man is able to say with the psalmist: "My heart was hot within me; while I was musing the fire burned" (Psalm 39:3). Here then is one unguent which the sinful soul ought to prepare for itself as the commencement of its conversion, and apply to its still fresh wounds; for the first sacrifice to be made to God is a troubled and contrite heart (Psalm 51:17).

This was that visible ointment where the feet of God manifest in the flesh were anointed by the woman who was a sinner. We read "that the house was filled with the odor of the ointment" (John 12:3). It was poured by the hands of a sinful woman upon the feet of our Lord. If we consider with what fragrance the Church is perfumed by the conversion of one sinner, and how powerful an odor unto life each penitent becomes, if his repentance is complete and public, we shall be able to say without hesitation that "the house was filled with the odor of the ointment."

Yet there is a perfume much more precious than this, as the materials of which it is composed are of a more excellent kind. For the materials of the former do not require to be sought from afar. We find them without difficulty within ourselves; in our own little garden plots we gather them easily and in great abundance, as often as the necessity requires. For who is there who does not know himself to have sins and iniquities, and often too many, and always at hand, unless he desires to deceive himself upon this?

But as for the sweet spices which compose the second perfume, our earth does not produce them at all. We must seek them in a land that is far off. For is not "every good gift and every perfect gift from above," and does it not "come down from the Father of Lights?" (James 1:17). For this second perfume is compounded of the benefits which Divine goodness has bestowed upon mankind. Happy is he who, with care and pains, collects them for himself, and sets them before the eyes of his mind, with acts of thanksgiving proportioned to their greatness.

Assuredly, this second perfume has been bruised and pounded in the mortar of our breast with the pestle of frequent meditation, boiled together from the fire of holy desire, and finally enriched with the oil of joy. The result is a perfume far more precious and more excellent than the former. Sufficient as proof of this is the testimony of Him who says: "Whoever offers praise glorifies Me" (Psalm 50:23). Nor can we doubt that the remembrance of benefits is an incitement to praise our Benefactor.

The benefit of this perfume is said to "glorify" God. While the former is poured upon the Lord's feet, the latter is poured upon His head.

I remember that I spoke to you of two perfumes.[6] The one perfume was penitence, which comprehends many sins; the other of devotion, which contains many benefits. Both of them are salutary, but not both agreeable. For the first has a stinging power which makes itself felt, because the bitter remembrance of sins moves the soul to compunction and causes pain, whereas the power of the other is soothing. It gives consolation and relieves spiritual distress by bringing into view the goodness of God.

But there is a perfume which far excels these. I have called it the perfume of piety, because it is that which results from the necessities of the poor, the cares of the oppressed, the disquiets of the sorrowful, the faults of the sinners, and finally from all of the misfortunes of those who are unhappy, even though they be our enemies. These materials seem to be despicable, but the perfume which is distilled from them surpasses all other sweet odors. It is a perfume which cures, because "blessed are the merciful, for they shall obtain mercy" (Matthew 5:7).

The perfume of piety

Who do you think is that happy man who has pity and lends to the needy (Psalm 112:5). Who is he who is accustomed to have compassion upon others, who is quick to help them, judging it better to give than to receive? Who is he who finds it easy to forgive, hard to be angry, and almost impossible to take revenge? And who in all things regards the interests of his neighbors even as his own? O happy soul, whoever you are, who has such a disposition that is so imbued with the dew of mercy, and so endued with charitable affection, rendering thyself all things to all men, regarding yourself as but a broken vessel, that you may be at the service of others, and assist them in their need, whensoever and wheresoever it may be. Who indeed is finally dead to himself, that he may live to the benefit of all.

If such are you, O happy soul, then you plainly possess this third and best of perfumes, and from your hands drops all its sweetness. For in the worst of times it will not dry up, nor shall the fire of persecution exhaust it. God shall ever be mindful of every sacrifice that you make, and shall render perfect your burnt offering.

THE SWEET NAME OF JESUS[7]
(Hymn attributed to Bernard)

Jesus, the very thought of Thee,
   With sweetness fills my breast;
But sweeter far Thy face to see,
   And in Thy presence rest.

Nor voice can sing, nor heart can frame,
   Nor can the mem'-ry find
A sweeter sound than Thy blest name,
   O Savior of mankind.

O hope of every contrite heart,
   O joy of all the meek,
To those who fall how kind Thou art!
   How good to those who seek!

But what to those who find? Ah, this
   Nor tongue nor pen can show—

The love of Jesus, what it is,
    None but His loved ones know.

Jesus, our only joy be Thou,
    As Thou our prize wilt be;
Jesus, be Thou our glory now,
    And through eternity.

"Your name is oil poured out" (Song of Solomon 1:3). Throughout the pages of Scripture, you read about many names given to the Bridegroom. But all of these I shall sum up in only two names. I think you will find all the names ascribed to Christ either as the grace of His kindness, or else the power of His majesty.

The Holy Spirit tells us this in the mouth of His friends: "These two things I heard, that power belongs to God, and mercy to You, O Lord" (Psalm 62:11f. Vulgate). With reference to His majesty we read: "Holy and reverend is His name" (Psalm 111:9). With reference to His love, we read: "There is no other name under heaven given among men, whereby we must be saved, than the name of Jesus" (Acts 4:12). Further examples make this clearer still. "This is His name whereby He shall be called, The Lord of Righteousness" (Jeremiah 23:6). This is a name suggesting His power. But when is said, "You shall call His name Immanuel" (Isaiah 7:14), he indicates His love. Christ said of Himself, "You call me Master and Lord" (John 13:13). There the first speaks of the name of love and the second of power. But it is love's concern to feed the mind, just as much as to feed the body. So again the prophet says: "His name shall be called Wonderful, Counsellor, the Mighty God, the Everlasting Father, the Prince of Peace" (Isaiah 9:6). The first, third, and fourth signify majesty, while the other signifies love.

Which then of these is "as oil poured forth?" In some mysterious way the name of power and majesty is tranfused into that which is the name of love and goodness, an amalgam that is poured forth abundantly in the person of our Savior, Jesus Christ. For instance, is not the name of God poured forth as "God with us"? For He is Immanuel.

The two names of Jesus

So the name of Wonderful is tranfused into that of Counsellor, the Mighty God into those of the Everlasting
Father and the Prince of Peace; likewise the Lord our
Righteousness is also the Lord gracious and full of compassion (Psalm 111:3-4).

Where, therefore, is that voice that warned with thun-
der, "I am the Lord!" that resounded with such terror to
the people of old? In its place the voice that I am familiar
with begins with the sweet name of "Father" (Matthew
6:9). This now gives me confidence to believe my peti-
tions that follow will be answered. Servants are now
called friends (John 15:14). Now the resurrection is not
even announced to disciples but to brothers (Matthew
28:10).

A name
revealed to all

I am not surprised, then, that when the time is fully
come there will be an outpouring of His Spirit, as God
promised to Joel, upon all mankind (Joel 2:28). For I read
that a similar event took place among the Hebrews in
another age (Numbers 11:26). But you may be anticipating what I am saying. For, you ask, what lay beyond God's
first answer to Moses, "I Am Who I Am" and "I Am has
sent Me to you" (Exodus 3:14). I question if Moses himself
realized or would have grasped it, had the name not been
poured forth in revelation. Once poured out, he could understand it. But it was not only poured out and sent forth,
but it was poured inwardly. The citizens of heaven already
possessed it, and the angels knew it. Now that intimate
secret which the angels knew was revealed as it was poured
out to men. Henceforth, they could justly proclaim from
the earth: "Your name is as oil poured out" (Song of
Solomon 1:2), unless the obstinacy of a thankless people
would prevent it. For He had said, "I am the God of
Abraham, Isaac, and Jacob" (Exodus 3:6).

A precious, yet
universal name

How dear then is that name, and yet how common
also, otherwise it would not have been poured out on me.
For I am a sharer of that name, which if it had not had
healing power, would have profited me nothing. But as a
sharer, I have a heavenly inheritance. I am a Christian,

even Christ's own brother. If I am what I say I am then I am called to be an heir of God, and co-heir with Christ (Romans 8:17). And is it any wonder that His name is thus poured out when He Himself was so poured out. For when He emptied Himself, He took upon Him the form of a servant (Philippians 2:7). Did He not even say, "I am poured out like water" (Psalm 22:14)? The plenitude of divine life was poured out and lived on earth in bodily form (Colossians 2:9) so that we who bear a mortal frame should also benefit of that plenitude. Thus being filled with that life-giving odor should say "Your name is as oil poured out." Such then is what is meant by the outpouring of the name, such is its manner, and such is its extent.

A name like oil.

But we may ask, why the symbolism of oil? For this I have not yet explained. I do not believe it is an arbitrary gesture that the Holy Spirit would compare the name of the Bridegroom with oil. Unless you can convince me otherwise, I see that likeness in the threefold property of oil: it illuminates, it nourishes, and it anoints. Is this not also true of the Bridegroom's name? When preached, it gives light. When meditated upon, it nourishes. When invoked, it alleviates the wounds of mind and soul. Let us consider each of these points.

A name that illuminates

How can we possibly explain the worldwide light of faith, that has spread so rapidly as a great flame, except by the preaching of the name of Jesus? Is it not by the light of this sacred name that God has called us into His marvellous light (1 Peter 2:9)? Does it not irradiate through all our darkness and empower us to see the light? (Psalm 35:10). Paul speaks to such as we, when he says: "You were sometimes darkness, but now you are light in the Lord" (Ephesians 5:8). It is this same name that the apostle was also commanded to bear before the Gentiles, kings, and the people of Israel (Acts 9:15). This name illuminated his country and people, as he carried it as a torch, when he preached in all his travels that the night was almost over and the dawn was near at hand. "Let us, therefore, cast off the works of darkness and put on the armor of light: let us walk honestly as in the day" (Romans 13:12f.). To all he displayed he was as a lamp in its lampstand (Matthew 5:15, Revelation 1:12). To every place he preached Christ and of Him crucified (1 Corinthians 2:2). What splendor radiated from that light, dazzling the crowd, when Peter uttered that name. It strengthened the feet and ankles of the cripple, shooting like a light of fire, when he said: "In the name of Christ Jesus of Nazareth rise up and walk" (Acts 3:6).

A name that nourishes

But the name of Jesus is not only light; it is also nourishment. Do you not feel nurtured every time you utter that name? What nourishes the mind more in meditation? What can more restore exhausted powers, reinforce virtues, encourage good and righteous habits, or foster the soul in chaste affections than that name? Every food of the mind is dry and tasteless if it is not dipped in that oil, and seasoned by that salt. No book or writing has any value to me if it does not contain in it the name of Jesus.[8] For the name of Jesus is like honey to my mouth, or as melody to the ear, or as song of gladness in my heart.[9]

A name that heals

Again, the name of Jesus is like a medicine. Do we feel sad? (James 5:13). Then let Jesus come into your heart. Then let His name leap from your lips. You will find that blessed name has lifted the clouds of sadness, giving you serenity and peace once more. Does anyone fall into sin? Does one even feel tempted to commit suicide? Let him invoke that life-giving name and his desire to live will be renewed. We all experience hardness of heart, the apathy of boredom, the bitterness of mind, the cold indifference of spirit. But have they ever failed to yield before the presence of that saving name? Have not those tears which were dammed up by pride broken through when that name of power has been called upon? Have not our apprehensions been driven away once more at the thought of Jesus? Indeed, where is the man living in doubt and uncertainty who has not had assurance once more restored to him by recourse to the name of Jesus? Was ever anyone so full of discouragement and so beaten down with adversity, to whom the sound of that Name did not give new resolve?

Indeed, for all the ills and afflictions to which flesh is heir, this name is medicine. As proof of this we have the words of the Lord Himself: "Call upon Me in the day of trouble: I will deliver you, and you shall magnify Me" (Psalm 50:15). For nothing so restrains the impulse to anger, so represses the rise of pride, than the power of the name of Jesus. It cures the wound of envy, it bridles the impulse of luxury, it extinguishes the flame of lust. It also cools the thirst of covetousness, and banishes the urge to think impure thoughts. When I utter the name of Jesus, I not only set before my mind a Man who is meek and humble in heart (Matthew 11:29), kind, prudent, chaste, merciful (Titus 1:8), and conspicuous in every honorable and saintly quality, but I also set before me the man who is Almighty God. He it is who heals me, and restores me to spiritual health by His character, and He is the One who helps me so powerfully. All of this is communicated to me, whenever His name is uttered, the name of Jesus. Because He is Man, I can strive to imitate Him. Because He is Almighty God, I can lean upon Him. The examples of His earthly life, I gather like medicinal herbs, and because of His divinity I can blend them. Then the result is a potion no pharmacist can ever prescribe.

Hidden in this sacred name, as in a vase, you my soul have a saving antidote which is proof against all sickness. So carry it always close to your heart, have it always ready to hand, in order that all your actions and all your affections are directed toward Jesus. To do this, you are invited as follows: "Set Me as a seal upon your arm" (Song of Solomon 8:6). This is a theme that we shall treat again. For now, you have a remedy for heart and hand. For you have in the name of Jesus the power to correct wrong actions, to perfect those that are imperfect, and the guard to protect your affections from corruption. In this name you will be made whole again.

HOW WE SHOULD LOVE CHRIST[10]

Life is futile without Christ.

"If anyone love not the Lord Jesus Christ, let him be anathema" (1 Corinthians 16:22).

Truly I ought to love the one through whom I have my very being, my life, and my understanding. If I am ungrateful, I am unworthy too. Lord Jesus, whoever refuses to live with You is clearly worthy of death, and indeed is dead already. For whoever does not know You is a fool. Whoever does not devote his mind to Your service is unreasonable, and he who cares to be anything except for You is good for nothing, and is nothing. Indeed, what is man except that You have taken knowledge of him (Psalm 144:3)? It is not for Your own self, O my God, that You have created all things. And he who desires to exist for himself and not for You begins to be as nothing among all things that are. What is it that the wise man says, "Fear God and keep His commandments for this is the whole duty of man" (Ecclesiastes 12:13)? If, then, this is the whole duty of man, without this man is nothing.

A prayer of surrender

Turn Yourself, O my God, toward me, so that You will enable me to be humble. Take wholly to Yourself the brief remainder of the years that belong to my poor life, for all the years which I have lost because I have been preoccupied with losing myself, despise not, I entreat, a humble and contrite heart. My days have declined as a shadow, and they have perished without fruit. It is now impossible for me to recall them. But make me, in Your goodness, at least to meditate upon them before You in the bitterness of my soul. You see that wisdom is the whole desire and purpose of my heart. If there is anything in me that is not employed in Your service, remove it. O God, You know my simplicity. If it is the beginning of wisdom in recognizing my ignorance, then I realize that this is Your gift. Increase it in me I pray, so that I shall not be ungrateful for the least of Your benefits, but shall strive to supply that which is still lacking in me. It is, then, for these Your benefits, that I love You with my feeble powers.

But there is a fact which moves and excites and inspires

me much more than this. For above all things it is the cup that You drank, O Jesus, merciful and kind, and undertook the great task of our redemption. This is a stronger motive than any other by which to love You.

Learn, then, O Christian, from Christ the manner in which you ought to love Christ. Learn to love Him tenderly, to love Him wisely, to love Him with a mighty love. Tenderly, that you may not be enticed away from Him. Wisely, that you may not be deceived and so drawn away. Strongly, that you may not be separated from Him by any force. Delight yourself in Christ who is Wisdom, beyond all else, in order that worldly glory or fleshly pleasures may not withdraw you from Him. Let Christ, who is the truth, enlighten you, so that you may not be led away by the spirit of falsehood and error. So that you may not be overcome by adversities, let Christ who is the Power of God strengthen you. Let charity render your zeal ardent; let wisdom rule and direct it. Let constancy make it enduring. Let it be free from lukewarmness, not timid, nor lacking indiscretion. Are not those three things prescribed to you in the Law, when God said: "You shall love the Lord your God with all your heart, with all your soul, and with all your strength" (Deuteronomy 6:5)?

It seems to me that if no other suitable meaning comes to mind for this triple distinction, then remember that the love of the heart answers to the earnestness of affection. The love of the soul answers to the purpose or judgment of the reason. And the love of strength can refer to the constancy and vigor of the mind. Love, then, the Lord your God with the entire and full affection of the heart. Love Him with all the vigilance and all the foresight of reason. Love Him with the full strength and vigor of the soul, so that for His love you will not fear even to die.

The forms of love

As it is written: "Love is strong as death, jealousy as cruel as the grave" (Song of Solomon 8:6). Let the Lord Jesus be to your heart sweet and pleasant, so as to attack the false attractions of the carnal life. Let His sweetness overcome all others as one nail drives out another.

Love of the heart

Love of the soul

To your understanding and to your reason let Him be a wise leader and a guiding light, not only to enable you to avoid the snares and deceits of heresy, but to preserve the purity of your faith from their cunning devices. Be careful also to avoid excessive and unwise enthusiasm in your conduct.

Love of the mind

Let your love be strong and constant, neither yielding to fear nor exhausted by sufferings.

Let us love tenderly, wisely, ardently, knowing that the love of the heart which we call tender is indeed sweet, but easily led astray if it is not accompanied by the love of the soul. While the love of the soul may be rational, yet it is also apt to be weak, unless courage and ardor go with it to strengthen it.

Affection can be weak

Notice, however, that the love of our hearts tends to be carnal, that is to say, in the way in which our hearts are affected towards Christ, according to His life after the flesh. A person who is filled with that love is easily touched with any discourse which dwells on that subject. There is nothing that he listens to more willingly, or reads more attentively, or recalls more often to memory, or meditates upon with greater enjoyment. His sacrifices of prayer receive from it a new exercise.

But as often as he prays, the image of the God-Man rises before him either in His birth or in His infancy, or in His teachings, or in His death, resurrection, and ascension. All of these similar images necessarily stimulate the soul to the love of holiness, driving away fleshly vices and putting away temptations and calming desires. But I consider it a principal reason why God—Who is invisible—willed to rend Himself visible in the flesh, and to dwell as a Man among men, or did so to enable the natural affections of carnal men to be drawn out by degrees toward a pure and spiritual affection.

For example, were not those who said to Jesus, "Behold, we have left all and followed you" (Matthew 19:27), still in this first degree of love? Yes, they had left all for the sole love of the bodily presence of Jesus, so that they were not able even to listen with equanimity to the announcement of His redeeming passion and death as near at hand. Even afterwards it touched them with profound sadness to look up to the glory of His ascension. For this reason, He said to them: "Because I have said these things unto you, sorrow has filled your heart" (John 16:6). So it was that only by His physical presence were their hearts detached from carnal loves. For it is certain that there is no love of Christ at all without the Holy Spirit, even if this love is of the flesh and without His fullness.

The measure of this higher love is that its sweetness seizes the whole heart, and draws it completely from the love of all flesh and from every sensual pleasure. It frees it from all the temptations of the flesh.

The love of the soul is higher

Of course, this devotion to the humanity of Christ is a gift of the Holy Spirit and a great gift. Yet I must call such love carnal, at least in comparison with that other affection which has regard, not so much for the Word as flesh, as for the Word as wisdom, as righteousness, as truth, as holiness, goodness, virtue, and all other perfections of whatever kind. For Christ is all these, inasmuch as by God "He is made unto us wisdom, and righteousness, and sanctification, and redemption" (1 Corinthians 1:30).

Take, for example, the love that two men have equally toward Christ. The one sympathizes piously with His sufferings and is moved by them to a lively sorrow and is easily softened by the memory of all that He endured. He feeds upon the sweetness of that devotion and is strengthened by it for all salutary, honorable, and pious actions.

On the other hand, the other man is always being fired by a zeal for righteousness, having in everything an ardent passion for truth; and he earnestly desires wisdom, preferring above all things the sanctity of life, and a perfectly disciplined character. He is ashamed at ostentation, abhors attraction, knows not what it is to be envious, detests pride, and not only avoids but dislikes and despises every kind of worldly glory. He vehemently hates and perceives in himself every impurity of heart and of the flesh. Last, he rejects instinctively all that is evil, and embraces all that is good. Comparing thus these two types of love, is it not obvious that the second is better? This, then, is to love God with all the soul.

Love in the strength of the Holy Spirit is best.

However, if, to this love, there is the added force given by the powerful assistance of the Holy Spirit, so that neither troubles nor sufferings, however violent, or even the fear of death, can ever cause the desertion of righteousness, then God is indeed loved with all the strength, and that is spiritual love.

KNOWING GOD[11]

"Tell me, O You whom my soul loves, where You feed, where You make Your flock to rest at noon" (Song of Solomon 1:7).

The Word, who is the Bridegroom, frequently appears to zealous souls under more than one form. Why is this? I think doubtless it is because we are not able to see Him as He really is (1 John 3:2). Only in heaven is the form of Him abiding, because the form in which we shall know Him will then also be permanent. For He is and receives no change or any alteration from anything which is, or has been, or shall be. Take away the Past and the Future, and where then is there any place for change or vicissitude? Everything passes from the condition of what has been, towards the condition of becoming, only through the point of being. It is this *being* that has potentiality. But God has not "been" (in this creaturely sense); therefore He Is from all eternity, and because He will not "become", He Is to all eternity (Exodus 3:14). Because of this reality, God is the Existence that is uncreated, unlimitable, and unchangeable.

SEEING GOD

Those who would behold God neither—desire, nor are capable of beholding anything more desired—than Him. When, then, can the eagerness of their gaze be satiated, the sweetness in which they delight be withdrawn, or the truth be exhausted? In a word, when can eternity come to an end? For if both the will to behold, and the full ability of beholding, be equally enlarged to all eternity, what can be wanting to complete felicity? What, I ask, remains to be experienced, or even to be wished for by those whose desire is always to behold Him and in whom that desire is being eternally satisfied?

Such a beatific vision is not for the present life, but is reserved for the final state of existence. It is reserved for those, at least, who are able to say: "We know that when He shall appear we shall be like Him; for we shall see Him as He is" (1 John 3:2). Even in the present life He appears to whom He wills, but in the manner as He wills, not as He is. There is no man, however wise or holy, there is no prophet who is or ever was able to see Him in this mortal body as He is. Yet those who shall be found worthy shall do so when their bodies shall be immortal.

The vision of God

Therefore He is indeed seen, but in a manner that seems good unto Him and not as He is. For though you have seen that great luminary, that is the sun which you behold every day, you have never seen it as it really is, but only as it lights up other things. Nor would you be able to behold it even in a certain degree if the light of your body, that is the eye, did not resemble in some degree the light of heaven in its inborn clearness and serenity.

So also he that is enlightened by that Son of righteousness which lightens every man that comes into the world, is able to behold him to the degree that he has been enlightened by Him and has been like Him in some degree. But still as he is not perfectly like Him, he is not able to see Him as He is. Therefore, the psalmist says: "They looked unto Him and were lightened, and their faces were not

We see God as we are enlightened.

ashamed" (Psalm 34:5). Thus it is in truth. Provided that
we are enlightened as far as we need, so that with open
face "beholding as in a glass the glory of the Lord, we are
changed into the same image from glory to glory, even as
by the Spirit of the Lord" (2 Corinthians 3:18).

It is therefore necessary not to approach God either ir-
rationally, or irreverently, but with respect and awe, lest
the irreverent observer of His Majesty be crushed and destroyed by His glory. He is not to be approached by a
change of places, but by an increase of excellencies, and
those not bodily, but spiritual, since the Spirit of the Lord
is our guide to Him. I say that it is by the Spirit of the Lord
that we draw near to Him, and not by the power of our
own spirit, although it is by our own spirit that this takes
place.

Thus the purer and more virtuous a spirit is, the nearer
it is to God, and to have attained absolute purity of virtue
is to have come into the very presence of God. For to be in
His presence is to see Him as He is. To do so is nothing
else than to be as He is, and so not to be dazzled and
idolatrously deceived. But that, as I say, will only be in
heaven.

God seen in many ways

In the present sphere of existence you discern something of Him by the great variety of created forms of life.
They are like the rays from the Sun of the Divine Being,
showing indeed that He exists, from whom they derive
their existence. This fact of His existence should lead you
forward to seek further after Him. As we have been taught
by the apostle, all those who have the use of reason can
clearly see that the invisible things of God are to be understood by the things which are made (Romans 1:20).

Again, the patriarchs saw God manifested in another
form. For He granted to them frequent and familiar communion with His presence, even though He was not actually visible to them as He really is, but only He deigned to
appear to them. Nor was it only in one manner that He revealed Himself to them all. For as the apostle declares: "at
sundry times and in diverse manners" (Hebrews 1:1) He
did so. Nor was that manifestation common to all. Yet it

was not made without appearances that were visible to the sense, nor words unheard by the ears.

But there is still another manner in which God was seen. It differed from the others in that it was inward. It was the way in which God deigned of His own accord to make Himself known to a soul that sought longingly for Him, and lavishing on that search the entire love of the affections. "My heart was hot within me, and while I was musing the fire burned" (Psalm 39:3). After a soul has been thus pressed by such frequent aspirations after God, or rather by such continual prayer, and afflicted by these very longings, it sometimes happens that God has pity on the soul and makes Himself manifest. I think this was the experience of the prophet Jeremiah when he said: "The Lord is good to them that wait upon the Lord, to the soul that seeks after Him" (Lamentations 3:25). "Delight thyself in the Lord . . . and keep His way," (Psalm 37:4, 34). Again, "Though He tarry, wait for Him; for He shall surely come, He shall not tarry" (Habakkuk 2:3). "As the hart pants after the waterbrooks, so longs the soul after You O Lord" (Psalm 42:1).

But be very careful not to allow yourself to think that vision of God will be induced by any imaginary, bodily experience, as the Word and the soul of the believer are so united. I say this, because the apostle reminds us that "He who is joined to the Lord is one spirit" (1 Corinthians 6:17). That union is made in spirit because God is a Spirit, and He is moved with love for the beauty of the soul that He sees walking in the Spirit, and he does not desire to live carnally. Filled with such an ardent love for God, such a one will not rest content to see her Bridegroom in a manner that is common to all. That is why such may experience in a way peculiar to only a few, the experience of dreams or visions. To such He comes, not with a sound in the ears, but as penetrating the heart. He comes not full of words, but full of power. He comes to the affections as sweetness itself, ineffably so. The features of His countenance are not formed and definable, yet they exercise formative powers. They do not strike upon the vision of the

The vision of God cannot be induced.

retina, but they rejoice the heart. They come not with the charm of form or color, but with the affection they create and deepen.

KNOWING GOD THROUGH INWARD THOUGHTS

If you also gaze into your own inner life, and the Holy Spirit is pleased to illuminate the ways in which He brings fruit in our lives, by His constant action, then I think we shall not remain ignorant of these mysteries. "For we have not received the spirit of the world but the Spirit which is from God, that we might understand the gifts bestowed on us by God" (1 Corinthians 2:12). If like the psalmist we find that it is good to cling to God (Psalm 72:28), and that we long to depart and be with Christ (Philippians 1:23) with an intense desire and a burning thirst, then we will indeed meet the Word as the Bridegroom. However, Christ will not reveal Himself to everyone in this way. He does so only to the one who has intense devotion, deep longing, and the sweetest affection. Then the Word will come to visit clothed in every aspect as the Bridegroom, in all His beauty.

Bitterness of spirit

But the one who has not yet reached this state is the one who is still smarting from the bitterness of his former deeds, or still in the grip of temptation. This person really needs a physician, not a bridegroom; His kisses and embraces are but oil and medicines for the healing of his wounds. All who have experienced this know full well that the Lord Jesus is a physician indeed, who "heals the broken-hearted and binds up their wounds" (Psalm 147:3).

Lukewarm in spirit

Other men grow weary of studying spiritual doctrine and become lukewarm. Their spiritual energies are drained away, and they walk in sadness along the ways of the Lord (Luke 24:17). They do the tasks asked of them with tired and arid hearts. They grumble endlessly, and complain all day and night, as Job did, saying: "When I lie down, I say, 'When shall I arise?', and then I long for the evening to come again" (Job 7:4). If, when we are in such moods, the compassionate Lord draws near to us on the way we are traveling (Luke 24:17), and being from heaven, He begins to speak to us of heavenly truths (John 3:31), singing our favorite hymns from the songs of Zion, discoursing on the city of God, on the peace of that eternal city, and on the eternal life, then indeed we are changed. Then all the weariness of the body, all the aversion of spirit, all are driven away.

But it confuses us to find such a close resemblance between our own thoughts and those of the truth Himself. What is in our own heart and what have we received from without? We need then to hear the words: "Out of the heart come evil thoughts" (Matthew 15:19), or the question, "Why do you think evil in your hearts?" (Matthew 9:4). The apostle says: "Not that we are sufficient of ourselves to think of anything as coming from ourselves," meaning any good being intrinsic to us, "but our sufficiency is from God" (2 Corinthians 3:5). So when we yield to wicked thoughts, the thoughts are our own. If we think on good things, then it is God's Word.

Confused in spirit

But who can guard his thoughts so closely and assiduously that he is able to exclude all the heart's illicit desires? I believe this is more than mere mortals can ever do, unless the light of the Holy Spirit gives them a special gift, namely the discernment of spirits (1 Corinthians 12:10). For according to Solomon, no matter how vigilantly a man may guard his heart (Proverbs 4:23), and watch every motion of his inner being, he will never be able to judge or diagnose exactly between good and evil within himself. "For who can understand sins?" (Psalm 18:13). Happy, then, is the man who has the Word as an inseparable companion, Who is always accessible, whose joyous discourse is an unceasing pleasure that always frees him from the troublesome vices of the flesh, and enables him to live profitably in an evil age (Ephesians 5:16).

Discernment of spirit

KNOWING GOD THROUGH TEMPTATIONS

"Make your ways known unto me, O Lord, teach me your paths" (Psalm 25:4). What he means by paths he reveals in another passage: "He leads me in the paths of righteousness" (Psalm 23:3). Thus the man who longs for these things will seek ceaselessly for righteousness, judgment, and the place where the Bridegroom dwells, namely in glory. So the psalmist says: "Righteousness and Judgment are the preparation of Your throne" (Psalm 89:15), and "O Lord, I love the beauty of Your house, and the place where Your glory dwells" (Psalm 26:8).

Need for light; not to be deceived

However, here on earth You feed Your flock but not to their full satisfaction. Nor is it possible for You to rest, as You must stand and keep watch because of the terrors of the night (Song of Solomon 3:8). There are also those other shepherds whose flocks feed on poisonous pastures; they are fed neither by You nor with You. I feel, therefore, that because of the invisible powers and spirits of seduction that lie in ambush (Psalm 10:9), we must, in the clear light of noontide, detect the tricks of the devil and be able to discern between our Lord and the angel of light who is Satan (2 Corinthians 11:14). For we cannot defend ourselves from the attacks of the noontide devil (Psalm 91:6), except with the aid of the noontide light.

Four kinds of temptation:
1. Discouragement

Therefore, realize that there are four kinds of temptation, described by the psalmist as follows: "His truth shall be your shield and buckler. You will not be afraid of the terror by night; nor for the arrow that flies by day; nor for the pestilence that walks in darkness; nor for the destruction that wastes at noonday" (Psalm 91:4-6). This is called nocturnal fear (Song of Solomon 3:8), either because adversity in the Scriptures represents darkness, or else the reward for which we are ready to suffer adversity has not yet been revealed. Beginners on the way to God, therefore, must watch and pray particularly against this first temptation. Otherwise, they can be overcome suddenly by a lack of spirit, and in the midst of the storm regret they ever started on the good work of faith.

When this temptation has been overcome, the next to fear is that of the praise of men. For our praiseworthy life may provide compliments. Perhaps this is "the arrow that flies by day" (Psalm 91:5), namely vainglory. For fame is said to fly, and that by day because of its deeds done in the light. However, when this temptation is blown away like hot air, we may be confronted with a stronger one, namely the offer of riches and honors of the world. For the man who despises praise may still hanker after position. Our Lord Himself experienced this order of temptation. First it was suggested to Him that He should cast Himself from the pinnacle of the temple for the sake of mere vanity. Then He was shown all the kingdoms of the world that were offered to Him (Matthew 4:8). Again, like the example of our Lord, you must refuse what is offered.

2. The praise of men

If not, you will fall for the third temptation, which is "the pestilence that stalks about in darkness" (Psalm 91:6). This is hypocrisy. For this originates in ambition; its dwelling is in darkness. For it hides what it really is, and it pretends to be what it is not. Always active, it retains the appearance of piety as a mask to hide behind, and it trades virtue for the purchase of honors.

3. Hypocrisy

The last temptation is that of the noontide devil. He lies in ambush for the mature Christians, who have been tried and tested by the other temptations. So what further weapons has the evil one against them? But what he cannot do openly, he will attempt to so so by subterfuge. So when he sees that open evil is repulsed, he will attack through a counterfeit good. Those like the apostle, who say "we are not ignorant of his devices" (2 Corinthians 2:11) will survive, being careful to avoid the trap set them.

Thus the greater virtue a man may seem to have attained (1 Corinthians 10:12), the more he must be convinced of the need to watch vigilantly for the noontide devil. Whenever this painted falsehood tries to take us

4. The attack of the Devil

unawares, may the true Noontide which shines from the heavens send forth His light and His truth even to us (Psalm 43:3). May we learn to distinguish darkness from light, so that we are not like those prophets who "put darkness for light, and light for darkness" (Isaiah 5:20).

KNOWING GOD IN HUMILITY

Humility enforced by God

"If I have found favor in Your sight, show me now Your ways that I may know You" (Exodus 33:13). Instead of granting him this request, God gave him an inferior vision, yet one which nevertheless would help him to attain eventually the one he longed to have. For anyone who would seek the heights, must like the bride (in the Song of Solomon) be rebuffed with an answer that seems harsh, yet which is really helpful and dependable. For anyone who strives to ascend the spiritual heights must have a lowly opinion of himself. For if he is raised above himself, he may lose a sense of proportion about himself; unless he is humble, he will not have a grip upon himself. It is only when humility warrants it that great graces can be obtained. Thus the one who is to be so enriched must first be humbled by correction, so that by humility he can benefit from such graces. So when you are humiliated, look on it as a sign that grace is on the way (Psalm 86:17). For just as pride goes before a fall (Proverbs 16:18), so humility goes before being honored. In Scripture you read how the Lord acts in two ways: He resists the proud, and He gives grace to the humble (James 4:6).

Humiliation from others

However, it matters little, if we are ready to be humbled by God, if at the same time we are not ready to maintain a similar attitude when He humiliates us through another human instrument. Thus we have the example of David when he was humiliated by a servant, yet he took no notice of the curses heaped upon him (2 Samuel 16:10). Truly he was a man after God's own heart who chose to be angry rather with the one who would praise him than with the one who would abuse him.

Knowing this was from God, he could say: "It was good for me that I should be afflicted (humiliated) that I might learn Your statutes" (Psalm 119:71).

Can you not see that humility makes us righteous? I say humility deliberately, and not humiliation. For many are humiliated but not humbled. Such react to humiliation with bitterness, and they are guilty. Some meet it with patience, and they are innocent. Others again meet it with cheerfulness, and they are just. Innocence is indeed part of justice, but only the humble possess it perfectly. So only he who can say, "it was good for me to be afflicted," is truly humble. And he is humble who turns humiliation into humility. Merely to endure humiliation is good to no one. It is only an obvious embarrassment. On the other hand we know that "God loves a cheerful giver" (2 Corinthians 9:7).

Distinction between humility and humiliation

So when you want to see an example of a truly humble man, glorying rightly in his circumstances, look at the Apostle Paul. He says that gladly would he rejoice in his weaknesses that the power of Christ would dwell within him (2 Corinthians 12:9). So you may take it as a general rule, that anyone who humbles himself will be exalted. Significantly, not every kind of humility will be exalted, but only that which is embraced gladly. It must be free of the spirit of compulsion, or of sadness. I have said all this to explain why the Bridegroom decided the bride's desires for a loftier experience should be restrained. It was not to frustrate her but to give an occasion for deeper humility, and thus prepare her for more sublime experiences.

KNOWING GOD IN KNOWING OURSELVES

You will remember I spoke of two kinds of ignorance; one of ourselves and the other with regard to God. We must beware of both dangers. Now there are various kinds of ignorance, not all of which are to be condemned, nor are detrimental to salvation. If you are ignorant of the craftsman's art or unacquainted with any of the liberal arts, they do not prevent you from being saved. Were not the men in the epistle to the Hebrews men who were dear to God, not because of knowledge of literature but because of a good conscience and a sincere faith? (Hebrews 11). They all pleased God in their lives by the merits of their lives, and not by their knowledge.

The limited influence of knowledge

You may think I have sullied too much the good name of knowledge, and cast aspersions on the learned and denied the study of letters. God forbid! For I am quite aware of the benefits its scholars have conferred on the Church, by both refuting her enemies, and instructing the simple. But I recall too that "knowledge puffs up" (1 Corinthians 8:1). "And the more knowledge, the more sorrow" (Ecclesiastes 1:18). All knowledge is good in itself, provided it is founded upon the truth. But because of the brevity of life, you need to "work out your own salvation with fear and trembling" (Philippians 2:12). So primarily and principally, take the trouble to learn about the doctrines on which your salvation is more intimately dependent.

Knowing in order to do good

There are some who long to know, simply for the sake of knowing, and that is a shameful curiosity. Others long to know to show off before others, and that is shameful vanity. To such as these the words of the satirist apply: "Your knowledge is worthless unless your friends know about it" (Persius, *Satires*, 1:27). There are others who long for knowledge to make a fat profit from it, or to make honors from it; and this is shameful profiteering. But there are those who long to know in order to be of service to others; and this is charity. Finally, there are those who long to know in order to benefit themselves morally; and this is prudence. Only the last two categories avoid the abuse of knowledge, because they desire to know for the purpose of doing good. Food that is badly cooked is indigestible and upsets the stomach. So too, a glut of knowledge that is stuffed into the memory (that stomach of the mind), unless it has been cooked on the fire of love, and thoroughly digested by the disciplines of the soul, it will also be damaging, instead of being nutritious.

Know yourself.

Before anything else, then, a man should know himself. It is this knowledge that results in humility instead of in self-importance, and therefore is a true basis upon which to build one's character. And there is no better way to find humility than to learn to know oneself. There must be no self deceit, but one must face up to himself resolutely, without flinching. There he will find himself in the clear light of truth, and realize that he has forfeited the likeness of God. How then can he escape from being truly humbled by this self-knowledge, when he sees the burden of sin that he carries, with all the oppression of earthly cares and their complexity that he carries, as well as the corrupting influences of sensual desires that he has? For then he sees his blindness, his worldliness, his weakness, his involvement in repeated errors. Then he also sees how he is exposed to a thousand dangers, trembling in the midst of a thousand fears, confused by a thousand difficulties, defenseless before a thousand suspicions, and worried by a thousand needs. Indeed, he is one who finds virtue repugnant and who welcomes vice. How can such a man lift up his head proudly, or afford to have haughty eyes?

So for myself, as long as I look at myself, my eyes are full of bitterness. But if I look at the blessed vision of God, with the aid of divine mercy, then this soon tempers the bitter vision of myself. This vision of God is no small thing. It reveals God who hears our prayers compassionately, and as One who is truly kind and merciful, never indulging in resentment (Joel 2:13). For His very nature is to be good, and to always show kindness. Thus by this kind of experience, and in this way, God makes Himself known to us for our good. Thus when a man is in difficulties, he will cry out to God who will hear him (Psalm 91:15). For He declares: "I will deliver you and you will glorify Me" (Psalm 50:15). In this way your self-knowledge will be a step towards the knowledge of God. He will then become visible to you as His image is being renewed in you. And then you, "beholding the glory of the Lord, will be changed into His likeness from one degree of glory to another; for this comes from the Lord who is the Spirit" (2 Corinthians 3:18).

Twofold knowledge   Now you can see how both these kinds of knowledge are so necessary for your salvation. For you cannot be saved without both of them. If you lack self-knowledge you will have neither the fear of the Lord, nor will you have humility. And whether you can ever do without the fear of the Lord or humility, you can judge for yourself. But if you have first made sure of this twofold knowledge, you will be less likely to become conceited by any other learning you may add to them. Indeed, what advantage can we ever derive from any amount of our learning, than the assurance that we are numbered among the sons of God? Not even all the fullness of the earth can be compared with this privilege, even if we were to take possession of it all (Matthew 16:26). But if we are ignorant of God, how can we hope in one in whom we do not know? And if we are ignorant about ourselves, how can we be humble, thinking of ourselves better than we ought to think (Galatians 6:3), when we are really nothing? For we know that neither the proud nor the hopeless will have any part in the inheritance of the saints of light (Colossians 1:12).

Let us, therefore, very carefully see how we can banish both these forms of ignorance. For these two forms of ignorance are the sources of all sin. For just as the fear of the Lord is the beginning of wisdom, so pride is the beginning of sin. Just as the love of God is the way to the fulfillment of wisdom, so despair leads to the committing of all sins. And just as the fear of God arises within you from the knowledge of yourself, and the love of God comes from knowing God, so on the contrary pride arises from the lack of self-knowledge, and despair arises from the lack of the knowledge of God.

THE DISCIPLINE OF LOVE

"He brought me into the banqueting house, and His banner over me was love" (Song of Solomon 2:4).

These words seem to suggest that when the bride had achieved her longing for the sweet and intimate communion with her Beloved, she returned at His departure to her maidens so refreshed and animated in spirit that she looked drunk. When they saw her they asked for the cause of it all. But she was not drunk in wine, but in love. The disciples too, were thought to be drunk with wine, when in fact they were filled with the Spirit (Acts 2:15). Does it not suggest to you that the banqueting hall was the house in which the disciples were assembled, when suddenly a sound came from heaven like the rush of a mighty wind, and it filled all the house where they were sitting" (Acts 2:2), and fulfilled Joel's prophecy (Joel 2:28).

Even so you, too, may in spirit enter into the house of prayer alone with God and stand in the presence of the Lord. You may touch the altar as if it were the gate of heaven with the hand of holy desire. It is as if you were in the presence of the choirs of the saints, and your devotion penetrated heavenward, for "the prayers of a righteous man avail much" (James 5:16). Bewailing miserably your misfortunes, you sigh with groans too deep for words. Yet, if you do so in confidence, asking you will receive (John 16:24), and knocking you will not go empty away (Luke 11:8). Indeed, when you return to us, you will be full of grace and love, unable in your ardor to conceal the gift you have received. In doing so you will be popularly received, so be careful then not to glory in yourself, but only in the Lord (1 Corinthians 1:31).

If, then, you obtain while you are praying this ecstasy of spirit in the mystery of God (2 Corinthians 5:13), you will return with a glowing ardor of divine love, overflowing with a zeal for righteousness, and fervent zeal in all spiritual duties and studies. Then you will say "my heart burned hot within me" (Psalm 39:3). From the abundance of love experienced you can clearly indicate that you have been "into His banqueting house, where His banner over you is love" (Song of Solomon 2:4).

The experience of ecstasy

Two forms of ecstasy

But holy contemplation has two forms of ecstasy, one in the intellect and one in the will. One is enlightened, and the other is fervent. One is of knowledge, and the other is of devotion. These qualities of tender affection, a heart glowing with love, with holy ardor, and a vigor of spirit that is filled with zeal, are clearly only acquired in the banqueting house. And everyone who rises from prayer with an abundance of these can truly say that "the King led me into His banqueting house."

Zeal needs discretion

But zeal without knowledge is unbearable (Romans 10:2). So where there is zeal, it also needs discretion, that moderator of love. Since zeal without knowledge is ineffective, such will be lacking, and may even be harmful. So the more eager the zeal, the more vigorous the spirit, the more generous the love, so too, there will be the need for more discreet knowledge to restrain the zeal, to control the temper, and to moderate the love. Hence the bride, returning to her maidens, needs to see that she has received the fruit of discretion, in case she returns overbearing and indeed insufferable. Discretion indeed is not so much a virtue as it is the moderator of virtues, their guide, a director of the affections, and a teacher of right living. Take it away, and virtue can even become a vice.

Doing the immediate thing

"He set love in order before me." Would then, that the Lord Jesus should set in order before me the little source of love that He has given me, so that while my interest will be extended to all His concerns, yet I will more diligently care above everything else for what He has specifically set before me to do. Yet while this should be my primary concern, may it not become so preoccupying that I may ignore the many other things that do not revolve around my interests. Failing to do this I shall only partially observe the discipline of love. If however I show a genuine concern for that which is my special charge, and yet show a still finer sympathy for a greater work, then I will fulfill the ordering of love in both ways. Thus you can also rejoice in the achievements of someone else.

"He has set love in order before me." Love exists in action and in feeling. For love in practice, an explicit command has been given to men (Deuteronomy 6:4, 5). Love then in practice is a command and love as an affection is the reward. Yet this command is an impossible one. Therefore in commanding impossible things, God would make men humble. Then on that day we shall know that God has saved us, "not by works of righteousness which we have done, but by His mercy He saved us" (Titus 3:5).

I am not saying that with our affections we should do our work with only an arid heart. But there is an affection which the flesh breeds, and one which the reason controls, and one which wisdom matures. The first one is that which the apostle says is not subject to the law of God (Romans 8:7), nor can it be. But the second agrees with the law of God because it is good (Romans 7:16). The third is far removed from either of these two, for it tastes and experiences that the Lord is good (Psalm 34:8). It eliminates the first while it rewards the second. While the first is pleasant but shameful, the second is strong, but without emotion. But the third is rich and delightful.

Three forms of affection

If you love the Lord your God with your whole heart, whole mind, whole strength, and leap beyond that with ardent love for your neighbor, then you will experience your own true self. For you will perceive that you possess nothing at all for which you love yourself, except that you yourself are possessed by God. So you pour out upon Him your whole power of loving. Indeed, I repeat, you experience who you really are when, by loving yourself by His love, you discover you are wholly unworthy of even your own love except for the sake of God, without Whom you are nothing.

As for your neighbor, whom you are obliged to love as yourself, you have to experience him as he really is. To do so, you will have to actually experience him as you do yourself, for he is what you are. So you, who cannot love yourself other than as God loves you, have likewise to love him by the same means. But to experience him as he is, is to experience him as he now is (for he is nothing) but as to what he will become. He is still almost nothing, since it is clear that if he does not return (like the Prodigal son), he is totally and eternally nothing.

THE RECIPROCAL AFFECTION OF THE BRIDE[12]

The words of the Bride

"My Beloved is mine, and I am His" (Song of Solomon 2:16).

Until now we have been pondering upon the words of the Bridegroom. Now we shall hear the words of the bride. To do so we pray that her words will be expressive of God's glory and to our salvation (Acts 14:11). For without God's guidance of our words, they cannot be considered and discussed by us. For as they are sweet to the senses, so they are fruitful and deep in mysteries when divinely guided. To what shall I compare them? They are like a banquet, excelling all other delicacies by a threefold superlative; they are delicious to taste, in delighting the affections; they nourish the mind in their solid worth of truth; and they are rich in their healing power, over against the pride and inflation caused by false knowledge (1 Corinthians 8:1). So it is with every word of the bride. But if anyone imagines that with his smattering of knowledge he can succeed, he will find that his intellectual faculty is overwhelmed and his whole mind reduced to bondage (2 Corinthians 10:5). He can only cope if he is humble to acknowledge: "Such knowledge is too wonderful for me; it is high, I cannot attain to it" (Psalm 139:6). So let us start with the simple, sweet words of our text: "My Beloved is mine, and I am His."

Words of love

The bride begins with love and goes on to speak of her Beloved, declaring that she knows no other that is so loved (1 Corinthians 2:2). It is, therefore, quite clear of whom she is speaking; but it is not so clear to whom she is speaking. For we are not allowed to suppose that He is present or that she is directly talking with Him. This appears plainly from her call to Him immediately afterwards, as if he were at a distance and she beseeches Him to return to her: "Turn, my Beloved." From this we are led to believe that, after He had spoken, He withdrew again according to His custom. Nevertheless, she continues to speak of Him for He is never absent from her mind. So He continues to be upon her lips for He has never departed from her heart. As what comes from her lips comes from her heart, for it is "out of the abundance of the heart that the mouth speaks" (Luke 6:45). She therefore speaks of her Beloved as One Who is truly loved and truly deserving to be loved and that is why she loves so much. We do not then really need to ask her to whom she is speaking. It is not to her handmaidens who are constantly in attention.

Rather, it is better to suppose that she is speaking to herself and not to anyone else in order that her words which seem abrupt and unconnected with what has been spoken before become a soliloquy. "My Beloved," she says, "is mine, and I am His." Nothing more? That, then, is why the discourse hangs suspended, so that anyone who listens is also held in suspense and not instructed, but waiting to be so. Receiving no communication, his interest however is aroused.

Words of soliloquy

What is it then that she is saying: "My Beloved is mine, and I am His?" We do not understand what she says, because we do not feel what she feels (John 16:18). O holy soul, what is your Beloved to you? What are you to Him? What is that mysterious and mutual love which seems so reciprocally made for each other, which comes with such kindness and familiarity? For you it is Him, and for Him you are. You are to Him what He is to you, or is there some difference? Speak plainly to us for the sake of our understanding (John 10:24). Do not keep us in suspense. Is your secret to be only for yourself? (Isaiah 24:16).

It is not that the prophet would remind us that it is the affection that has spoken and not the intellect and, therefore, that is why we can scarcely understand. What then is the reason for this communication? Surely there is none, except that the bride is transported with delight and enraptured with intense joy and earnest longing to see her

Words of affection

beloved again. For when all words cease she cannot keep silent but must express what she feels in some other way. It is to express her feelings that she must break out of her silence, for "out of the fullness of the heart the mouth speaks" (Luke 6:45).

The language of the affections

Thus the affections have their own language, in which they disclose themselves even against their own will. Thus fear expresses itself with timid words, grief with mournful words, and love with joyful words. What are the lamentations of those who are in trouble? What are the sobs and sighs of mourners? What are the sudden and ungovernable screams and cries of those who are scared or stricken with fear? What are the yawns of the bored and the smugly satisfied? Are all these caused by habit or aroused by the intellect or commanded by reflection or shaped by premeditation? Clearly, all such expressions of feeling are not the products of a deliberate purpose, but are caused by sudden and spontaneous impulse. Thus a vehement and burning love, especially towards God, does not stop to restrain itself to consider the order, grammar, the style or the length of word that it employs, when it cannot contain itself. Thus the bride when she is burning with an ardent and holy love, seeking to control some of the intensity of her feelings, will still burst forth with the first words that come into her mind. How else do we expect her to act other than from a heart that is so full?

So reflect again upon the words of this marriage psalm. Look and see whether in all tryst and conversations together the Bridegroom has ever spoken to her with the same tenderness or with such delightful words as she now speaks to him. Of course He has, and that is why she is so satisfied with good things (Psalm 103:5). It is not at all strange that she should utter a cry rather than words. For if she appears to form words, they would be inarticulate rather than polished or well chosen. In fact the bride takes upon herself the words of the psalmist: "My heart is inditing a good matter" (Psalm 45:1). She speaks thus, because her heart is so filled.

Remember again the words of this marriage Psalm. Has **The language of** the Bridegroom ever said to her, "My Beloved is mine, **a loved heart** and I am hers" (Song of Solomon 2:16). Clearly so, for her wishes are satisfied to the full, and it is with a burst of joy that these words come into her lips too. There is no prayer in his marriage psalm, and there is no conclusion to be drawn from it. What then? It is an outburst of feeling. In such an utterance, what logic of sentiments, what rules of phraseology are you looking for? What is the grammatical structure that you are imposing upon it? Clearly you cannot argue about it like this at all. For the song bursts forth from within, without your will or knowledge. It gives forth an odor that may be good or bad, according to the quality of the vessel that it comes from. So a good man out of the good treasure will bring forth good things. And an evil man, evil things (Matthew 12:35). But the bride of our Lord is a vessel of good things and so the odor which comes from her is sweet.

I thank You, Lord Jesus, that You have deigned to allow me at least to smell that fragrance. Yes, Lord, for it is also permitted to me, like the dogs, to eat the crumbs which come from the rich man's table (Matthew 15:27). This utterance of the feelings of Your beloved is to me, I must confess, very agreeable. "And of his fullness have we all received, gratefully" (John 1:16), even though it may be in very small measure. For it causes the memory of your abundant sweetness to suffuse me with the ineffable perfume of Your love and condescension. This is what these few words of the bride do for me: "My Beloved is mine, and I am His." So let her be transported out of herself for Your sake, and may she be sober for our sakes.

THE SOUL, SEEKING GOD, IS ANTICIPATED BY HIM[13]

"By night on my bed I sought Him, whom my soul **The desire for** loves" (Song of Solomon 3:1). **God is the grateful** **good.**

It is a great good to seek God. I believe that there is no

greater blessing of the soul than this. For it is the first of
the gifts of God, and it is the final stage in its progress. No
other virtue can be added to it. None can climax it. What
virtue can be attributed to anyone who does not seek
God? What limit can be prescribed to anyone who is seeking Him? "Seek His face evermore" (Psalm 105:4). Nor do
I think that when a soul has found Him will it cease from
seeking. For God is sought, not by the movement of the
feet, but by the desires of the heart. When a soul has been
so blessed as to find Him, that secret desire is not extin-
guished, but on the contrary, it is increased. Is the consummation of the joy the extinction of the desire? No,
rather it is as oil poured upon a flame, for desire is as it
were a flame. Joy will be fulfilled. But the fulfillment will
not be the ending of the desire, nor therefore of the seeking. If you can, think of this earnest love of seeking God as
being without fear of His absence, and of having this desire for Him, as without anxiety or trouble of mind. His
presence excludes the one, and the abundance of His
graces prevents the other.

**Our desire of God
has been antici-
pated by Him.**   Now see why I have made these introductory remarks.
It is because every soul among you which is seeking God
should know that it has been already anticipated by Him,
and has been sought by Him before it began to seek Him.
Without this knowledge, great blessing might lead to
great harm, if, when one has been filled with the good
gifts of God, the soul treated these gifts as if they had been
received not from Him, and so does not render to God the
glory of possessing them.

**God alone is to
be praised**   Doubtless, this is why some who may appear to be very
great before men, because of the graces which have been
confined upon them by God, were also counted as the
least before God, because they did not return to Him the
glory which was due on their account. In this way He who
is the best of men may become the worst. For it is a certainty that such a person becomes as blamable as before as
he was praiseworthy, if he ascribes to himself the praise
which really belongs to God. This is one of the worst of

crimes. Someone will perhaps add, "God forbid that I should have such a mind. I fully recognize that by the grace of God I am what I am (1 Corinthians 15:10). Instead, suppose that someone should try to take for himself some spark of glory for the grace that he has received, is he not therefore a thief and a robber?" Be warned then by the words: "Out of your mouth will I judge you, you wicked servant" (Matthew 19:22). For what can be more wicked than the servant that usurps to himself the glory which belong to his Lord?

"By night on my bed I sought Him whom my soul loves." The soul seeks the Word, but it had been previously sought by the Word. Otherwise, when it had once been driven out or cast forth from the presence of the Word, it would have returned no more to obtain the sight of good things which it had lost, if it had not been sought by the Word. Our soul, if abandoned to itself, is a spirit which goes to and fro, but does not return. Listen to a fugitive and wandering soul, and learn what it complains of, and what it seeks: "I have gone astray like a lost sheep; seek Your servant" (Psalm 119:176). O man, do you really desire to return? But if that depends upon your own will, why do you entreat help? Are you asking from someone else what you already have in abundance in your own self? What if the will of the soul is to return?

The Word antici-pates our search

The will lies inoperative, if it is not supported by the power to do so. Or "to will is present with me," says the apostle, "but how to perform that which is good I find not" (Romans 7:18). What is it then that the psalmist seeks in the passage which I have quoted? He plainly seeks nothing else than to be sought; which he would not seek if he had not been sought. Yet again he would not seek if he had not been sought sufficiently. This latter grace indeed is what he entreats: "Seek thy servant." He asks that there might be given to him the desire to attain according to the good pleasure of God.

Our wills need to be empowered

"I have sought," says the bride, "Him whom my soul loves." It is to this that the goodness of Him Who has anticipated you in seeking you and loving you first, it is to this that His goodness is calling and arousing you. You would not seek Him at all, O soul, nor love Him at all, if you had not first been sought and loved by Him.

Love seeks.

You have been anticipated by a twofold benediction, that of love and of seeking. Love is the cause of the seeking. The seeking is the fruit and the clear proof for the love. You have been loved, so that you might not fear that you were sought for to be punished. You were sought for, that you might not complain that you were loved to no purpose. Each of these two great and unmistakable favors has given you courage. It has removed shyness and timidity. It has touched your feelings and inclined you to return to Him. Hence arises that zeal and ardor in seeking Him whom your soul loves. Just as you were not able to seek Him, until you had first been sought, so now you have been sought so that you may not complain that you are loved in vain. Both of these great and obvious favors have given you courage. They have removed shyness and timidity. They have touched your feelings and disposed you to seek Him. From this comes the zeal and ardor to seek Him whom your soul loves. Because you cannot seek unless you are sought, now that you have been sought you are unable to do other than seek Him.

Our unfaithfulness to God

Never forget where you come from. In applying what I have said to myself (which is the safer curse), is it not you, O my soul, who has left your first husband, with whom it went well with you? Have you broken the faith which you first pledged to Him and gone after other lovers? (Hosea 2:5-13). Now that you have committed fornication with them and then been cast aside by them do you have the effrontery to return to Him, to whom you have behaved with so much pride and insolence? Do you really seek the light when you are only fit to hide yourself in the darkness? When you deserve the blows of correction, do you dare to run into the Bridegroom's arms? It would be a wonder if you don't find a Judge to condemn you instead of a Husband to receive you.

Yet happy is he who shall hear his soul replying to these reproaches: "I do not fear because I love, and I am loved. Nor could I have loved unless he had first loved me. So let those fear who have no love, but for the soul that loves there is nothing to be feared. How can those who have no love do otherwise than be under the constant apprehension of retribution? But because I love, I no more doubt that I am loved than I doubt in my own love. Nor can I possibly fear His countenance, whose affection for me I have felt so assuredly. Nor can I possibly fear to look upon Him since I have sensed His tenderness. In what have I known it? Simply in this, that He has not only sought me as I am, but He has shown me tenderness, and caused me to seek Him with confidence.

Love casts out fear

How can I then not respond to Him when He seeks me, since I am only responding to Him in His affection toward me? How can He be angry with me for seeking Him, when He has forgiven the contempt that I have shown toward Him? If He sought me when I was in contempt of Him, why should He have contempt of me when I seek Him? The spirit of the Word is benign and gentle. Gentle is His greeting to me. He makes me aware of His kindness toward me, He whispers to me and convinces me of the earnest love of the Word for me, which cannot be hidden from Him (Matthew 5:14). For he searches the deep things of God, and knows what are the divine thoughts to be thoughts of peace, and not purposes of vengeance. How can I then fail to be encouraged to seek Him, when I have had experience of His mercy, and am persuaded of His reconciliation with me?

My brethren, to think seriously of these truths is to be sought by the Word. To be persuaded of them is to be found by Him. But not all are capable of receiving that Word. What shall we do for the little children among us? I mean those that are at the stage of beginners and are so far from understanding, even though they already possess the beginning of wisdom and are subject to one another in the fear of Christ. How can we help them to see that it is the

Let the Word rebuke us.

Bridegroom who deals thus with them, when they themselves cannot yet perceive what is happening to them? I reply, let them read in the Scriptures that which they fail to discern in the heart of a fellow man and will therefore not believe. For it is written in one of the prophets: "If a man put away his wife, and she go from him, and become another man's, shall he return to her again? Shall not that land be greatly polluted? But you have played the harlot with many lovers, yet you return again to Me, says the Lord" (Jeremiah 3:1). These are the words of the Lord which you dare not doubt or hesitate to obey. So let them believe what they have not yet experienced, that by the merit of their faith they may one day gain the fruit of experience.

I think enough has been said about what it means to be sought by the Word. This is necessary, not for the Word, but for the soul's sake. We must add, however, that the soul which has experienced this knows Him both more fully and more happily by this experience. So it remains for me to treat in another discourse how souls that thirst for Christ seek Him by whom they have been sought. Or rather we should learn it from the one who is mentioned in this passage as seeking him whom his soul loves. For this is that Bridegroom of the soul, Jesus Christ our Lord, Who is above all, God blessed forever, Amen.

[1]Bernard of Clairvaux, *On the Song of Songs IV*, Cistercian Fathers series 40, Introduction by Jean Leclercq (Cistercian Publications, Kalamazoo, 1980), pp. xi, xii.

[2]*On the Song of Solomon*, Sermon Three.

[3]*On the Song of Solomon*, Sermon Seven.

[4]*On the Song of Solomon*, Sermon Eight.

[5]*On the Song of Solomon*, Sermons Ten and Eleven.

[6]*On the Song of Solomon*, Sermon Twelve.

[7]*On the Song of Solomon*, Sermon Fifteen.

[8]Augustine in his *Confessions* says the same thing. Reading the *Hortensius*, he says: "There was only one thing in that eloquent language that distressed me; it was that the name of Christ was not to be found there . . . and any writing in which that Name was wanting, however learned, polished and true it might be, would not wholly satisfy me."

[9]This passage is reminiscent of the hymn "How Sweet the Name of Jesus Sounds," quoted above, p. 178. It echoes the thoughts of Bernard, if perhaps it was composed by some other, anonymous twelfth century writer.

[10]*On the Song of Solomon*, Sermon Twenty.

[11]*On the Song of Solomon*, Sermons Thirty-one to Thirty-seven.

[12]*On the Song of Solomon*, Sermon Sixty-seven.

[13]*On the Song of Solomon*, Sermon Eighty-four.

Part IV

SPIRITUAL FRIENDSHIP

VIII
LETTERS OF FRIENDSHIP
To William, Abbot of St. -Thierry, c. 1125[1]

ROTHER BERNARD WISHES HEALTH AND THE love which comes out of a pure heart, a good conscience, and faith unfeigned.

Since no one knows the things of a man save the spirit of man which is in him (1 Corinthians 2:11), and man sees only the face while God reads the heart, I wonder then about your affection for me. For how are you able to distinguish between your affection for me and mine for you? How can you judge, not only the feelings of your own heart, but also those of another person? For it seems to be the error of the human mind, not only to think good as evil and evil as good, or confess true things with the false and conversely, but to regard sure things as doubtful and doubtful things as sure.

In our relationship, perhaps this is true what you say, that you are loved less by me than you love me. But I am quite sure of this, that you really do not know this to be so! How then can you be so certain about what you really cannot be certain about? Paul did not trust his own certainty when he said, "I judge not mine own self" (1 Corinthians 4:3). Peter mourned for the presumption with which he had deceived himself, when he said of himself, "Though I should die with Thee, I will not deny thee" (Matthew 26:35). Likewise the disciples, not trusting their own consciences, replied one after the other concerning the denial of their Lord, "Is it I, Lord?" (Matthew 26:22). David confesses his own ignorance of himself in his prayer, "Remember not my sins of youthful ignorance" (Psalm 25:7). But you, with marvelous confidence, declare so positively, not only about your own heart but mine, "though I love more, I am loved less."

2   These were, in fact, your words. I wish they had not been given, because I do not know whether they are really true. For if you know, how do you know that I am more loved by you than you are by me? Is it from what you have added in your letters? Do those who come and go between our houses never bring you a pledge of regard and affection from me? What pledge, what proof of love, do you require from me? Is this the trouble that disturbs you, that to none of your many letters to me have I ever replied? (This was the first letter of Bernard's to William.) But how could I think that the rightness of your wisdom could take any pleasure in the scribblings of my inexperience?

For I knew who said, "My little children, let us not love in word nor by tongue, but in deed and in truth" (1 John 3:18). When have you ever had need of my help and it has failed you? O, You who search the hearts and the minds! Who alone, as the Son of Righteousness, lights the hearts of Your servants with the differing rays of Your grace. You know how I feel, that I love him by Your gift, and because he merits it. How much I love him You know and I know not. You, O Lord, who gives the love that we have, I for him and he for me, You know how much you have given. And by what right does any of us dare say to whom you have not revealed it, "I love more, I am loved less," unless he already sees his light in Your light; that is to say that he recognizes in the light of Your truth how bright the fire of love may be?

3   In the meantime, I am content, O Lord, to see my own darkness in Your light, until You will visit me sitting in the darkness in the shadow of death. By You, the thoughts of men shall be revealed. The secret things of darkness will be made manifest, and the shadows will be dissipated. Darkness and light shall remain in Your light.

I feel, indeed, that by Your gift, I love him. But I do not

see yet in Your light, whether I love him sufficiently. Nor do I yet know if I have reached that degree of affection, for which there can be no greater than that one should lay down his life for his friend. For who will boast that his heart is pure, or that it is perfect? O Lord, who has lighted in my soul a lamp by whose lamp I see and shudder at my own darkness, my God, enlighten also that very darkness, so that I may see and rejoice in my affections perfectly regulated within me, that I may know and love what ought to be loved, and to the right degree and for the right reasons.

May I not be desired to be loved except in You, and no more than I ought to be loved. Woe to me also if either I was more loved by him than I deserved, or he was loved less by me than he was worthy to be. Nevertheless, if those who are better ought to be loved the more, "for those are the better who love more," what else shall I say? For I do not doubt that I love him more than myself, whom I know to be better than myself. But I confess at the same time, that I love him less than I ought to do, because I have less capability of doing so.

But my father, the greater your love is, the less you 4 ought to despise the imperfection of mine. Because although you love more, having a greater capability, yet you do not love more than your capacity enables you. It is thus with me, although I love you less than I ought, yet I love you as much as my capacity permits, and I can only do what I have received the capacity of doing. Draw me, then, in your train that I may reach to you, and with you receive capacity more fully and love more abundantly.

Why then do you endeavor that I should attain and complain that I am not able to do so? Accept me as I am, not as such as you had hoped to find in me. Indeed, you see in me something that I do not know, which I have not, and which you pursue as that which is not me. Therefore, you do not attain it, because I am sufficient for this, and as you rightly complain in your letter, it is not I that fail you, but God in me. Now, if all this verbiage pleases you that I have ventured upon here in this letter, tell me and I will repeat it, since obeying you I shall not fear the reproach of presumption.

The little preface which you have ordered to be sent to you I do not have now at hand, nor did I think it necessary as yet to draw it up. I pray that He who is given you to will, may in His good pleasure accomplish to you and to your friends whatsoever you will rightly seek. For you are my pious and most reverent father, who is fully worthy of all my regard.

EXCERPT FROM ANOTHER LETTER BY BERNARD TO WILLIAM, c. 1130

From his friend Brother Bernard of Clairvaux all that a friend can wish for a friend.

1   You have given me this formula of salutation when you wrote, "to his friend all that a friend can wish." Receive what is your own and perceive that the assumption of it is a proof that we are of one mind, for my heart is not distant from him with whom I have language in common. I must now reply briefly to your letter.

You wrote that you wished to know what I desired you to do, as if I were aware of all that concerns you. But this plan, if I should say what I think, is one that neither I could counsel nor you could carry out. I wish indeed for you what, as I have long known, you wish for yourself. But putting on one side, as it is right, both your will and mine, I think more of what God wills for you, and to my mind, it is both safer for me to advise you to do that, and much more advantageous for you to do it.

My advice then, is that you continue to hold your present charge, to remain where you are, and study to profit those over whom you are set, nor flee from the cares of office while you are able to be of use. Because woe to you if you are over the flock and do not profit them. But deeper woe still if, because you fear the cares of office, you abandon the opportunity of usefulness.

To Guigues, De Castro, the Prior, and to the Other Monks of the Grande Chartreuse, c. 1125[2]

Brother Bernard of Clairvaux wishes the continued health to the most esteemed among fathers, and to the dearest among friends, Guigues, Prior of the Grande Chartreuse; also to the saintly monks who are with him.

I have received your letter as joyfully as I have eagerly and longingly desired to have it. I have read it and I felt that the letters which I pronounced with my mouth were like sparks of fire in my heart. They warmed my heart within me, as if they came from that fire which the Lord sent upon the earth (Luke 12:49). How great a fire must glow in those meditations from which such sparks fly forth!

I confess that your inspiring greeting came not from man, but were like words that descended from Him who visited Jacob in his dream. It was not for me merely a conventional greeting, but it was one plainly from the very heart of love. It came so sweetly and so unexpectedly. I pray that God will bless you, who has had the goodness to anticipate my own greetings, so that I am encouraged to reply to you since I received your letter. Although I had thought often of writing to you, I had not presumed to do so. For I hesitated to disturb you with my eager scribbling and so interrupt the holy quiet which you have in the Lord and in the religious silence which isolates you from the world.

I did not want to interrupt, not even for a moment, those mysterious whispers from God by pouring out my words into ears which are always occupied with the secret praises of heaven. I was afraid to become as one who would trouble even Moses on the mount, or Elisha in the desert, or Samuel as he watched in the temple, if I tried to turn away even for a second minds that were so occupied with Divine communion. If Samuel cries out: "Speak Lord, for your servant hears" (1 Samuel 3:10), why should I presume to make myself heard? I feared that you might not want to listen to me and instead might say: "Excuse me, I cannot hear you now; I prefer rather to give ear to words sweeter than yours." I want to "hear what the Lord will say to me; for He will speak peace unto His people, and to His saints, and to those who are converted in heart" (Psalm 85:8, Vulgate). Or, worse still, to say: "Depart from me, the evil dispose, and I will study the commandments of my God" (Psalm 119:115). For how could I be so presumptuous as to distrub the much-loved spouse that rests sweetly in the arms of the Bridegroom as long as she wills to do so? Should I not hear her say immediately: Do not disturb me; I am only for my Beloved and my Beloved is for me; He feeds among the lilies (Song of Solomon 2:16).

2   But what can I not dare to do, she loves to dare, and with all confidence she knocks at the door of a friend. For I do not believe that love thinks she will be repulsed, knowing that love is the mother of friendships. Nor does love fear to interrupt for one moment your rest, however pleasant it may be, in order to speak to you of love's own task. For when love wills, she causes you to withdraw from being alone with God. When love so desires she will also make you attentive to me. So not only did you regard it as unworthy of you to endure benignly, but more, you urged me to break the silence. I esteem the kindness and the worthiness with which you think I praise the Lord. I am glad of this wonderful testimony and esteem myself happy in a friendship that serves in the praise of God.

Indeed you have received me even before, if I may judge by your letter. Now with a closer and more intimate friendship, you do so again. I find that he has brought back to you favorable reports concerning me, which doubtless he believed, although without sufficient cause. As a faithful and pious man, God forbid that he should speak otherwise than what he believes. And truly I experience in myself what the Savior says: "He who receives a righteous man in the name of a righteous man, shall receive a righteous man's reward" (Matthew 10:41). I have said that the reward of a righteous man, because I am re-

garded as righteous, is only through receiving one who is
righteous. If he has reported in me something more than
what is true, he has not spoken other than out of simplicity and goodness of his own heart. You have heard, you
have believed, you have rejoiced, and have written accordingly, giving me much joy, not only because I have
been honored with a degree of praise in the high place in
the esteem of your Holiness, but also because all the sincerity of your souls has made it known to me in no small
way. In brief, you have shown me how your spirit is motivated.

I therefore rejoice and thank you for your sincerity and 3
goodness. I am grateful for the encouragement that you
have shown to me. It is indeed true and sincere love, and
must be considered to proceed from a heart that is entirely
pure, having a good conscience, and faith unfeigned with
which we love our neighbors as ourselves. For he that
loves only the good that he himself has done, or at least
loves it more than that of others, does not really love good
for its own sake, but only on account of himself. He who is
such cannot do as the psalmist says: "Give thanks unto the
Lord, because He is good" (Psalm 118:1). He may give
thanks indeed because the Lord is good to him, but not because he is good in Himself.

Therefore let him understand that this reproach from
the same psalmist is directed against him: "Men will praise
Thee, when you do well to your own soul" (Psalm 49:18).
One man praises the Lord because He is mighty; another
because He is good to him; and again, another simply because He is good. The first is a slave and fears for himself.
The second is a mercenary, and thinks he deserves something for himself. But the third is a son, and he gives praise
to his Father. Therefore, both he who fears, and he who
desires, are each working for his own advantage. Love
which alone is in him is truly from a son who seeks not his
own.

Therefore I think that it was said of love: "The law of
the Lord is pure, converting the soul" (Psalm 19:7). For it
is that alone which can turn away the mind from the love

of self, and the love of the world, to direct it only towards God. Neither fear nor selfish love converts the soul. They change sometimes the outward appearance or the actions, but they never affect the heart. Doubtless even the slave sometimes does the work of God, but because he does not do it of his own free will, he still remains in his hardness of spirit. The mercenary person also does it, not out of kindness, but only as attracted to do so by his own particular advantage. So where distinction of persons is made, there lie personal interests. Where there are personal interests, there is a limit of willingness. This leads doubtless to the meanness that rusts the soul. Let the very fear by which he is constrained by the law to be a slave lead him. Let the greed and desire by which the mercenary is bound be a law to him, since it is by it that he is drawn away and enticed. But neither of these is without fault or is able to convert the soul. Love converts souls when it fills them with disinterested zeal.

4   Now I should add that this love is blameless in him who has become accustomed to retain nothing for himself. He who keeps nothing for himself gives to God all that he has. And that which belongs to God cannot be unclean. Thus that pure law of the Lord is none other than love, which seeks not what is advantageous to herself, but what profits others. But law is said to be of the Lord, either because He Himself lives by it, or because no one possesses it except by His gift. Nor is it absurd to say that even God lives by law, since this law is no other than love. For what can it be but love which preserves in the supreme and blessed Trinity that lofty and unspeakable unity which it has? It is law, then, and love is the law of the Lord, which maintains in a wonderful manner the Trinity and Unity and binds It in the bond of peace. Yet let no one think that I take love here to be a quality or a certain attribute in God. Nor do I say that in God (which God forbid) there is something which is not God. Rather I say that it is the very substance of God. I am saying nothing new or unheard of, for St. John says, "God is love" (1 John 4:16). It is right then to say that love is God, and at the same

time the gift of God. Therefore Love gives love, the reality that gives the gift. Whether the Word signifies the Giver, it is the name of the substance, and whether the thing is given, it is the name of the gift. This is the eternal law, Creator and Ruler of the universe. All things have been made through it and nothing is left without law. So He who is the Law of all things is Himself none other than the law which rules Him, a law uncreated as He.

But the slave and the mercenary have a law. It does not 5 come from God, but is what they have made for themselves. One is by not loving God, the other is by loving something else more than Him. They have, I say, a law which is of their own nature and not of the Lord, to which, nevertheless, their own is still subjected. Nor are they able to withdraw themselves from the unchangeable order of the divine law, although each should make a law for himself.

I would say then that a person makes a law for himself when he prefers his own will to the common and eternal law, perversely wishing to irritate his Creator. That is to say, God is a law unto Himself, and is under no authority but His own. Likewise, the man who would be as God will be his own master, and will make his own will a law to himself. Alas! What a heavy and insupportable yoke has thus been put upon all the sons of Adam. How it weighs upon, and bows down our necks, so that our life is drawn near to the grave. "O wretched man that I am, who shall deliver me from the body of this death?" (Romans 7:24). Thus I am so weighed down, unless the Lord helps me, my soul would almost go down to the grave (Psalm 94:17). With this load man is burdened, groaning and saying: "Why have you set me as a mark against You, so that I am a burden to myself?" (Job 7:20).

Where Job says I am made a burden to myself, he shows that he is a law unto himself, and the law is no other than what he himself has made it to be. But when, speaking to God, he commences by saying, "You have set me as a mark against You," he shows that he has not escaped from the divine law. For this is the property of that eternal and just law of God, that he who would not be ruled with gentleness by God shall be ruled as a punishment by his own self. All those who have willingly thrown off the gentle yoke and the light burden of love have instead to bear unwillingly the insupportable burden of their own will.

6   Thus God's law in a wonderful way makes him who is a fugitive from its power both an adversary and yet still a subject. On the one hand, he has not escaped from the law of justice, which deals out according to his merits. On the other hand, he cannot commune with God in His light, or peace, or glory. He is subjected to power, and excluded from Divine blessing. "Oh Lord, my God, why do You not take away my sin and pardon my transgression?" (Job 7:21). So when I can throw down the heavy weight of my own will, I shall breathe more easily under the light burden of love. Then I will no longer be overwhelmed by servile fear, nor allured by selfishness. Instead, I will be impelled by Your Spirit, the Spirit of liberty, which is that of Your children. Who is it who witnesses to my spirit that I, too, am one of Your children, since Your law is mine, and as You are, so am I also in this world?

For it is quite certain that those who do this which the apostle says, "owe no one anything except to love one another" (Romans 13:8), are themselves neither slaves nor mercenaries but sons of God.

Sons are not without law. This is written: "The law is not made for a righteous man" (1 Timothy 1:9). Yet it needs to be remembered that the law promulgated in fear by a spirit of slavery is one thing, but the law given sweetly and gently by the spirit of liberty is another. Those who are sons are not obliged to submit to the first, but they are always under the rule of the second. Do you want to understand why it is said that the law is not made for the righteous? "You have not received," he says, "the spirit of slavery again in fear." Why then are they always under the rule of the law of love? "You have received the spirit of the adoption of sons" (Romans 8:15).

Listen, also, how the righteous man confesses that he is

at the same time not under the law. "I became," he says, "to those that were under the law as being under the law, although I myself was not under the law. But to those who were without the law, I was as being without law, since I was not without the law of God but in the law of Christ" (1 Corinthians 9:20, 21). From this, it is inaccurate to say that the righteous have no law, or the righteous are without law. The law indeed was not made for the righteous. It is not imposed upon unwilling subjects. It is given freely to willing hearts by Him to whose sweet inspiration it is due. Therefore the Lord also beautifully says, "Take My yoke upon you" (Matthew 11:29). It is as if He would say, "I do not impose it upon you against your will. Take it only willingly. Otherwise you will find no rest, only labor for your souls."

The law of love, then, is good and sweet. It is not only 7
light and sweet to bear, but it renders bearable and light the laws even of slaves and mercenaries. But it does not destroy these. It brings about their fulfillment, as the Lord says: "I have not come to destroy the law, but to fulfill it" (Matthew 5:17). It moderates the one, and it reduces the other to order, and so each is lightened. Love will never be without sin, but this is a good kind of fear. It will never be without any thought of interest, yet it is a restrained and moderated interest.

Love therefore perfects the law of the slave when it inspires a generous devotion. It perfects the law of the mercenary when it gives a better direction to self interested desires. Thus, devotion mixed with fear does not annul these. But it purifies them, taking away the fear of punishment from which servile fear is never exempt. This fear is "clean and filial, enduring forever" (Psalm 19:9). For "perfect love takes away fear" (1 John 4:18). This is to be understood as the fear of punishment, which is never lacking, as we have said, in slavish fear.

As for cupidity, it is then rightly directed by the love which is now joined to it. Ceasing altogether to desire things which are evil, it begins now to prefer those which are better. Nor does it desire good things, except in order to reach those which are better. When, by the grace of God, it has fully obtained this, then the body and all the good things which belong to the body will be loved only for the sake of the soul. Then the soul will be loved only for the sake of God, and God loved alone for Himself.

8   However, as we are still in mortal bodies and are born with the desires of the flesh, it is necessary that our desires or affections should originate from the flesh. However, if it is rightly directed, advancing step by step under the guidance of grace, it will at length be perfected by the Spirit. Because as the apostle says, "That is not first which is spiritual, but that which is natural, and afterwards that which is spiritual; and it is needful that we should first bear the image of the earthly and afterwards that of the heavenly" (1 Corinthians 15:46, 49).

First, then, a man loves his own self for self's sake, since he is flesh. He cannot have any taste except for things in relation to himself. But when he sees that he is not able to subsist by himself, that God is indeed necessary to him, he begins to inquire and to love God by faith.

In the second place, he thus loves God for his own interest, and not for the interest of God Himself. But when, on account of his own necessity, he has begun to worship Him, and to approach Him by meditation, by reading, by prayer, and by obedience, then he comes little by little to know God with a certain intimacy. In consequence, he begins to find Him sweet and kind.

Having thus tasted how sweet the Lord is, he passes to the third stage, and thus loves God no longer on account of his own interest, but for the sake of God Himself. Once he is there, he remains stabilized.

But I do not know if in this life man is truly able to rise to the fourth degree. For it is the state where he no longer loves himself, except for the sake of God. Those who have attempted this (if there be any) may consider that it is attainable. To me, I confess, it appears impossible.

It will no doubt be so one day, when the good and faithful servant shall have been brought into the joy of His Lord, and filled with the fullness of the house of God.

Being so exhilarated, he shall in a wonderful way be forgetful of himself. He shall then lose the consciousness of what he is, and become absorbed altogether in God. Then he shall attach himself unto Him with all his powers, and thenceforth shall be one Spirit with Him.

I consider that the psalmist referred to this when he said: "I will go in the strength of the Lord: I will make mention of Thy righteousness, even of Thine only" (Psalm 71:16). He well knew that when he entered into the spiritual powers of God, he would be freed from all the infirmities of the flesh. He would no longer have to think of them, but would be occupied only with the perfections of God. Then for certain, each of the members of Christ will be able to say to himself what Paul said of their Head: "If we have known Christ according to the flesh, yet now henceforth know we Him no more" (2 Corinthians 5:16). There in heaven no one knows himself according to the flesh, because "flesh and blood will not inherit the kingdom of God" (1 Corinthians 15:50).

It is not that the substance of flesh will not be there, but every fleshly necessity will be done away. For the love of the flesh will be absorbed into the love of the Spirit, and the weak human passions which exist at present will be absorbed into divine powers. Then the net of love which is now drawn through a great and vast sea, and does not cease to bring together every kind of fish, will at length be drawn to the shore. Then it will retain only the good, rejecting the bad. In this life love fills the vast spaces of its net with all kinds of fishes. It suits itself to all, according to the time, identifying and partaking of the good and evil circumstances of all. So it is a custom not only to rejoice with them who rejoice, but to weep with them that weep. But when it shall have reached the shore (of eternity), casting away as evil fish all that it bore with grief before, it will retain only those which are sources of pleasure and gladness. Then Paul will no longer be weak with the weak, or be scandalized with those who are scandalized, since scandal and weakness will be removed far away.

We ought not to think that he will still let fall tears

over those who have not repented here below. For it is certain that there will no longer be sinners, so there will be no one to repent. Far be it from us to think that He will mourn and deplore those whose portion is everlasting fire with the Devil and his angels. For in that City of God the streams of that river will make glad their hearts (Psalm 46:4). The gates of that city the Lord loves more than all the dwellings of Jacob (Psalm 87:2). In those earthly dwellings, although the joy of victory is sometimes tasted, yet the combat always continues and sometimes the struggle is for life. But in that dear country there is no place for adversity or sorrow. So with the psalmist we sing: "The abiding place of all those who rejoice is in Thee" (Psalm 87:7, Vulgate), and again: "Everlasting joy shall be unto them" (Isaiah 61:7). How then shall there be any remembrance of mercy where the justice of God shall alone be remembered? How can the feeling of compassion be exercised, when there shall be no place for misery, or occasion for pity?

10   I am compelled to prolong this already lengthy discourse, dearly beloved and much longed-for brethren, by the very strong desire I have of conversing with you. But there are three things which show me that I ought to come to an end. First, because I fear to be burdensome to you. Second, because I am ashamed to show myself to be so loquacious. And third, because I am so pressed by my personal cares.

In conclusion, I beg you to have compassion upon me, and if you have rejoiced because of the good things which you have heard of me, sympathize with me also, I pray, in my very real temptations and cares. He who has related these things to you has no doubt seen some very few things and has overexaggerated these small things as though they were great. In these your indulgence has easily believed, for you have been willing to hear the best. May you be blessed indeed with that love which "believes all things" (1 Corinthians 13:7). But I am confounded by the truth which knows all things. I beg you to believe me in what I say of myself, rather than listen to others who have only seen me from the outside. "No man knows the things that are in a man save the spirit of man which is in him" (1 Corinthians 2:11). I can assure you that I do not speak of myself by conjecture, but out of full knowledge. I am not really such as I am believed and said to be. I need to have you know this and to confess it frankly. So I need to have your special prayers. May this become such as your letter sets forth, for there is nothing more that I desire.

---

[1]William, a simple monk, having heard of the sickness with which Bernard was seized soon after he became Abbot of Clairvaux, went to see him with a companion. From the conversations they had then, the two became close friends.

[2]Written by Bernard to the Carthusians about 1125. Its interest lies in being the original material which Bernard later expanded into his *Treatise on the Love of God*.

IX
SPIRITUAL FRIENDSHIP

BOOK I OF THIS
CHAPTER IS PROBABLY SET
at the Abbey of Wardon, Bedfordshire, a
daughter house of Rievaulx where Ivo was a
monk. It was probably this same Ivo to whom Aelred had
sent his earlier work *On Jesus at the Age of Twelve*. On an
official visit, Bernard notices that Ivo is silent in the animated discussions of the community. Drawing him aside,
Aelred enters into the following dialogue with him on the
nature of friendship. Both had read Cicero's work on
Friendship and questioned if a pagan who does not know
Christ can ever really understand spiritual friendship.

Many years later, after Aelred had written *The Mirror of
Charity* in which he also discussed friendship, Books II and
III were written. They record a discussion in Rievaulx
with two friends of the monastery, Walter and Gratian.
The biographer of Aelred, Walter Daniel, tells us that it
was he that was referred to. Gratian is unknown; presuma-
bly he was another monk at Rievaulx.

Both Walter and Gratian are pessimistic about the
practice of spiritual friendship, as many of us are today.
But for Aelred, friendship and godliness are so profoundly
integrated that he carries through all three debates with a
deep conviction of its need and possibility. This runs so
strongly within him that, of all his works, this is the most

carefully argued and most well-written. For it suggests no subject was dearer to his own heart.

BOOK I: THE NATURE OF FRIENDSHIP

Aelred: Here we are. You and I, and I hope a third is also present—Christ Himself. Since no one else is here to disturb us, open your heart, and let me hear what you have to say.

Ivo: I deeply appreciate your concern for me. The Spirit of love Himself has shown you my heart. I do want to be instructed more fully about friendship in Christ.

Christ as our friend

Aelred: I am unable to teach you anything about friendship, but we can discuss it freely. You introduced the subject rightly when you see friendship in Christ beginning and being perfected in Christ. But how do we enter into a discussion about this subject?

Ivo: Not by describing friendship as a relationship in a vacuum.

Cicero's definition of friendship

Aelred: "Friendship is mutual harmony in human and divine affairs," argues Cicero, "together with benevolence and charity."

Ivo: What did Cicero mean by "charity" and "benevolence"?

Aelred: Perhaps he meant by "charity" affection, and by "benevolence" he meant expressing that affection by deeds.

Ivo: That seems right. But it could apply to the pagans and the Christians alike. I am convinced, however, that true friendship can only exist between those who are really living in Christ.

Aelred: Yes, the definition is perhaps imperfect, but it may be cleared up in our discourse together. Love of a friend is like a garden, where we can rejoice in his joys, and weep in his sorrows (Romans 12:15). Even the philosophers of this world have noted that friendship is not transitory; its virtues are eternal. For says Solomon, "He who is a friend loves at all times" (Proverbs 17:17). If it ceases, then it proves it never was real friendship, according to Jerome (*Letters,* 3:6).

Ivo: Yet we do not expect such a high standard. Real friendship is very rare. Indeed, Cicero notes that "in so many past ages, tradition scarcely extols more than three or four pairs of such friends." Even now, under Christianity, real friends are very few.

Aelred: Yet the Christian should not despair and give up. "Ask and you shall receive" (Matthew 7:7) is the promise of Matthew's Gospel.

It is not surprising that pagans have no such hope. Through faith in Christ, the early church records not three or four, but thousands of such examples of friendship, for "the multitude had but one heart and one soul . . . having all things in common" (Acts 4:32).

Ivo: Is there no difference, then, between charity and friendship? Are we not compelled to love both our friends and our enemies? (Matthew 5:44; Luke 6:27f.). Yet we can only call those our friends to whom we can entrust our hearts.

Aelred: Carnal friendship begins with lustful eyes and ears turned outward. It is the affection of the harlot for every passerby (Ezekiel 16:25). Likewise, worldly friendship is prompted by the desire to have temporal and material advantages. It is fair-weather friendship that seeks only what is profitable. Such a false beginning may develop into a more genuine kind of friendship, but it is still a temporary affair.

Spiritual friendship has no profit motive. It is desired for the dignity of its own sake. Its fruition occurs simply because the Lord of the gospel commands that we should bear "fruit" (John 15:16f.). That is to say, that we should love one another.

True friendship means, then, the exclusion of every vice. It is only this which provides for real community. Such a friendship is directed by prudence, ruled by justice, guarded by fortitude, and moderated by temperance. We shall consider this further, but have we said enough on the true nature of friendship?

Ivo: Yes, indeed! But tell me, how did friendship first begin with mankind? Did it happen accidentally, or by necessity, or was some law imposed on the human race?

Aelred: As I see it, the human soul by creation has desired friendship. Experience intensified its desire, and the sanction of law confirmed it.

God said, "It is not good for man to be alone; let us make him a helper like himself " (Genesis 2:18). How beautifully was the equality of the sexes recognized, for equality is the characteristic of true friendship. Yet alas, by the Fall, the experience of such sweetness and affection was corrupted by avarice and envy, strife, rivalry, hatred, and suspicion. The original, universal friendship God intended for mankind—like wisdom also—became corrupted. It needed to be regulated and empowered by the strength of the Law.

Ivo: Why do you associate wisdom with friendship?

Aelred: Because friendship is really nothing else but true wisdom.

Ivo: By this, do you mean to say about friendship what the friend of Jesus says about love: "God is friendship" (1 John 4:16)?

Aelred: That would be an unusual way of putting it, yet that is what Scripture sanctions, saying, "He that abides in friendship abides in God and God in Him" (1 John 4:16).

BOOK II: THE MATURITY AND FRUITFULNESS OF FRIENDSHIP

Walter: Do you remember the conversation you once had with your friend Ivo on spiritual friendship?

Aelred: Indeed I do remember my dear Ivo. His consistent love and affection will always remain with me, even though he is now dead. For his spirit will be all the time with me. His devout countenance still inspires me, and his charming eyes still smile upon me. His words yet linger, even though I have lost the notes of the conversation we had together.

Friendship sustained by memory

Walter: To be honest, I heard that you received these very notes only three days ago. So I am eager to review the whole discussion with you.

Aelred: All right, then, but it is only for your private scrutiny.

Walter: After all these years, it is so wonderful to read it all again. But this splendid discourse on the nature of friendship only makes me want to ask all the more about the purpose and value of friendship.

Aelred: Since friendship bears fruit both in this life and in the life to come, I cannot presume to explain all about its benefits. Scarcely any happiness can exist for mankind without friendship. Man is like a beast without it. "Woe to him who is alone, for when he falls, he has no one to lift him up" (Ecclesiastes 4:10).

Benefits of friendship

What blessing, security, and joy there is in having someone in whom you can trust and speak man to man, woman to woman. How assuring to be able to confide your spiritual progress to him or her. How joyful to have someone with whom you can share your plans, and be united as one.

Such a friend, says the wise man, "is the medicine of life" (Sirach 6:16). The healing of wounds by such a friendship, and the "bearing of one another's burdens" (Galatians 6:2) is so effective. Such a friendship prolongs life, for it is the best medicine of life. Indeed, it is the best gift of life. How much more, then, is the friendship of God. For our Savior in John's Gospel says, "I will call you not servants but my friends" (John 15:15).

Walter: I admit you move me deeply and intensify my desire to have such friendship. But above all, I desire to see how the love of God in spiritual friendship may be more fully developed. I know that, among the stages of spiritual maturity, true friendship is the very highest.

But here comes Gratian, whose eagerness for friendship makes me call him friendship's own child.

Gratian: Thank you, though I feel like an intruder into this august conversation. For if I am really "friendship's child," and you are not just jesting with me, then I should have been here at the start of this talk together. But carry on, Father Aelred.

Aelred: Do not think, my son, that we have exhausted the subject already. But to bring you to where we are, notice how friendship is but a stage toward the love and knowledge of God. As the apostle says in 1 Corinthians 13, true love is always holy, voluntary, and true. Thus true friendship shines forth with special qualities of joy, security, and sweetness.

Friendship matures in Christ. Such friendship is therefore a marvelous thing, if to it are added all the virtues of honor, charm, truth, joy, sweetness, goodwill, affection, and action. All of these things have their beginning only in Christ. They develop only in Christ. They are perfected only in Christ. Such an ascent is not too steep, for it is inspired by the love of Christ.

By Christ's love, then, we can love our friend. This is the love that Christ gives, when He gave Himself to us as our Friend. In Him, charm follows charm and affection is poured out upon affection. As a friend cleaves to a friend, so in the spirit of Christ they are made one heart and one soul with Christ (Acts 4:32).

Man needs two elements to sustain his life: food and air. He can subsist for some time without food, but without air, he will die within a few moments. Spiritually, we may think of this as analogous to the kiss of Christ. The saintly soul cries out, "Let Him kiss me with the kiss of His mouth" (Song of Solomon 1:1). The result is the union of affections between Christ and the soul.

[Here Aelred discusses the "kiss" in three senses: bodily, spiritually, and contemplatively.] Bodily, the kiss is an expression of the lips; spiritually, it is the union of spirits; contemplatively, it is the kiss of the Spirit of God received in grace. Bodily, we need the kiss for some specific purpose such as reconciliation. Spiritually, the kiss is characteristic of the covenant of friends whose spirits are mingled and united. But "the kiss of Christ" offered through the affection of the heart (not by the contact of the mouth) and the mingling of the spirit (not by the meeting of the lips) is really spiritual friendship. Then they can say with the psalmist, "Behold, how good and how pleasant it is for brethren to dwell together in unity" (Psalm 133:1).

The soul which grows accustomed to such a kiss sighs for more and more of such an experience of love. He takes delight in resting in His embrace, saying: "His left hand is under my head, and His right hand shall embrace me" (Song of Solomon 2:6).

Gratian: This kind of friendship, as I see it, is unusual. We are not accustomed to dream of friendship having such a character. I do not know what Walter has said so far, but for me friendship is nothing else but a complete identity of wills, and the mutual sharing of all that one has.

What are the bounds of friendship?

Walter: Compared with the first dialogue on friendship, I have learned so much more about its character. My problem is, how far should one go; what are the limits of friendship? Is the sharing of one's goods enough? Or should one also share one's country, or even go into exile, or expose one's self to what others consider dishonorable, or what else should one do for one's friend?

I have come to believe that none of these claims really define friendship. For Gratian's sake—who tends to be reckless—I would prefer to set some bounds.

Gratian: That is nice of you, but I would prefer to hear what Father Aelred has to say.

Aelred: Christ Himself set us the bounds when He said, "Greater love has no man than this, than that a man lays down his life for his friend" (John 15:13). Does that seem enough?

Gratian: Since no greater friendship is possible, why is that not enough?

Walter: But what if the pagans, in mutual harmony of evil, are willing to die for one another; can we grant that they know the epitome of true friendship?

Aelred: Heaven forbid, for true friendship cannot exist among such!

Gratian: Who, then, can have such friendship?

Aelred: I will tell you briefly. It can begin among the good, progress among the better, and be consummated among the best. This means you must detest all evil. The first man, Adam, would have been better off if he had accused his wife of being presumptuous instead of complying with her request to share the forbidden fruit (Genesis 3:6). Jonadab was no friend of Ammon in offering to help him attain his lust of incest (2 Samuel 13:3f.).

Such friendship. is rare

So you see, friendship can only exist among the good.

Gratian: What, then, is the reality of friendship among those of us who are not good?

Aelred: Since no one is absolutely good, we are talking relatively about this subject, in light of our fallenness. "Live soberly, and justly, and godly in this world" (Titus 2:12). It is with such that friendship can occur and develop.

Walter: I am tempted to believe we should avoid friendship. The Stoics felt this, for they thought it better to give this impossible ideal a wide berth.

Gratian: All right. What we are doing at this very moment is then a waste of time. If we can so easily withhold ourselves from the desire of friendship—the fruit of which is so holy, so useful, and so acceptable to God—how are we ever to be persuaded to practice it? As for me, I leave such cynicism to the fickle, to those whose love can readily turn to hatred.

Walter: Like Gratian, I used to think that doves lack gall. But Aelred will show us how such opinions can be refuted.

Aelred: Cicero speaks beautifully on this point: "To take the sun out of the world is to take friendship out of life, for we have nothing better from God, and nothing more pleasant." What wisdom can there lie in despising the need of friendship?

Paul, then, must have been a fool, for he was unwilling to live without concern for others. For the sake of real love—to him the sovereign virtue—he was weak with the weak (2 Corinthians 11:28f.) and sorrowful for his brethren (Romans 9:2f.). Sometimes he cherished his people like a nurse (1 Thessalonians 2:7). At times he was filled with grief (2 Corinthians 2:4; 12:21).

Was it also in vain that Hushai the Archite should preserve a loyal friendship with David? (2 Samuel 16:15f.; 17:5f.).

No, I must insist that those men are beasts who say men

should live indifferently to each other. Not to care, or be cared after, is quite wrong.

Yet heaven forbid that I should also think of friendship as merely a profession that is not costly. It costs love.

Walter: Well, if many are so deceived by the mere appearance of friendship, tell us what sort of friendship we should avoid, and what we should seek after.

Aelred: Since real friendship is only among the good, nothing unbecoming can be acceptable.

Gratian: However, perhaps we are still not clear about the difference between true and false friendship.

Aelred: There is immature friendship that is aimless and playful affection; it catches the attention of the passerby. But it lacks reason and is unstable. Such childish friendship is fickle, unstable, and mixed with impure motives.

Mature and spiritual friendship begins with the preservation of pure motives. Then it follows reason, and it is also disciplined.

Spiritual friendship is contrasted with the kind of friendship we consider advantageous to us. Yet if you include among the "advantages" such things as guidance in doubt, comfort in sorrow, and other benefits of that kind, then these are what should be expected of a friend. But such friendship will never come forth from the advantages, but rather the advantages will come forth after the friendship.

Such was the case of the benefits that came to David from Barzillai (2 Samuel 17:27f.). Likewise, we know that the sacred bond of friendship between David and Jonathan was not consecrated through hope of any ulterior motive, but from the contemplation of the virtue itself. The benefit came later (1 Samuel 19:20; 2 Samuel 9).

(*Ed.—Aelred concludes that nothing ought to be denied to a friend. Nothing ought to be refused on behalf of a friend, even one's very life. But since the life of a soul is of far greater excel-*

*lence than that of the body, any action which brings about the
death of the friend's soul must be totally denied.)*

Gratian: Please tell us now what cautions we should keep
in mind in limits to serving one's friend?

Aelred: The time has gone, unfortunately, and I am being
called to attend to other business.

Walter: I am reluctant to stop. But let us make sure
Gratian arrives on time tomorrow morning to continue
our discussion.

BOOK III: THE CONDITIONS AND CHARACTERISTICS OF UNBROKEN FRIENDSHIP

Aelred: What are you doing here?

Gratian: Surely you know why I am here.

Aelred: Is Walter not present with us?

Gratian: Let him see to himself. At least he cannot accuse
me of being late today.

Aelred: Do you want me to deal with the questions
suggested yesterday?

Gratian: I hope Walter comes soon. For he is quicker at
grasping things and better in asking questions. He also has
a better memory.

(Enter Walter)
Aelred: Do you hear that, Walter? Gratian is friendlier to
you than I thought.

Walter: How could he fail to be my friend, when he is
everybody's friend? But let us make the most of our time
now.

Love is the source of friendship.

Aelred: Love is the source of friendship. There can be love without friendship, but friendship without love is impossible. With love there is also reason which may keep it pure, while affection keeps love sweet. But the foundation of spiritual friendship is the love of God. To this divine love, all human love points. This, then, must be the foundation on which we build.

But not all whom we love are our friends. If your friend is to be the companion of your soul, then you have to choose carefully. For you will hide nothing from each other, and fear nothing from each other. So there are conditions for such friendship. A friend must be tested; and he must be stable. Nothing is more detestable than a man who injures a friendship. So choose with utmost care. For once he is admitted, he should be borne with, deferred to, and be united in soul and spirit.

Four stages of friendship

There are four stages in the development of friendship. First, there is selection; second is probation; third is admission; and fourth is perfect harmony.

Walter: I remember how you showed this definition in your first discussion with Ivo. But since then, you have discussed so many kinds of friendship that I would like to know what you think the character of true friendship is.

Aelred: As we have seen, true friendship only exists among the good. So this is the main characteristic for such.

Gratian: But what of friendship being a community of those with common likes and dislikes?

Aelred: Certainly I would accept this, provided it was a community of those who exercised disciplined affections.

Walter: But what of the four stages you mentioned?

The choice of friends

Aelred: First, let me begin with the selection of friends. Avoid the irascible, the fickle, the suspicious, and the talkative. For Scripture says: "Be not the friend of an angry man, and do not walk with a furious man, lest he become a snare to your soul" (Proverbs 22:24f.). Solomon adds: "Anger rests in the bosom of a fool" (Ecclesiastes 7:10). Who thinks he can really be a friend to a fool?

Walter: Yet you have exemplified deep devotion to a friend who was very irascible. We have heard you were never hurt by him.

Aelred: You must remember there are some people who are naturally bad-tempered. In overcoming their weakness, they may occasionally offend a friend by a careless word or act with indiscretion. So if we happen to have such a friend, then we must bear with him patiently.

Gratian: Yes, we saw that friend the other day being angry with you, yet you had such patience with him.

Walter: Gratian is bolder than I am in saying this.

Aelred: Of course that man you mention is very dear to me. But once he has become my friend, I can only continue to accept him. If I happen to be stronger than he is in the matter of temper, I can yield to him for his peace of mind.

Walter: Since Ivo passed away, this other friend has satisfied you; but we do not see how he can. Tell us then what are the five vices that destroy friendship.

Aelred: Well, slander is indeed an injurious vice that destroys reputations. Just as many are enamored by self-praise, so they will find satisfaction in reproaches cast against their neighbors. What can be more outrageous than the reproach which slaps the face of an innocent man?

Then there is the vice that reveals confidences. Nothing can be baser or more detestable between friends. Hence it is written: "He who discloses the secret of a friend loses his credit" (Sirach 27:24). A little later it adds: "To disclose the secret of a friend leaves no hope to an unhappy soul" (Sirach 27:24). "If a serpent bites in silence," says Solomon, "he is no better who backbites secretly" (Ecclesiastes 10:11). To slander in this way is to commit the treachery of Miriam which caused her to be covered with leprosy (Numbers 12:1f.).

Another factor in the choice of friends is to avoid those who are fickle. A privileged fruit of friendship is the security in which you can entrust and commit yourself to your friend. How can there be any security in one who is like putty?

Also, you need the mutual peace and tranquility of heart that a suspicious person can never give. His suspicion is like an inexhaustible supply of fuel to a fire that never goes out. This terrible vice undermines everything. It is a situation in which none can win.

Avoid also the talkative. "Do you not know," says the wise man, "the person over-ready with his tongue? There is more hope for a fool than for such a one" (Proverbs 29:20, Septuagint).

So the man you choose for your friend should be one who is not upset by anger, one who is not fickle, one who is not consumed by suspicions, and one whose deportment is not upset by gossip. Rather seek someone who suits your temperaments and habits.

Walter: Where can such a man be found?

Aelred: I admit it is not easy to find such a one. But there are some who learn to discipline themselves in these ways, and they are most to be treasured.

Walter: But suppose you find a friend who has none of these vices and later falls into them? Do you go on tolerating this?

Aelred: Well, of course you should begin by choosing wisely. Then you should take time in developing friendship. But if the friendship then has to be severed, do so gradually, rather than traumatically. Such a gradual dissolution will avoid bitterness, quarrels, and enmity. For it is a shameful thing to wage war against someone who has been your intimate.

But if someone really is your friend, then learn to be patient with his faults. For since friendship should be unending, "he that is a friend loves at all times" (Proverbs 17:17). If he offends you, continue to love him in spite of the heart. Safeguard his reputation. Never betray the secrets of a friend, even if he betrays yours.

Be patient with a true friend.

Walter: What, then, are the vices which you said might dissolve friendship gradually?

What vices destroy friendship?

Aelred: Those five vices are faults, especially the revelation of secrets and the hidden stains of suspicion; these are intolerable.

But there is a sixth vice. Namely, if your friend injures those whom you love and he persists in doing so. Thus King Ahasuerus suspended the friendship of Haman whom he had cherished above all other friends. He did so because he preferred the love of his wife and her people (Esther 7).

But between perfect friends who have been wisely chosen and tested and united in genuine spiritual friendship, no disagreement can possibly arise. The friendship which does lead to divisions shows it was never a true one. "Friendship which can end was never true" (Jerome, *Letters* 3:6).

Walter: What can dissolve friendships?

Aelred: There are four elements in particular that characterize friendship: love, affection, security, and happiness. Without these, friendship will not last.

Love implies rendering services with benevolence. Affection is an inward pleasure seen from the outside. Security is a revelation of counsels and confidences that is securely held. Happiness is shared together and pleasing in all circumstances. So you see, when these are lost, then friendship may be withdrawn.

Walter: I would like now a summary of what has been discussed so far.

Aelred: Very well. We have said love is the source of friendship; not just any kind of love, but that which comes with reason and affection together. Then we said that the foundation of true friendship is laid upon the love of God. Then we decided to pay attention to four stages upon which mature friendship is nurtured. Then we spoke of vices to avoid in choosing your friend.

The test of friendship
So now if you have grasped all this, let us pass on to the subject of the probation of friendship.

Walter: This is very opportune. For I am looking at the door in case someone bursts in to interrupt our wonderful session.

Aelred: There are four qualities which must be tested in a friend: loyalty, right intention, discretion, and patience.
Loyalty must be tested so that you can entrust yourself safely to your friend. Right intention needs testing so that nothing but God's goodness is expected from the friendship. Discretion also must be tested, so that a person may understand what is required of his friend. Patience, too, is needed, so that a friend may not be grieved when rebuked, nor despise or hate the one inflicting the rebuke. He also needs to bear suffering on behalf of his friend.
Loyalty is hidden in prosperity, so it only is really seen in adversity. "A brother is proved in adversity" (Proverbs 17:17), but "to trust an unfaithful man in times of trouble is like a rotten tooth and a weary foot" (Proverbs 25:19).
In regard to right intention, our Lord and Savior has Himself written for us the formula for true friendship when He says: "You shall love your neighbor as yourself" (Matthew 22:39). This is the mirror. And generally speaking, friendship among the poor is generally more se-

cure than among the rich. For poverty takes away the hope of gain in such a way as not to decrease the friendship, but rather to increase it.

The quality of discretion is needed in dealing with the trivial faults of one's friends. Otherwise one may get caught up in the controversies and daily quarrels because of a lack of such discretion. The absence of this virtue is like a ship drifting without a rudder.

The prudent man also needs patience to proceed gradually in his affections.

Suppose the whole human race were taken out of this world. What, then, would be the meaning of all the natural and cultural treasures of the world? Tell me now. Without having a companion, could you really enjoy all these possessions?

Possessions are joyless without friends.

Walter: No, not at all.

Aelred: This is what God has given us. He has provided us with eternal friendship which begins in this world, and is perfected in the next. He, then, is most blessed who rests in the intimate hearts of those whom he loves, loving all and being loved by all.

Walter: Excellently said and so true.

Aelred: It may seem difficult to conceive of such perfect friendship in this world. But the day before yesterday I was walking in the cloister, and the brethren were sitting around, forming a most loving group. In the midst of the garden of flowers, the love of such friends was itself like a spiritual garden of Eden. I was filled with delight, remembering the words of the psalmist: "How good and how pleasant it is for brethren to dwell together in unity" (Psalm 133:1).

Gratian: Are you telling us you can love all this crowd?

Distinction
between being
affable and
having a friend

Aelred: No, but we can embrace them all differently, without having all of them as intimate friends. Ambrose speaks of "laying bare our confidences, only to our friend" (*Duties*, 135). Ambrose adds, "But would it not be imprudent for many of those whom we love if we laid bare our souls before them and poured out our inner hearts to them?"

Walter: This conception of friendship is so sublime and idealistic that I do not even hope to aspire to it. For me and my friend Gratian, friendship is more like that described by Augustine. Namely, it is someone who I can jest with, sometimes quarrel with, learn from, long for in his absence, and then receive back joyfully.

Aelred: Yes, but this kind of friend also belongs to the carnal life of the world. We can trust that it is from such beginnings—along with a growing piety and consistent zeal for the things of the Spirit—that a more holy friendship will mature. With holier affections, it may then be translated to a friendship for God.

Other virtues
of friendship

Remembering the four virtues needed for friendship, we can add others: affability of speech, good manners, serenity, and the expression of a kindly eye. These add relish and charm to a friendship. Consider and treat your friend as an equal. Give yourself to your friend in such a way that you neither reproach him nor seek for any reward. Meet him with kindness, just as Boaz treated Ruth, and spared her any embarrassment (Ruth 2:8f.). So, too, we need to be adroit in anticipating our friend's need.

Walter: But if we feel we have nothing to give, and that we must not expect anything, what is the use of such spiritual friendship?

Aelred: Man would live a much better life if the words "mine" and "yours" were taken away from our vocabulary. It is holy poverty that bestows so much strength to friend-

ship. But cupidity makes such heavy demands on friendship.

Reverence is the best companion of friendship. For he
who takes away respect takes away the greatest adornment
there is from friendship. How well does reverence control
and put out fires which the tongue may ignite. But along
with reverence, admonition (which is also needed) must
be done in secret. As Ambrose said, "If you see any vice in
your friend, correct him secretly. If he will not heed you,
correct him openly. For correction is good, and it is often
better than a friendship which keeps silent. For the
wounds inflicted by a friend are more tolerable than the
kisses of the flatterer. Therefore, correct the erring
friend."

Since it is growing late, I hope you are now convinced   Conclusion
that friendship is founded on love. But as love includes
many people, let him choose from among them one whom
he can admit in intimate fashion to the mysteries of
friendship. But let such a person not be chosen capri-
ciously by impulsive affection, but by foresight and
reason. Let him choose from similarity of character and
the goodness he sees in his friend.

Then see that this person's loyalty and honor, as well as
his patience, are tested. Let confidence gradually
develop, together with mutual concerns, and similarity of
expressions. When you are confident he will look upon
friendship as a virtue and not as a trade, then you have discovered a real friend.

A GUIDE TO DEVOTIONAL READING

Our lives are both private and public. Yet the pressures of our culture are to believe that the public activities, duties, and responsibilities are more important. Function then becomes more valued than being. Meanwhile, our souls become starved, and the inner person within us cries out for fulfillment of deeper needs. We long for deeper, more real spiritual life. For we sense we are inauthentic when we are only professors and promoters in the shallows of life. We know that we must nourish this drive to know God.

This reading guide is not a comprehensive list of principles that you must read, master, and know in order to have a "how-to kit" for spirituality. It is, however, suggestive of what might introduce you to the classics of faith and devotion and other helpful material. There is an art in devotional reading that is not exegetical, informational, or literary in its emphasis. For spiritual reading is essentially formative of the soul before God. We need, then, to read this devotional literature in such a way that it helps us be inspired and in tune with God in "the inner man." It is writing which turns us heavenward and forms our character in Christ.

Curiously, however, in spite of the spate of new books and reprints of this spiritual literature, there is little guidance offered about how the art of spiritual reading can and should be cultivated.[1] The following guidelines are suggested to help you focus on this art.

1. Spiritual reading requires a primary emphasis on the devotional use of Scripture.

Do not allow the excitement of entering into devotional literature detract you from the priority you give to Bible study and meditation on the Scriptures. Remember, the Scriptures are the canon of the devotion of God's people. They saw the Scriptures as God's revelation and the Holy Spirit as the Guide for its writing.

Devotional reading by theological students is made difficult by the mixture of methods used. This mixture is inevitable and not bad, provided we begin to allow the text to speak to us personally instead of being detached from it to pursue more information or mere hypothetical knowledge.

2. Growing in the art of devotional reading is less a matter of techniques than it is a matter of attitudes of the heart.

It is like developing a "sixth sense" of reading which is distinct from reading for information or rational understanding. So the attitude is changed from seeking information to that of being inspired and transformed.

Informational reading is more a search for questions and answers. Devotional reading is more dwelling on meanings about life's deepest issues. The former looks for transparency, the latter is content to contemplate mysteries. Again, informational reading is more dialectical and comparative, and logic is important. But devotional reading is more docile and receptive rather than critical and comparative.

Informational reading tends toward being dissective. Data is taken to pieces by analysis in order to increase one's ability to learn. But devotional reading is living and dynamic and seeks to relate the material to life. For this reason, devotional reading is more personal, allowing the reader to interpret its insights in such personal forms of assimilation as a spiritual journal and the practice of prayer. In these ways, the effects of reading for the inner man are personalized and deepened to affect and shape character, nourish the soul, and permeate the whole of one's life.

3. Devotional reading is an art learned by facilitating conditions and circumstances rather than by improving cognitive techniques.

It is God's grace alone which prompts us to have any desires for God and, therefore, any thirst for spiritual literature. Since we cannot invent, create, or refashion "facilitating conditions" for our own sanctity, or cognitively become better listeners to God's guiding Word, "facilitating conditions and circumstances" means to help remove obstacles to the action of grace.

In the history of the Church, as well as in the history of the soul, we experience "the desert" as such a facilitating condition. We feel "the desert within" of loneliness, "the desert outside" of relationships. Desert silence and solitude may be an experience. We relearn the priorities and essentials of life in the spiritual experiences of the desert. We discover new dimensions there of self-knowledge. We need patience, fortitude, and acceptance of desert suffering. We discover dependence and need of God in new ways. There, we reverse the worldly values of self-reliance toward dependence upon God, the dynamic of spiritual life.

A reawakening of the consciousness of indwelling sin in the believer and a sensitivity to the reality of Satan also drive us to our knees. We rediscover the great Puritan classics on the pathology of the heart, its deceptions, its hiddenness, its inaccessibility to our control. Temptation is a constant reality which requires a moral watchfulness that can be alerted by the writings of those experienced in its subtleties. Repentance becomes a lived reality that needs support and comfort. For more material on these subjects, please consult Richard Baxter's book *The Reformed Pastor* and John Owen's book *Sin & Temptation*, two volumes in the Classics of Faith and Devotion series by Multnomah Press.

A desire to reset our course of life, after failure and dishonesty with our soul, intensifies our search to learn how others have done so. Spiritual restoration is not seen as a return to the *status quo*, but as a radical change in direction into unknown territory, where we can walk "more by faith and less by sight." Seeing life with deeper meaning calls for greater spiritual resources than we previously imagined we would ever need. See *Real Christianity* by William Wilberforce and published by Multnomah Press.

Such deeper surrender to the will and purpose of God, after the defeat of self-will, creates longing in the soul for inner peace, spiritual gentleness, serenity, and spiritual refreshment. A deeper understanding and experience of the love of God creates a desire to build up covenant relations in friendships that embody the reality of God in social relationships. Moved by God's grace and compassion, we look below the marred and shattered forms of human relations to the potentials of redemption.

4. Devotional reading has its own pace of assimilation.

Think about the speedy insights of the mind, the transformation of thought into action, or the assimilation of deed into character—each have their own relative paces. Devotional reading does, too. The motion toward godliness is the slowest pace of human actions. Inauthenticity occurs when we move too fast, inappropriate to the nature of the transformation. Devotional reading needs its own time which is not determined by the academic calendar nor the impatience we have for "instant results." Spiritual classics cannot be read in one evening like detective novels. Such slow motion requires a regular habit of fixed times for devotional reading and an unhurried leisure to learn the disciplines of meditation and contemplation.

Devotional reading also requires space in our lives. Literally this may lead to the habit of a particular environment being developed—one spot in our room that locates an "altar" of devotion. Physically, it may require comfort, a particular chair, an accustomed posture, where we learn most readily to relax, and where the atmosphere is made for such exercise of devotion. Devotional reading requires a quiet spot, habitually frequented in solitude.

5. Choose carefully the devotional work you want to read for the benefit of your own soul. Choose it, then, possibly with the advice of others.

Keep in mind that the book should be chosen to open the doors of perception for you in terms of new as well as existing needs and desires. An imitation of others may not be the best reason for your choice. Because its purpose is to nurture the unique conditions of your own life, individual choice is important. At the same time, bear in mind that books we reject today may be rediscovered later because we are then ready for their insight.

Personal adoption of a book is also helped by marking the text. This may record our first reactions of approval, of help, or of questioning and rejection. It may also help to keep a spiritual journal which we feed with quotations reflected upon and assimilated from the text. Such a reflective notebook may record the immediate reactions to the text, the state of mind we were in when we read a passage, and the duties faithfully performed as a response to what we read. Recordings of ordinary feelings and happenings set within the framework of the devotional readings keep the realities of ordinary life before us. We retain and remember our thoughts if we write them down on the text. This also makes the meaning of the message clearer and more readily available to us.

6. Choose spiritual classics from a broad spectrum of thinkers.

Range widely and without prejudice over the classics of devotion, be they Orthodox, Catholic, or Protestant. From our perspective of history and cultural change, we can read more appreciatively of other traditions. Their encapsulation within their own culture also helps us see how likely we are entrapped by our culture as well.

Do not let the great merits of the Reformation block your view of the past so that you think there is nothing between New Testament times and the beginning of the Reformation (early 1500s) that is worth reading! See the Multnomah Press classics *The Love of God* by Bernard of Clairvaux and *A Life of Prayer* by St. Teresa of Avila. Enjoy richly the devotions of the patristic, medieval, modern, and contemporary periods alike. Discover the communion of saints as a living reality in all periods of history. Do not let modernity make you temporarily parochial.

Discern the spirits wisely by penetrating to the presuppositions and assumptions of theological stance of your writers. Learn to distinguish false from valid mysticism.

7. Enjoy fellowship with soul-friends so that you mutually benefit in a group, in a shared reading program.

Such a group may meet every three or four weeks to hear and discuss books reviewed in turn by members of the group. Discernment and shared enrichment are thereby exercised together. Insights may be shared of a more personal nature as confidentiality is developed. Differing perspectives may correct or add to individual impressions. The common goal of growing in Christ is emphasized as a corporate maturity that excludes no one in the group.

8. Recognize that spiritual reading meets with obstacles to distract, discourage, or dissuade us from persistence in our reading.

Often we do not see clearly enough what the obstacles are, and we seem to lose interest or get distracted easily by other things.

A first obstacle to remove is the time-bound and cultural or theological perspective of what we are reading. The imagery of a book like Teresa's *Interior Castle* or Bunyan's *Holy War* is bound to a particular time and culture. Nevertheless, the truths and insights contained in such works are timeless. The message of surrender and desire in the one book, or of watchfulness in temptation in the other, are timeless. Try not to be prejudiced with such labels as "old fashioned," "relevant for today," "traditional," or even "classic."

A second obstacle is the more subtle obstacle of aesthetic resistance to a text. We may not feel poetically inspired, or we may dislike allegory, or be impatient with the turgid, heavy style of a sermon. Or we may be entranced so much by the romantic imagery that we lose sight of the truth being conveyed. For being enraptured, just as much as being turned off, we may remain spectators, not really involved spiritually and personally in the text and its meaning to us. We remain connoisseurs with no real personal involvement. Many scholars are just doing literary criticism with little or no care for the spiritual food needed by the soul.

A third obstacle is moving further into the scholastic games that can be played with the text of Scripture: such are one-upmanship, where we create novelty of interpretation; name-dropping, when we review all that everyone else has said about the text; or negative listening, where we ignore all that is said positively and only draw attention to what is not said and what we think *should* be said. Such reading is shallow, in spite of its apparent scholarship, and rejects the docility and abiding in the text which we have already described as necessary for devotional reading.

A fourth obstacle is the ensuing despondency that sets in when we compare our state negatively and unfavorably with the spiritual condition of the writer. We can feel so miserable about our sinful condition that we are tempted to ignore spiritual books that show us our desperate need for God. Yet we learn precisely in this way that God can do nothing with our self-sufficiency, self-reliance, and self-respect. Acceptance of our limitations, repentance, and pleas for redemption from God—these are the bases for spiritual growth.

Finally, discouragement will rear its ugly head, even when there are signs all around us of encouragement and blessing. Patience with God's ways, trust in God's control of our circumstances, persistence when spiritual exercises seem fruitless, are all needed. The seed has to die to bear much fruit. Whether God leads us into the desert or into the garden in our devotional reading, let us follow Him. Accept mortification, as much as blessing, in your spiritual reading.

9. Seek a balance in your reading, both between modern and ancient writings. Be sure that you nourish and strengthen a wide range of your affections by good reading.

Remember, contemporary literature is untried, lacks vintage, and often reflects the fads of the marketplace. As C. S. Lewis has said:

> "A new book is still on trial, and the amateur is not in a position to judge it. . . . The only safety is to have a standard of plain, central Christianity ("mere Christianity" as Baxter called it), which puts the controversies of the moment in their proper perspective. Such a standard can only be acquired from old books. It is a good rule, after reading a new book, never to allow yourself another new one till you have read an old one in between. If that is too much for you, you should *read an old one to every three new ones.* "[2]

Examine also the need of balanced reading. In this same essay, Lewis gives us his preferences. Match, he argues, the somewhat "astringent" *Imitation of Christ* by Thomas à Kempis, with the "joyous" *Centuries of Meditation* by Thomas Traherne. Perhaps sandwich in between them the anonymously written *Theologia Germanica* which Luther loved. For Lewis, frequent companions were Richard Hooker's *Law of Ecclesiastical Polity*, George Herbert's poems, *The Temple*, William Law's *A Serious Call to a Devout and Holy Life*, and Francis de Sales' *Introduction to the Devout Life*. Some books, once read, may build important foundations. One such book includes Boethius' *On the Consolations of Philosophy*, which gave Lewis a firm awareness of the solidity of eternity that was more than measureless time. For every young inquirer or convert, Augustine's *Confessions* was Lewis' choice for inspiring the reality of the soul's relationship before God. However, Lewis' boon companions were G. K. Chesterton as his intellectual mentor on the sanity of the Christian faith, and George MacDonald, who fed his imagination with true devotion.

Lewis, however, would not have us slavishly imitate his fancies; he would encourage us to find devotion in heavy theological "stuff" as well as theology in the experiences of the simple things. He made friends with books in the whole range of affections we need to develop and exercise before God. Today, we tend to suffer from illiteracy of too much rapid, superficial reading—or rather mere glancing at books. Digestion, assimilation, and then a lifetime companionship with a book is a good test to see whether or not it is really a classic of faith and devotion.

James M. Houston

---

[1]Two useful Catholic aids to such material are: Susan Annette Muto, *A Practical Guide to Spiritual Reading* (Denville, N.J.: Dimension Books, 1976). John Weborg, *An Introductory, Annotated Bibliography in Spirituality*, Synthesis Series (Chicago: Franciscan Herald Press, 1979).

[2]C. S. Lewis, *God in the Dock*, ed. by Walter Hooper (Grand Rapids: Eerdmans, 1970).

Scripture Index

Old Testament

Subject Index